S0-BRU-484

Bernard Berenson in his study at 'I Tatti', Settignano, near Florence, 1955

SYLVIA SPRIGGE

BERENSON

A Biography

Illustrated

HOUGHTON MIFFLIN COMPANY BOSTON

THE RIVERSIDE PRESS CAMBRIDGE

N
8375
B46
S65

11/1/60 Gft 76 3,76

SECOND PRINTING

© SYLVIA SPRIGGE 1960
ALL RIGHTS RESERVED INCLUDING THE RIGHT TO
REPRODUCE THIS BOOK OR PARTS THEREOF IN ANY FORM
LIBRARY OF CONGRESS CATALOG CARD NUMBER: 60-7386

The Riverside Press
CAMBRIDGE · MASSACHUSETTS
PRINTED IN THE U. S. A.

42013

CONTENTS

ILLUSTRATIONS

The frontispiece and plates number 8, 18, 19, 21
and 22 are reproduced from photographs provided
by Messrs Conzett & Huber of Zürich, publishers
of *DU* magazine.

LIST OF ABBREVIATIONS USED
IN THIS BOOK

S.S.P.	*Sketch for a Self-Portrait*
O.C.	Own Correspondence
U.L.	Unfinished Life (by Mary Berenson)
R. and R.	*Rumour and Reflection*
A. and H.	*Aesthetics and History*
I.P.R.	*Italian Painters of the Renaissance*
S. and K.	*Seeing and Knowing*

CHRONOLOGY OF BERNARD BERENSON'S PUBLICATIONS IN ENGLISH

1894 *The Venetian Painters of the Renaissance*, New York and London, G. P. Putnam's Sons and The Knickerbocker Press.

1895 *Lorenzo Lotto—An Essay in Constructive Art Criticism*, New York and London, Putnam and The Knickerbocker Press.

1896 *The Florentine Painters of the Renaissance*, New York and London, Putnam and The Knickerbocker Press.

1897 *The Central Italian Painters of the Renaissance*, New York and London, Putnam and The Knickerbocker Press.

1901 *The Study and Criticism of Italian Art*, London, George Bell & Sons.

1902 *The Study and Criticism of Italian Art*, Second Series, London, George Bell & Sons.

1903 *Drawings of the Florentine Painters*, London, John Murray.

1907 *The North Italian Painters of the Renaissance*, New York and London, Putnam and The Knickerbocker Press.

1909 *A Sienese Painter of the Franciscan Legend*, London, J. M. Dent & Sons.

1913 *Catalogue of a Collection of Paintings and Some Art Objects*, Philadelphia, John G. Johnson.

1916 *Venetian Painting in America: The Fifteenth Century*, London, George Bell & Sons.
      The Study and Criticism of Italian Art, Third Series, London, George Bell & Sons.

1918 *Essays in the Study of Sienese Painting*, New York, Frederick Fairchild Sherman.

1926 *Three Essays in Method*, Oxford, The Clarendon Press.
      Speculum Humanae Salvationis, Oxford, The Clarendon Press.

1930 *Studies in Medieval Painting*, New Haven, Yale University Press, London, Oxford University Press

1932 *Italian Pictures of the Renaissance*, Oxford, The Clarendon Press.

1948 *Aesthetics and History in the Visual Arts*, New York, Pantheon.

1949 *Sketch for a Self-Portrait*, London, Constable.

1952 *Rumour and Reflection*, 1941–1944, London, Constable.

1953 *Seeing and Knowing*, London, Chapman & Hall.
      Caravaggio, His Incongruity and His Fame, London, Chapman & Hall.

1953 *The Arch of Constantine*, London, Chapman & Hall.

1960 (In preparation) *The Passionate Pilgrim. (Travel Diary extracts to 1958)*, Thames & Hudson.
      And very many articles, listed, together with all the translations in *Bibliografia di Bernard Berenson* by William Mostyn Owen, Electa, Milan, 1955.

FOREWORD

O NE snowy afternoon in mid-January 1945, after a long jeep ride down from the Italian war front which was then stuck about ten miles north of Ravenna, I persuaded the two officers with whom I was driving down to Rome to stop a moment about half-way, near a village called Settignano just before Florence, so that I might deliver a small book of poems and essays to a man there from his old friend in England. The man was Bernard Berenson, the small book was called *Windfalls*, and the old friend and poet was Robert Trevelyan, a neighbour of ours at home, in Abinger.

Burnt-out tanks, overturned trucks, bombed houses and unending lorry loads of German prisoners met the eye all along the snowy and then muddy road from Ravenna to Florence. Up at Settignano, as we sat in the uncarpeted fire-lit drawing-room in the dusk, with barely a picture on the wall, a certain sadness was suddenly dispelled by the appearance of a most welcoming cheerful lady carrying a candle. She had a broad brow crowned with rebellious greying hair, intelligent eyes, and she gave an impression of flowing comfortable dress about her, and of a rush of fluent English accented with some foreign quavers very difficult to identify, not Italian, not German, but what?

This was 'Nicky' Mariano, Mr Bernard Berenson's secretary, assistant and great friend, upon whose shoulders the whole of the big household rested, and who was much beloved by all who ever visited 'I Tatti' since her arrival there in 1917. She was half Baltic and half Italian, with a fluent knowledge of four languages and of a great deal more besides.

In January 1945 the war in Italy was not yet over. Before the final defeat of Hitler's armies there were four more months to go. Two great armies had passed this way, and the retreating Germans had blown up all the bridges except the Ponte Vecchio; also all the approaches to that bridge and the town's water and gas works. Florence and its hillsides were without light and almost without water. Into the semi-darkness more candles were brought and a

11

lamp. Then an Italian butler, who looked more distinguished than a Cabinet Minister, pushed in a trolley laden with tea things, and we were all refreshed.

In the doorway there suddenly appeared, with hardly any noise of footsteps, a very slight, small, elderly, bearded man, strikingly handsome, who carried his hands in front of him, one resting in the other. We all got up. This man carried with him, as some people do, a presence, which made everyone, men and women, get up even when he came into his own drawing-room. It was noticeably a cheerful and a purposeful presence, unaccompanied by any talk until Nicky had completed the introductions. His whole face and figure gave an impression of tranquillity and at the same time of lively curiosity. I did not know it then, but within the next ten years some two hundred articles were to be written in the popular Press of the world on the subject of first meetings with Bernard Berenson. Perhaps the civilized world after the two frightful conflicts was thirsty for elderly survivors who preserved not only a personal poise but a way of life and of hospitality that was, in these troubled and revolutionary times, still able to enforce a standard of nimble and polite conversation.

But there was, of course, far more to it than that. Berenson's name had been a household word in the world's chief museums and private collections for over half a century. He was the author of a score of books, some of which have become classics for the art student. He was a seer, a sage, some said; in any case a man born to look at pictures and works of art, with a rare power of understanding and appreciation:

> *Zum Sehen geboren*
> *Zum Schauen bestellt.*[1]

If pictures could react (with friendliness, hostility or indifference) as sharply as people did to this man's presence, they would, one felt, most certainly talk to him.

The *Sehen* and the *Schauen* had its own rhythm. It began, by long habit, in the countryside itself, for he was a great walker and a man completely at home with the light and the twilight, with the outlines and shapes of the scene, with the atmosphere at all times of the day and at all the turns of the seasons. The changing seasons gave him

---

[1] 'Born to see, destined to gaze.' Goethe, *Faust*, Act II, Scene 5.

sharp and keen pleasure, and continual refreshment. He could never have lived in the town and its modern mechanism passed him by. But he travelled miles in order to see works of art in the cities of Europe and North Africa, and later of the United States.

People were indispensable, for Berenson was a great talker, original, intelligent, full of wit and full of knowledge. The most varied band of visitors and friends called and stayed—an unending stream of them, reminding one of a small court at a German or Italian principality, Weimar at the time of Goethe, or Mantua at the time of Giulio Romano. Human beings, not 'art', enjoyed top priority at 'I Tatti', and I think what he most dreaded was the pedant. He saw the art world dangerously full of pedants, busily dissecting (botanizing, he called it), writing and talking for each other's discomfiture; 'art crickets' chirping away in a great buzz, icono-graphers engaged in 'icononsense'. He became so suspicious of students 'reading art' at American or European universities, lest they be already irremediably enmeshed in pedantry, that the students themselves got cold feet. There was one such, the story ran, who took a week to recover after a morning's grilling at 'I Tatti'. His host would have been kindness itself in any other circumstance except this one, which was probably (one has seen it so often) a display of nerves, of pretension and of theory, where Berenson was asking for first-hand observation and experience.

I think Berenson was and remains Walter Pater's first important pupil. He acknowledged the debt to Pater wholeheartedly, without reserve, and curiously enough, as we shall see, to George Eliot. His debt to the luminaries of art appreciation, to Winckelmann, Ruskin, Jacob Burckhardt, Cavalcaselle, Giovanni Morelli and a few others he tempered with his experience of their shortcomings.

I cannot record any deep thrill or excitement upon that first encounter, myself in a very muddy war correspondent's kit, and my companions hardly more presentable, except that they were men from battle. I thought Berenson was in complete and graceful com-mand of the situation as he took Robert Trevelyan's book of poems, said he was an American and that this was the first breath of England in five years, and that he must embrace me for it. Then he talked with my companions, discovering at once beneath their uniforms that one of them in peace-time was a student of Byzantine history and the other a painter. I asked after his wife: 'Ah, my Mary,' he said, 'she is very ill, upstairs—she will not recover.'[1] A few weeks later Mary died, and I never met her.

We had to reach Rome before dawn, and there were friendly farewells and the invitation to come again. 'We have nothing, you know. The biscuits for tea came from America. The tea comes from your army. In the old days we used to put up friends all the time. Now that is not possible. We could not feed them. But come again.'

From Rome I wrote to thank him for the afternoon's hospitality, and received a letter back renewing the invitation to call when passing through Florence next time.

This became a regular habit. During the next nine years my work in Italy often took me north from Rome with a halt at 'I Tatti', and even when it did not, I would try to snatch a week-end when I could, to enjoy the host and hostess of this enchanting place, and the various members of the household who worked with Berenson on his books and essays, which continued to come out in a steady flow regardless of his eighty years.

The two hundred or so Renaissance pictures began to reappear on the bare walls after months of patient restoration by the best skill Florence could provide.[2] The most precious of these lovely, curious and important pictures had been stored for safety during the final battle for Florence in the neighbouring cellars of Baroness Ritter's villa, and they suffered no damage. Others were sent to the Florence house of Baroness Alda von Anrep, Miss Mariano's sister. When Marshal Kesselring ordered all but one of the Arno bridges to be blown up, and the entrances to the Ponte Vecchio to be blocked by the dynamited debris of houses on either side of it, Baroness Anrep's house was among those destroyed. The pictures suffered, but being in a strong room, not irremediably. Some, however, were actually looted and never traced. Berenson's bronzes suffered too, and were likewise restored with great skill.

Friends in ever-greater numbers came to call and to stay. I soon learned that the whole house with its great library of art, history, literature and travel books in half a dozen languages, its pictures

---

[1] Mary Berenson came of a Philadelphia Quaker family. She was the daughter of Mary Whittall, a famous evangelist; her sister Alys was Bertrand Russell's first wife, and her brother, Logan Pearsall Smith, was the author among other works of a biting collection of aphoristic essays published under the titles of *Trivia* and *More Trivia*.

[2] The restorer was Signor Giannino Marchig in Florence.

and bronzes, its photograph library and its fine gardens and farms had been bequeathed by Berenson to his former university, Harvard, and endowed by him, for the use of American, English and other students of the humanities.

I felt, as many people felt, a certain mystery in Berenson's origin. His nationality was American. He was a Harvard man. He had been born in Lithuania in 1865, and his parents had emigrated to Boston in 1875.

How could an American stay unmolested in Italy during a long war, in which Italy was at war with America? Why was Bernard Berenson leaving the whole of his villa and lands and his great library and his collection to Harvard? In the course of the years all the answers to these questions became clearer to me. His loyalty as a friend was enduring. I was not alone in this happy experience.

In 1953 I finally returned to England. It never occurred to me to write about Berenson, and when pressed to do so, I refused, saying I could only do so with his permission. He gave it unwillingly, and for a 'portrait'. He wished, he said, for a brief book like his *Sketch for a Self-Portrait*[1] 'seen from without', as his book had attempted a study of himself 'seen from within'. He wished the book to cover the period 1945–53, the years of our frequent meetings. Later he said that the first thirty-six years of his life had been by far the most important. By the time I had begun my difficult task, I too had discovered that. Finally he wished that the book should not be published in his lifetime, but that an old and good friend of his should read it through.[2] And his wishes have been observed. We often talked of matters arising in the book, and he was sometimes helpful. It was understood that his letters, which run into many thousands, for he was a great correspondent and received long letters from a wide circle of friends and acquaintances, would be edited later by his executors.

*   *   *

Great numbers of people knew this man. When some of them came to hear of this book they spoke or wrote down some of their living impressions of him. These I have used in the story as occasion arose.

[1] *Sketch for a Self-Portrait*, by Bernard Berenson, Constable, London, 1949.
[2] Count Umberto Morra, for several years head of the Italian Institute in London. Mr W. G. Constable of Boston also very kindly read it, and corrections suggested by both were made.

15

The story begins at the beginning, for I know no other way of telling it. It ends in the hillsides above Florence. The beginning lies very far away from Tuscany, in the fens and plains of north-eastern Europe, far from the lifelong scene of

> those cypress-wooded hills that mount
> Beyond Vincigliata and quarried Ceceri
> To where by San Clemente we so often have seen
> Tuscany spread its grave and gracious landscape out
> From Vallombrosa to the far Carraran peaks;
> A vision of enchantment, a delight more deep
> Than ever elsewhere spirit or sense may hope to know.[1]

[1] 'To Bernard Berenson', poem by R. C. Trevelyan in the *Abinger Chronicle*, Vol. I, No. 2, January 1940.

CHAPTER I

In the Pale of Settlement

For precept must be upon precept, precept upon
precept; line upon line, line upon line;

Isaiah xxviii. 10

No one except the Jews has heard of the Pale of Settlement for a very long time. It no longer exists as a boundaried place. Russia, since 1945, has again annexed most of it after a brief interval, between the first two wars of this century, when parts of it, like Lithuania, Esthonia and Latvia, enjoyed a breeze of independent existence. The annexation has not been recognized by Western Europe or the United States.

The Pale was the setting in which many Jewish families had lived for many centuries (some since the Crusades) at the time our story begins with the birth of Bernard Berenson on June 26, 1865, in the little town of Butremanz, twelve miles from the fourteenth-century city of Vilna, capital of Lithuania. Vilna had about 80,000 inhabitants in 1865, Butremanz under 5,000. Both the Berenson parents were Jewish.

Lithuania in 1865 lay inside Czarist Russia, and more precisely in the northernmost part of the Pale of Settlement, which was a long stretch of territory running all the way from the Baltic to the Black Sea. At one time or another between the tenth and eighteenth centuries all the grand duchies and kingdoms in the region, comprising Lithuania, Poland, Hungary, Bulgaria and Rumania laid claim to frontiers running from the Baltic to the Black Sea. The Pale of Settlement alone, which was no country, covered the great strip.[1]

It was a defined area set aside for Russian Jews by the Czarist government, after the Polish–Russian and Polish–Swedish wars during the eighteenth century. At the third partition of Poland in 1795 Russia annexed it altogether. In 1919 Russia lost it. Vilna, like

[1] Chaim Weizmann called it 'that prison-house of the Jews created by Czarist Russia'.

17

Odessa far away in the south, already contained some of the very oldest European Jewish communities, originally from the Rhineland. It had become the centre of the Jewish religious printing presses, almost a Holy City for the Talmudists. Vilna contained some palaces of the Polish nobility, the Roman Catholic Cathedral of St Casimir built in the late 1300s and a library and museum—all that remained of a Jesuit Academy founded in 1578 and closed down in 1823. There were monuments to Catherine II, to Pushkin, and an Imperial Society of Physicians from which, of course, Jews were excluded. They formed a state within the State. Among those who came from or were brought up in the Pale were Leo Trotsky, Chaim Weizmann (the first President of the Israeli Republic); Debussy; Soutine and Chagall the painters; Heifitz and other famous violinists, and many notable chemists and physicists who afterwards settled in the United States. It was a different kind of emigration altogether from that of the Kafka and Freud type of the big cities of Central Europe. These people of the Pale were not metropolitan, nervous, introspective.

With its little country ghettos near the big villages where the Polish Catholic peasants lived, this part of the Pale became one of the most famous halting-places of a gifted and much persecuted race on its long journey through the centuries.

The country ghettos of the Pale were immensely remote. Vilna itself was miles out of the line of any tourist (even if he included, which he rarely did, Moscow or St Petersburg on his grand tour). The little towns of the Pale held small promise of reward to any itinerant merchant, except perhaps to the bookseller. Jewish life in the northern Pale was healthy, rigorous, puritan, full of hard work, full of ritual and full of disputations, on a high, medium or low level, according to the disputants. In the 'Hassidic' southern Pale thousands of the Jews were illiterate. When one asked Berenson what the first ten years of his life had really been like, he would say: 'Read the first chapter of Weizmann's autobiography, and read Jerôme and Jean Tharaud's *L'Ombre de la Croix*. It was exactly like that. They capture it marvellously, though the Tharauds were never there.' But they pieced together story after story brought by refugees who arrived from there in Budapest after the First World War.[1]

Bernard's parents were very young when he was born. His mother,

---

[1] The Tharauds were teaching in the French Institute in Budapest in 1919. They wrote many books about the Jews, becoming progressively more anti-Semitic. This one is more in the nature of a report.

Julia Mieliszanski,[1] was eighteen and his father, whose name was Albert Valvrojenski,[2] was nineteen. This name was changed to Berenson some time before emigration, mainly because Valvrojenski was considered too difficult to pronounce abroad. Mary Pearsall Smith, whom Bernard married in 1901 and who died in 1945, left an Unfinished Life of her husband, in which she suggests with all the stubborn insularity of a Philadelphia Quaker, that the name Berenson was chosen 'because the bear was the symbol of the tribe to which Bernard belongs', much as small Boy Scouts are called Wolf Cubs. Elizabeth (or Bessie) Berenson, Bernard's only surviving sister in the fifties of this century, remembered that the name had been changed, but could no longer remember the original name. She suggested that the reason for the change was greater clarity. Jewish people frequently took such names, or diminutives or patronymics, before emigration; names like Baer, Wolf, Sperling, Fuchs, Vogel, Loewe, Loewen (whence Lewis, Lewisohn, etc.) as well as names of towns and names of trades.[3]

Both Bernard and his sister remembered their mother as a small, capable, green-eyed, curly-haired creature. The whole family loved and respected her. 'She brought us up to be meticulous about our persons, and was very neat herself and orderly', Bessie would say. And she taught all her children to hold themselves straight. She knew and recited the new Yiddish poetry to her children, which had old high German traditions in it.

Because Bernard Berenson's appearance in later life had great distinction, people would surmise that he must be descended from a long line of rabbis. As far as he knew, he was not. His sisters knew no more than he did. There is no family tree, no family history at all. His origin is as obscure as that of Horace.

It is too late now to try to find out who the Valvrojenskis of Butremanz were, or even more important, who Julia's parents were. Too many revolutions and armies have passed that way, back and forth, since 1865, for there to be any records left.[4] Weizmann's father, like Berenson's, worked in the timber trade.

[1] Registered thus in Bernard Berenson's entry form at Harvard, under 'Mother's maiden name'.   [2] Given thus by Mary Berenson in U.L.

[3] A Jewish friend pointed out that Albert in Yiddish (which was the spoken language among Jews here) is 'Ber'.

[4] One of the later emigrants from Butremanz, Mr Max L. Alpert of Boston, wrote to the author on September 21, 1956, from Boston: 'The majority of people who left Butremanz came to Boston, and for many years we had a Butremanz Society here'.

In the timber districts the able-bodied men of the community, including Albert Valvrojenski, would go off in the last days of autumn, laden with winter supplies of food and extra clothing. On the first day of the journey some of the children would accompany the men a little way, down the rough tracks and along the many lakes, and return at night. There were wolves and bears and bison in the forests, and sometimes bands of outlaws. For the rest, it was a great flat plain with an occasional big wooden crucifix on the horizon. The timber business was a cold and exacting occupation, with bad years when the rains came late or intermittently, and the rafts would not move easily. There were far less comforts in those days than there are in the same trade in Canada today.

By November the men were deep in the forests and far from home. The trees would be marked, and the Polish peasants began the felling. The young Jewish sub-contractors supervised the Polish peasants who tied the long logs into rafts, and settled their proper placing both on the ice and alongside the frozen river banks, just where the waters would overflow in the great spring thaw. If all went well and the rains came in downpours at the end of the great freeze, the rafts of cut trees would be carried downstream, down the Niemen, the Dvina and the Bug or one of their tributaries, and be manoeuvred into canals and towards rivers which carried the wood in as westerly a direction as possible, for export to countries less well provided with forests than Russia.

Much of the wood round Vilna went to Tilsit and Riga. The wood worked by the Weizmanns a little farther south bumped its way down the water to a canal at Brest Litovsk, and thence into the Bug and the Vistula, to Danzig on the Baltic. There was fun to be had for the youngsters in the spring leaping from raft to raft, and Berenson remembered such days in which one had to be nimble and well-balanced. He recalled those spring days in Lithuania as 'big and fresh and dewy'.

He covered great distances in the never-ending plain at speed. Skies and clouds in that broad flat horizon were, and remained all his life, visions of intense pleasure. They sailed over him, he said, the huge cloudy symbols of a high romance; castles, mountains, strange animals, armies and navies in the skies, never alike from one moment to another, enjoyable above all at sunrise and at sunset, and often to be seen reflected in the water of the lakes round the village. None named the trees and flowers and birds in the woods for him. Free of any botanical interest, he looked at shapes and colours, light and shade, and listened for the ripple of lake water and the song of birds. It was, as all country life is for children, the best introduction to life itself.

One blessing the Jews enjoyed in the Pale until the nineteenth century by comparison with most Jewish communities outside it: there had been no serious persecution of the Jews in the Pale itself until 1863, two years before Bernard's birth, and the year of the rising in Poland. The participation of the Jews in the rising had outraged the Czar. He withdrew certain privileges enjoyed by the Jews and introduced conscription to the Russian army. Many Jewish families bribed their way out of this conscription which was a savage one, lasting no less than fifteen years. But in 1874 things were tightened up and exemption became exceedingly difficult. Then, in 1881, one young Jew was implicated among several Russians in the assassination of Czar Alexander II. The first pogroms inside the Pale began. Hundreds of thousands then abandoned their homes in the Pale altogether in search of toleration and work in America, South Africa, and (in many thousands) in the Whitechapel district of London.

But even that compelling reason was not the one which caused the young Valvrojenskis to leave Butremanz. By 1881 they had already been gone six years.

*   *   *

Not all Jews in the Pale worked in timber. Some worked in the professions, for which a university degree was a necessity. This was very difficult to get. All kinds of disability clauses governed the admission of Jews to the Russian universities. Even entry to secondary school in Vilna or Pinsk was a matter for celebration. In the northern Pale all the Jewish male children went to the nearest Jewish schools or Chederim from the age of five—usually a bare and draughty barn of a place in which the children sat on the earthen floor. The teacher made little money out of his task. No Jews in the country ghettos of the Pale were rich. They lived patriarchally, three generations in one house, and that one small; a few fowls in the yard, and a small vegetable plot. They could not buy land, only forests for cutting, and this they did co-operatively. In the Pale they were still strangers, even century-old strangers, in a strange land. It was not a place in which there was either time or inclination

21

for architecture or the visual arts. Against the last there was still a strong religious prejudice, lest it spill over into 'graven images'.

A people who had no art and little music to kindle the spirit, and only the poetry of David, Isaiah and Solomon for comfort in the endless snowy plains and fens of Eastern Europe would, if opportunity offered, be artists in the choice of words. If anyone excelled, he excelled in talk. Speech, good recitation, and then good disputations: these were the manly arts. In the 1860's, moreover, there had been a literary revival in Yiddish writing, and a translation into modern Hebrew of ancient Jewish folk-tales, songs and rhymes. In 1870 Bernard went to the Cheder.

*   *   *

There was much ritual in the daily attendance at the Cheder, where the new boy on his first day would eat the letter Alef, the first letter of the Hebrew alphabet, made in the form of a bun. The old Testament was thoroughly conned. The Pentateuch and the Psalms were recited verse by verse. By the age of ten a boy was expected to read and write Hebrew fluently. One wonders how the girls were educated. The ritual of a boy's first recitation from the Scriptures was to set him high on a platform in his new caftan, his ritual curls under a small round cap, while all listened intently to see how well and intelligently he could intone the set passage. If he excelled, the praise and the gifts were lavish. This day of recitation might come at any time after two years' attendance at the Cheder, according to the boy's ability. The 'Bar Midwa', or entrance into adulthood, was a later ceremony usually undertaken at the age of thirteen.

There was nothing lugubrious about it all, for the very opening lesson in the Talmud had been 'The first gift of God is life, His finest creation'. Life was a gift to be welcomed and treasured, but never without ritual. At the age of thirteen the eldest boy could take the headship of the family in his father's absence. In Berenson's case it probably happened earlier.

The ritual of headship of the family carried small duties with it, such as sitting at the head of a table of elders and saying grace at meals. In the spring of 1873, when the men came back from the forests just in time for the Feast of Passover, Bernard, at the age of seven, would be taking his part for the first time in the annual rejoicing and ceremonies connected with the greatest feast of the year. The Passover rites and those of the Day of Atonement were rich in ritual detail, even to the sound of the candles as they spluttered each time the wick reached some of the women's tears in the wax, for weeping was ritual for the women as they kneaded the wax for the Atonement candles, remembering their dead. The Jews of the Pale, like all old and remote races, were swift to link the visible with the invisible, the familiar with the miraculous. Custom, ritual and morality became interchangeable, which, of course, they are not, among non-Jews.

A world of ritual lay in the day's and the season's work. There was the ritual evening prayer of Minchah, and another ritual morning prayer; both could only be said by ten voices together, a fact which made the Jewish traveller ever eager to meet other Jewish travellers at dawn and towards sunset. There was the autumn Feast of Tabernacles when white sheets were ritually hung upon a tent of sticks in memory of the long years in the wilderness, and against the white sheets all the bright coloured fruits of the harvest, like a Mantegna garland, but probably not so neat. Even today in the little gardens of Hampstead houses in North London, where many Jews live, these tents appear in autumn, garlanded with fruits.

There were weddings such as Bernard's parents and many of their friends must have had, in which ritual ordained that the bride walk seven times round her betrothed, he round her, and likewise the parents, after which the bridegroom put the ring on the bride's finger, they drank from the same glass and the glass was ritually broken. The violins played and the men in their silk caftans formed a joyous procession to the feast prepared by the women (Chagall has painted fragments from this kind of scene in almost all his pictures). There, at the feast, a Talmudic problem is ritually set and argued with both ferocity and subtle irony. The alternation of feast and fast, rejoicing and high argument, songs of praise and lamentations of despair; all were governed by a ritual which alone could invest this immense energy with the significance of newborn life, marriage, death, and divine purpose. At the birth of a child, the father or some near male relation if he were away in the forests would hurry to the synagogue as soon as the labours of childbirth began, and there untie the precious leather scroll of the Torah saying: 'Lord, deliver my wife, as I have just untied Thy law'.

The boy child must grow the ritual locks which are 'the livery of the Lord'. Berenson kept his till the age of twenty-two.

The ritual of the Sabbath was almost as severe as that in a Scottish Presbyterian household at the same period but more jovial. There was better food, wine and much singing. No secular reading, no work of any kind. Even the lamps and fires remained ritually unlit for those who could not afford to pay for these services to be performed by a Christian peasant. One just froze that day.

Weizmann says that these country ghettos were almost completely ignorant of the natural sciences. Occasionally a scientific textbook would arrive and pass from hand to hand, but mostly the 'modern' books were French, English and German classics in German, or in Russian translations, and Russian literature. Hebrew occupied the place of Latin and Greek, and was, besides, a sacred language. Before the days of Zionism to speak it would have been to desecrate it. Yiddish was the language of everyday, a patchwork tongue of many dialect words gleaned from places through which the Jews had wandered, but based mainly on middle high German. Everyone spoke some Polish and Russian, and many knew German.

In the more liberal Jewish households in the northern non-Hassidic part of the Pale—and such was the Berenson household—the foreign classics were read.[1] In all the families, one gathers, daily life was regulated in many of its details in accordance with Hebrew law, and therein lay the very strength and resilience of this wholly monotheistic people. The Jews had obeyed the first Commandment, despite Baal, Ashteroth and Moloch, and despite the quick rewards attending the Emperor-worship of Rome. In the Pale they lived, as Jewish communities had always lived, with the memory of much wandering and much learning down the centuries, knit by a strict ritual and buoyed by the hope of better times to come.

All this could easily turn to mysticism in times of stress. Holiness and wisdom were highly prized. Advice was ritually sought on all secular matters (with offerings of food), from the nearest Zadik, and the Zadiks were wise men who lived in places where they could always be found, surrounded by their large families. It was believed that they inherited their wisdom, for the office had grown hereditary

[1] I have not ventured into all the details of the Misnagdin disciplines of the northern regions of the Pale. By the time Berenson was born the Chabad Movement appears to have made the attempt in these regions to bridge the gulf with the South, and to have assimilated some of the Hassidic mysticism into its own intellectual religion.

from father to son. A Zadik from the Pale is said to keep open house to this day in the borough of Brooklyn, New York.[1]

The winter in this north-east corner of Europe was very long. On winter evenings there was little to do but listen to the old, the Grandparents, the Zadiks or the Rabbis, often arguing fiercely about fine points of the law, quarrelling, or just telling stories. Zadiks and Rabbis held separate court.

Weizmann recalls how his grandfather told the children of 'the mighty figures of Israel', and how the talk in the 'sixties would often turn to the famous journey ten years before, of old Moses Montefiore to St Petersburg to plead for a cessation of pogroms in Kiev and for better conditions for the Jewish settlements in the Pale, and how, on his return to Vilna, the Jews unharnessed his horses and drew his carriage triumphantly through the streets.

Bernard's great favourite in his little patriarchal home was his maternal grandmother. He remembered her death, just before he was five.

'Her departure stunned me. She had meant more to me than all other people put together, including my mother. I not only missed her day and night, but could not understand what had happened . . . my grandmother's death made me ponder and enquire. All I seemed able to learn was that after one died one went before awesome judges who assigned one to terrible punishments for sins. Were animals too subject to such treatment? No. Why? They had no souls. I envied the animals. When dead they were dead, and that was an end of it. Yes, Death was the evil of evils. How could it be avoided? Sticks and stones do not die. Better then to be a stick or a stone. But they have not lived at all. No, no! Anything rather than not to have lived. With that utterly childish conclusion I was for ever liberated from death.'[2]

Soon after this loss (which was accompanied by a strange dream about his grandmother[3]) a little girl who had been his constant play-

---

[1] Sir Isaiah Berlin, to the author, March 1954. I am much indebted to him and to his mother for having read this chapter. Mrs Berlin was very familiar with life in the Pale in the 'seventies, although she lived in Riga after her marriage.

[2] *Sketch for a Self-Portrait*, by Bernard Berenson, p. 106, Constable, London, 1949. Future reference under *S.S.P.*   [3] *Ibid.*, p. 107.

mate also died. Then school became the chief business of life, and there he excelled. One day, it must have been just after that first important Passover when he was seven, he announced to his mother that he was now grown up. It was a memorable year. At the end of life he still recalled it, saying that he had become aware at the age of seven of 'a vein of spiritual energy'. Most boys and some girls have such moments. Only they forget.

The realization of it was likely enough to take some form of dedication, as it often took among boys in the Highlands of Scotland, who also learned the psalms of David at their mother's knee in almost as rugged circumstances.

'From childhood I have had the dream of life lived as a sacrament', he wrote, and 'the dream implied taking life ritually as something holy'.[1] It would be difficult to detect in this anything priggish or affected, having regard for the ritual setting, the ritual circumstances of life in the Pale and the epoch. Chance and necessity might blight the high endeavour, but one thing would remain—a profound sense of ritual, or order and regularity, of a time for study and a time for play which are the characteristics of Hebrew law. All his sisters shared these characteristics. If the ritual of the Pale life was to be abandoned, as likely as not some new ritual would be sought, and that one a more secular one.

*   *   *

In 1875 the Valvrojenski home was accidentally destroyed by fire.[2] The prospect of emigration suddenly assumed the proportions of reality. The older Jews in the Pale would often meditate the centuries-old dream of the Dispersion—the dream of the great return to the Promised Land.[3] But the younger members of the communities, threatened now by severe conscription laws, talked more practically of emigration to the United States, or to nearby Germany, which in those days had glamour, efficiency and modernity, when compared with the primitive confusion, backwardness and growing oppression of the Russian rule in the Pale.

---

[1] *S.S.P.*, p. 106.   [2] U.L.
[3] Zionism was not popular in the Valvrojenski household. In later years Berenson wrote 'I hated Zionism until Hitler's attempt to destroy the Jews. Now the experiment of a Jewish State is a necessity that can't be avoided . . . the Hebrew language may be swamped by Arabia, and then Israel will sink into another and poorer Lebanon. *Absit omen.*' (O.C., 27. x. 54.)

Young prospective emigrants saved to buy a ticket from the ticket merchants who wandered about the Pale offering berths on emigrant steamers across the ocean. A deposit was paid which carried the emigrant to a British port, and there, if he could afford it, he paid the rest, boarded another steamer and went on to whatever destination was marked on the ticket. A very large part of the first Jewish citizens of Whitechapel in London came to England from the Pale of Settlement in this way, unable at the time to afford the remaining two-thirds of the deposit which would have carried them all the way from the Pale to the New World.

Besides the ticket money, the emigrants tried to save for the little bag of gold which was essential for the new life and above all for the new career.

Some cousins were also going to emigrate. Now Albert and his wife, Bernard aged ten, Abe his younger brother and Senda his younger sister set off. The tickets bore the destination—Boston. Chance, nothing more, but a chance which Berenson was always to cherish. The oldest puritans in Europe were about to arrive among the descendants of the Pilgrim Fathers, puritans of a later age, in a place where these too had once sought a new life—and found it.

No Jewish families who left the Pale ever returned to it. Far away, in their new countries, they always retained some mark of the pristine ritual and simplicity of their lives here, which they themselves could hardly explain.

CHAPTER II

'Into the New World'

Machinery just meant
To give thy soul its bent,
Try thee and turn thee forth, sufficiently impressed.

ROBERT BROWNING, *Rabbi ben Ezra*

BOSTON had a huge fire in 1872, in which some sixty-five acres of buildings were destroyed, with a loss of eighty million dollars. When the Berensons arrived in 1875 the city was in the throes of reconstruction. Its population was a quarter of a million. Today the city and its surrounding hillsides number nearly three million inhabitants.

The 'eighties were a time of great new commercial expansion, but not for these young emigrants. The Berenson emigration to Boston can hardly be called a successful operation. So hard were these early years that Bernard Berenson would never speak of them. A discreet silence covered the whole period between the fresh and dewy boyhood in Lithuania and entry to Harvard. Yet these were intense, full years, and without some knowledge of them it is impossible to understand how the young emigrant from the Pale of Settlement ever entered the famous New England University on the banks of the Charles River.

Home was virtually in a railway siding, first at 32 Nashua Street[1] in a grim little house, and then at 11 Minot Street round the corner. At the bottom of both streets, all along Lowell Street, was a railway track. The noise of shunting was never far. The Berensons remained there for thirty long years, until Bernard's first earnings changed their lot.[2]

The new immigrants helped each other in the awful problem of how to earn. One way, among the Jews, was to trade in old metal,

[1] Where the cab-rank now is, outside North Station. No. 32 no longer stands, as part of a wide motor causeway has caused the clearance of some of Nashua Street. See Plate II.　　　　　　　　[2] See Plate II.

mainly cast-off pots and pans, while taking round new pots and pans. The business required travelling pedlars and stationary dealers. Albert Berenson became a travelling pedlar, tramping the highways and byways into all the pretty villages which still survive in the motorized countryside round Boston. His cousin Louis, also an immigrant, became a dealer. He too changed his name to Berenson.[1]

Some time in the mid-'eighties Albert would take a boy with him, the son of another immigrant from Zosle near Butremanz in Vilna province, a youth called Louis Aron Lebowich, who years after set up his own insurance business in 18 Tremont Street in Boston. Mr Lebowich retained an undying devotion to Berenson's father. The small, quick walker, with his trim pointed beard, would talk 'beautifully' as they walked,[2] especially about French history and philosophy, about Voltaire and Rousseau. By then Albert had completely shed what remained of his Jewish orthodoxy. The orthodoxy had become, as with so many Jewish immigrants, secularized. He was a Free Thinker, or, in his eldest son's sharper view, a Nihilist. The other son, Abe (Mr Lebowich maintained), was 'a rough lad whom no one could get on with'. He died in early manhood.

Sometimes Albert would talk of his peddling experiences during the previous years before Lebowich joined him. Albert Berenson told young Lebowich how he had once reached a fine country house at Concord, not far from the rude bridge where

> Once the embattled farmers stood
> And fired the shot heard round the world[3]

which started the gunfire of the American Revolution against George III on April 19, 1775. Lebowich recalls that the New England ladies of these houses especially enjoyed the visits of *this* pedlar because 'he talked so well'. So, for that matter, did Louisa Alcott, the daughters of Emerson and other neighbours. At this Concord house one day in the early 'eighties, Albert Berenson was greeted with the remark: 'Guess who is in the drawing-room! A young man called Bernard Berenson', whereupon Albert gathered

[1] 'Lawrence Berenson (Bernard's lawyer) was a grandson of a cousin of B.B.'s father, who emigrated from Lithuania and took the same name as B.B.'s family did.' (Letter from Nicky Mariano to the author, February 29, 1956.)

[2] Mr Lebowich to the author, in Boston, June 1955, and all that follows concerning Albert Berenson.

[3] Ralph Waldo Emerson, *Hymn Sung at the Completion of Concord Monument*.

his outspread wares as hurriedly as he could, loaded them on to his little barrow outside and fled. He was a modest man, Mr Lebowich said, shy of disturbing his children's progress in the New World. His was the problem of many American settlers among whom first and second generation of the same family avoid each other, for the shame of poverty and of a foreign accent in the new tongue.

On another occasion, Albert told the young Lebowich, he was in a train with his sacks of tin wares when a cluster of schoolgirls tumbled down the centre corridor of the long carriage. Among them Albert recognized his daughter Senda, then attending the local public (or State) school, and once again he hastily collected his bags and fled to another compartment, not wanting to embarrass her with the revelation to her schoolmates that her father was a pedlar. It is doubtful whether the vigorous, athletic Senda herself would have been in the least bit embarrassed. She later became physical drill instructor at Smith College and married a resident professor there.[1]

Boston City Records[2] tell how Albert's pedlar's licence was renewed in 1880, when he moved with the family from 32 Nashua Street to 11 Minot Street, round the corner from Nashua Street; Louis Berenson was then registered as a tin-ware dealer at nearby Salem Street, Number 95, and Albert and the young Lebowich used to turn in the scrap metal they collected on the long treks at Louis' shop in Salem Street.[3]

Even sixty-five years after these events, Mr Lebowich remembered that Albert and his eldest son did not get on well,[4] certainly not well enough to go on these journeyings together. In any case the Berenson parents were determined not to interrupt their children's free schooling. In this respect the young Lebowich seems to have been less fortunate, though he later passed his accountancy examinations.

Bernard never went on the peddling expeditions. When not at the public (State) school, he was at the top of the little house in

---

[1] In 1948 Mrs Senda Abbott, well on in the eighties, and her slightly younger sister Elizabeth, thought nothing of climbing in and out of a rough jeep in Rome when the author took them on several sightseeing expeditions.

[2] City directory of that year consulted in the Boston Athenaeum.

[3] Mr Lebowich, to the author, in Boston, June 1955.

[4] Berenson was once reminded of his father (in a letter of 1891 to Mary from Naples) when an American friend burst into 'a dreadful laugh . . . so much like my father's . . . but there the resemblance ends for my father's face, five years ago, was still beautiful'. U.L., VI. 10.

Minot Street with his books. His mother attended the 'reformed' synagogue in Boston. He was already reading the New Testament at school, and one day he was baptized into the Episcopal Church by a famous Boston preacher, Phillips Brooks. But looking back from the warmer, richer religious experience that came to him ten years later in Italy, he recalled this New England venture into Christianity as a too rational step. It had been taken with good intent, but it had turned out badly, and was to be submerged in a great wave of scepticism of a late Victorian and not a Latin brand.

For Mr Lebowich, Bernard's father was a bright beacon in a hard world. Lebowich still, in old age, maintained that Albert Berenson was unappreciated at home, unlistened to, so that often he would just go on talking to himself in a kind of *sotto voce*. It is probable that Albert's early devotion to Voltaire and Rousseau remained static and unfruitful. His uncongenial labours can have left him little time or energy for reading and for further development of the lines of his thought. Voltaire and Rousseau mocked on, in a vacuum.

Albert opened a dry goods store at 11 Minot Street, but it was unsuccessful, and he took to the road again. The struggle of these years was desperate. Mrs Berenson turned one room into a dining-room for regular diners. She also took in sewing. The family was growing, for two more children had arrived, Rachel[1] and Elizabeth, and there were now seven mouths to feed. In the memory of one of the regular diners at Minot Street, 'Mrs Berenson presided there with a special kind of distinction, and the dinners became popular because of her nice ways, as well as because the food was good'.

But she always attended to her children and insisted on great neatness and cleanliness. That was a part of Bernard's modest nursery.

If the curtain has been lifted here, which Berenson himself never lifted privately or in print, it is only because his own landscape gains immensely in brightness by comparison with Minot Street. It is on such a plain bare canvas that the luminous design has to grow, and grow it did. Often in later years the only reference to these days was of a sense of calling, of having been brought up for great things. Mrs Berenson, like all mothers with a much loved and remarkable son, would certainly have been his ally in his pursuit of what he began to feel as 'dream of a life lived as a sacrament'.[2] Everything is mys-

[1] Later the wife of Ralph Barton Perry, Professor of Philosophy at Harvard.
[2] *S.S.P.*, p. 106.

terious about such a goal; the departure, the journey, the arrival, if arrival there can be.

To people long settled in areas of poverty, dreams of revolution come easily, but not to new emigrants. Berenson saw no reason for revolution in the vicissitudes of Minot Street. His father's failure to compete in the industrial expansion that was Boston's in the seventies and eighties of the last century was a plain fact. In the Pale, Albert's work had been collective, prescribed. In the New World every effort was individual and chancy. Whatever might happen, his eldest boy must never be an extra burden to the hard-pressed Minot Street household. Other members of the family, the cousins, 'made the grade'. Today, the Berensons in Boston flourish mostly in what is called in America the 'liquor business'.

Mrs Berenson gave her studious boy a room at the top of the house in Minot Street. It was hot in summer, icy in winter. The discovery of the Public Library was the first great event for him in Boston. Once he had discovered it, housed in an Italianate building at the Tremont Street corner of Boylston Street (as it then was), he called there twice a week to exchange books. From the age of eleven to eighteen he was a constant visitor there. At first the assistants would not believe he could read all the books he borrowed (and returned). In the end they had to believe it. It was prodigious how much he read. Now that the Old Testament was no longer the only book, the whole world seemed to open up. From mere statistics about the new continent he had landed in he leapt to astronomy, to history, to literature and then to art. He covered continents, not just Western Europe. He paused long in Arabia, even to borrowing an Arabic grammar and reading sentences of the Koran in its own language. He memorized a great deal. He got outside himself very early and stood to watch the intimate effects of all this on himself. In many ways this ability to stop and take stock was, and remained, a most important, indeed a vital acquisition. He became intensely interested in knowledge for its own sake, and his ambition was to get to the University. There were two: Boston University and Harvard, both on the wide Charles River, about five miles apart. The latter seemed unattainable. The former was almost free and one could attend daily.

When does a boy suddenly stop reading to shout 'Eureka! I have found something!' Berenson remembered several of these occasions all his life. The first one occurred when he had sufficiently mastered English to have plunged suddenly into Young's very suicidal *Night*

32

Thoughts. He was about fifteen, and at the moment deep in astronomy and a 'preoccupation with inter-stellar space'. He had been reading Coleridge, and felt

> . . . visited all night by troops of stars
> or when they climb the sky or when they sink.[1]

For Young in the eighteenth century, as for Fred Hoyle in the twentieth century, the stars rose 'from fluid dregs to masses rude and then to spheres opaque'. Young felt the skies had mathematical glories, still unfathomed. As for man, he wrote, 'his greatest strength is shown in standing still'. Immobility in face of the moment when

> Final Ruin fiercely drives
> Her ploughshare o'er Creation

was cold comfort for the young Berenson. The sentiment is akin to Logan Pearsall Smith's 'The Moon, that awful unheeded warning and forecast of our ultimate fate'. Edward Young, the poet-rector of Welwyn in Hertfordshire in the middle of the eighteenth century, in spite of a thousand contradictions, many platitudes and much bad taste and bad poetry, *could* cast a boy into the depths of despair; even in 1880.

Young Berenson, deep in Young's *Night Thoughts*, was in fact wrestling with the telescopic view of human beings. To a later generation the horror took the form of helmeted 'space men', of mass 'culture' and mass movements, of massive atomic annihilation. To Pascal infinite space itself had been frightening; to many a poet the inwardness of the problem had been real.

Light came to Bernard suddenly and unforgettably from a remarkable essay, which is almost forgotten today. In Berenson's own words:[2]

'George Eliot's Essays cured one of the cult of awe-inspiring stretches of time and space, and were the first to present me with the idea that art-values deserved as much consideration as those of life or of morals in shaping or directing actuality. Nothing I had yet encountered struck me as so startling, so improbable, so paradoxical even. How could such an absurdity be accepted by a boyish intellect as

[1] *Hymn before Sunrise in the Vale of Chamouni*, by S. T. Coleridge.
[2] *S.S.P.*, pp. 116–17.

42013

Puritanical in outlook as mine. It stuck fast, however, like a seed sending out numberless roots and the problem has never ceased to occupy me since.'

George Eliot died at Christmas 1880, when Bernard was fifteen, just about the time to which this paragraph refers.

The 'cure' was a lifting of the mind from unprofitable speculation about immensity, despair and irresponsibility, to the immediate and invigorating study of the art of doing things well. George Eliot's essay on Young's *Night Thoughts* professionally examines that writer's long ascendancy over the English scene. She exposes the flatness of his satire and epigrams, she mocks at his frightful inversions and the superfluous words that spoil the music and then she makes her point that Young quite lacks the art that conceals art, the *ars celare artem*. She can discern his processes, instead of being startled by the result.

Odd how the Latin phrase stuck, and how it crops up again with new vigour and meaning five years later, of all places, at Harvard, as we shall see. *Ars celare artem* is a Latin tag, unfathered, I think; a motto that was grist to Bernard's mill. It is an exciting motto. George Eliot is sage in her use of it. As for Young, she concludes that he lacks 'the living touches by virtue of which the individual and particular in Art becomes the universal and immortal'.[1]

She compares Young with Cowper to the advantage of *The Task*, and there young Berenson, pursuing Cowper with her, would come upon the same range of ideas.[2] Cowper's *Discipline and Art*; George Eliot's *Art that Conceals Art*: these appeared not only as desirable frames of mind, but they were closely associated with the way some literature was developing in the last two decades of the century, across the long stretch of water in distant, unvisited, mysterious England. Moreover, here were the keys to Pater, and to the love of beauty for its own sake.

[1] The Works of George Eliot, Standard Edition; *Essays and Leaves from a Notebook*, pp. 37–8, Blackwood, Edinburgh and London, 1883.

[2] Where Cowper in *The Task* sings his 'native nook of earth' and its blessed freedom, he stops to consider England's 'rude climate' and 'still ruder manners'

> less soft
> And plausible than social life requires,
> And thou hast need of discipline and art
> To give thee what politer France receives
> From nature's bounty.

Berenson was becoming more and more familiar with the Victorian sages. One could hardly do otherwise in New England at that moment. The Old Corner Bookstore[1] which he often visited was full of their works. He read Carlyle and Ruskin, and he discovered Browning and Matthew Arnold for himself, and gave them his devotion and admiration. Through each and all of them there was a glow of something warm and rich, an experience down on the Mediterranean among temples, palaces, galleries and ruins of great nobility and significance, which must have been extraordinarily tantalizing to read about, four thousand miles away on the rocky North Atlantic shore, in a land without a ruin, with (as yet) little Renaissance painting, and with a pleasant but uniform Palladian type of small country house architecture.

For Berenson 'culture' became his desire, his goal and his aim, and for its own sake. There were times coming in which even to write about it seemed a desecration. The idea of 'passing it on', of improving anyone or anything but his own ever keener enjoyment of it, was utterly remote, and in fact repellent. He was in love with it now, and no more capable of writing about it than contented lovers usually are. Each new discovery led to another vista. As for schooling, it was so precarious that he clearly determined to rely most on the Public Library. He entered Boston Latin School in October 1881, and left it again in June 1882, ranking among the top seven boys in Class V, Division B, in all subjects, and came first in English, History, Geography and Zoology exams.[2]

*　　*　　*

The sage's 'aim is to make his readers see life and the world over again, see it with a more searching, or perhaps a more subtle and sensitive gaze. His essential equipment is some insight that is abnormally keen . . . if they do have an interest as sages, it is largely or entirely this impingement upon ordinary life which gives it to them'.[3]

[1] See Plate II.
[2] Mr John J. Doyle, Headmaster of Boston Latin School at present, kindly looked up the records, and sent them to the author in a letter, August 22, 1956. B.B. himself could offer no explanation of his late entry into Boston Latin School. He suggested to the author in 1956 that he was taken away eight months later in order to 'cram' for University entrance.
[3] John Holloway, *The Victorian Sage*, pp. 296–7, Macmillan, 1953.

Young Berenson absorbed much from his reading of the contemporary Victorian sages. But the youth was, it must be remembered, growing up not in England, not with mainly Latin and Greek to steer by, but in a great library, rich in European and Eastern books, in English translations and in English classics. He read all he could find about Russia. His family had been subjects of the Czars (though with very limited rights), and his curiosity was not satisfied until he had read the history, passive and violent, of that country, and tasted the brief blossoming of its powerful narrative and poetic literature. The notion of Byzantium was familiar to him long before he went to Harvard.

There was one Russian tale he re-read several times. It was Turgenev's *Dimitri Rudin,* an almost forgotten long short-story, a little masterpiece on the ancient and tragic theme of a wandering Jew, gifted with unparalleled powers of persuasion, with the ability to teach 'so that our hearts beat faster . . . with endless fire and tireless striving after an ideal'. Rudin drifts from pillar to post, unable to keep a position for any length of time for one reason and another, but mainly because the verbal fireworks of his language were too disturbing in the daily round of school or office. The young Jewish wanderer dies holding a flag on the barricades in Paris in July 1848, during the revolution of the National Workshops.

'It's a difficult thing, brother, to construct when one has no solid ground under one's feet,' says Dimitri Rudin, recalling his student days with his old friend Lezhnev, shortly before he goes to the barricades, 'when one has first of all to build a foundation for oneself.'[1] And there is another passage where Lezhnev and a group of Russian friends are discussing the absent Rudin: 'Russia can do without any of us, but not one of us can do without her. . . . Cosmopolitanism is rubbish, the cosmopolitan man is a nonentity—worse than a nonentity; without nationality there is neither art, truth, life, nor anything else. . . . It would take us too long to analyse why Rudins appear among us. . . . I drink to the health of the friend of my best years. I drink to youth, to its hopes, its endeavours, its faith and its honesty —to all that our hearts beat for when we were twenty . . . I drink to you, golden time, and I drink to the health of Rudin.'

Berenson pondered long over this tale. It came near the bone.

[1] Ivan Turgenev, *Fathers and Children and Rudin*, pp. 270, 278, translated by Richard Hare, Hutchinson International Authors, London, New York, Melbourne, Sydney, Cape Town, 1947.

PLATE II

Left: The Old Corner Bookstore in Boston (Mass.). A contemporary photo (1886) from the archives of the Boston Athenaeum

Right: Lowell Street, Boston, Mass. (with the rails of the goods train), off which run Nashua Street and Minot Street where the Berenson's lived from 1875–94. (Photo by courtesy of the Boston Athenaeum archives, taken in 1880)

Below: Park Street, corner of Beacon Street in Boston, Mass., 1885, from an old print belonging to the author

PLATE III Bernard Berenson (second from right) and contemporaries and friends at Harvard in 1887. Second from the left, George Santayana; in front, Charles Loeser. (Photo from 'I Tatti' lent by Miss Mariano)

Bernard Berenson, 1887
(Photo from 'I Tatti'
lent by Miss Mariano)

He too had a wonderfully persuasive gift of speech, as he must have discovered now he was beginning at the age of sixteen to earn a little pocket money by coaching backward boys at school and others cramming to get into a university. He too was equipping himself with all manner of knowledge. He too was native nowhere now, and yet was very much at home with the English poets, historians and essayists three thousand miles away who had been the inspiration of the local men of letters in New England. He had school Latin, and a little Greek, but in spite of the glow he puts in his autobiographical essay into his childhood in Lithuania ('I knew from infancy I was to be the first in my village and it bred in me the sense of being anybody's social equal that I have never lost'[1]), he had no position of any kind in Boston during those first eight years in the New World. He is much nearer the truth when he writes: 'Not that I had not touched squalor and sordidness, meanness and brutality. They seemed necessary conditions of existence, unavoidable and to be thought about as little as possible',[2] and also nearer reality when he later dubs himself the undergraduate 'on the ragged edge of the social body',[3] with nothing to recommend him but his 'Pandora box of personal gifts and characteristics'. In a post-Harvard essay he suddenly described those first ten years in Boston as 'living alone with one's thoughts and anguish and despair'.[4]

'The social body' was a strong force in Boston. It lived on the Hill, five minutes' walk across a corner of green and bosky Boston Common which lay within sight of the Public Library (in those days). Beacon Hill still has squares, streets and houses of the turn of the eighteenth century, some with enchanting Bulfinch frontages, light airy staircases, French windows on its balconies and, still today, civilized little tea-parties among old friends.[5]

In the Boston of Beacon Street and the Hill of the 'eighties the luminaries of a slender New England Athens were still living or visiting, though their time was drawing to a close. Thoreau and Nathaniel Hawthorne were no more. Longfellow and Emerson both died in 1882, James Russell Lowell in 1891, John Greenleaf Whittier in 1892, and two hundred miles south in New York, Walt Whitman died in the same year. Oliver Wendell Holmes died two years later. Henry James's short stories were beginning to appear in the *Atlantic*

---

[1] *S.S.P.*, p. 44. [2] *Ibid.*, p. 45. [3] *Ibid.*, p. 45.
[4] *Harvard Monthly*, November 1887. 'Essay on Matthew Arnold', by Bernard Berenson. [5] See Plate IV.

Monthly about this time. These delightful Regency-style houses and squares must have seemed a magic world of their own to the boy Bernard when he took a peep at them on exploratory walks. All Boston knew who lived and who visited there.

For the benefit of this Boston and of anyone else who cared to attend, the Professor of Fine Arts at Harvard, Charles Eliot Norton,[1] gave a weekly lecture in the town on Dante one year, on Mediaeval Italian Churches another. To these Bernard went. I think it must have been here that Isabella Gardner first met him. She had a way of spotting the gifted and the outstanding young men of her day at just such occasions, and inviting them round to her house on Beacon Street, where Professor Norton, among others, especially Whistler and Sargent, and later Paul Bourget, were helping her to form her collection of mainly contemporary American and French Impressionist works of art. Berenson could never quite remember where he first met her. Ellery Sedgwick, for thirty years Editor of the *Atlantic Monthly*, describes her as 'a sun in that heaven'[2] of his own boyhood. Isabella Gardner was the daughter of a successful New York grocer of Scottish descent called David Stewart. He had sent his daughter to a polite boarding school where she met a New England girl, sister of John L. Gardner. The Gardners belonged to the old Boston families, the 'Brahmins' as they used to be called. Isabella was invited to the girl's home, and John Gardner fell in love with her and married her. He had made his fortune in Pennsylvania coal mines. Boston approved and liked him, and remembered him as a most upright man.

Sedgwick says, 'Her taste seemed infallible . . . had she not picked out Berenson himself when he was a poor boy struggling through college and helped to educate him?'[3]

The college the eighteen-year-old Berenson was 'struggling through' in 1883 was Boston University, where he is registered for a year (1883–4) as coming from the Myers–Richardson school, which no longer exists.[4]

[1] See Plate IV.
[2] Ellery Sedgwick, *The Happy Profession*, pp. 168–70, Boston, 1946.
[3] *Ibid.*
[4] The Records Department of Boston University, in answer to the author's inquiry, June 1955.
It was 'one of the many private schools which spring up from time to time'. (Mr John J. Doyle, Headmaster Boston Latin School, in the letter referred to above, August 1956.)

Into the New World

Isabella Gardner was not characteristic of Boston's 'social body'. Indeed she was New York to the core—an innovating and profoundly disturbing element in that puritan and high-minded New England society. Innumerable stories are still told about her. What she did she did in the grand style or not at all.

America loves impertinence, and she carried it to new heights. Boston in the 'eighties was by turn antagonized and attracted by this extraordinary lady who wore rubies in her slippers, or appeared on occasion without any ornament at all; who said 'Don't spoil a good story by telling the truth',[1] who loved 'physical pre-eminence, the grace and symmetry of young athletes'[2] and whose devoted biographer, Mr Morris Carter (for many years Director of her museum at Fenway Court), wrote: 'To dominate others gave Mrs Gardner such pleasure that she must have regretted the passing of slavery'.[3] Everything about her presaged the film star of a later age, her energy, her temper, her bouts of self-denial, her feasts and her parties, which were the terror of the Bostonian parents of the young men who attended them at Beacon Street, or were invited to the night *festas* at her Brookline country house in the illuminated Japanese garden. She was reputed to have a most bewitching voice. She was not beautiful. Her mouth was too large, her eyes never quite came out clearly in Sargent's many portraits of her. At her parties Italian peasants in their traditional dress presented the guests with simple food in lordly dishes; orchestras entertained the guests (a weekly orchestra, piano or song recital is still given today at Fenway Court, in accordance with the terms of her will); and when her interest in Oriental art began, there were parties to which the guests were invited to come in Eastern dress, eat Eastern foods, hear Oriental music and admire Oriental works of art, newly purchased for her collection. Conversation was the art most highly favoured on these occasions.

The most important acquaintance in Mrs Gardner's life as a collector was undoubtedly Bernard Berenson, and the same must be said of her importance to him in the vital pre-Duveen period of his life from 1884 to 1906. His letters to her, preserved at Fenway Court (the Venetian palace she began building in 1898, when the Beacon Street house became too small), start in 1887 and only ceased when she died at a ripe old age on July 17, 1924. Yet

[1] *The Happy Profession, ed. cit.*   [2] *Ibid.*
[3] Morris Carter, *Isabella Stewart Gardner*, p. 26, Heinemann, 1926.

Berenson only once mentioned her in print and hardly ever in conversation.

Why this reticence on his part? The Boston associated with all that New England means in American history, in American literature and in American character, was the Boston he valued and adopted as far as he adopted any nationality.[1] Some kind of inner qualm lest his name and hers be linked, and all the rest of his New England association be forgotten, may have decided him never to speak of her. He had his own ritual, she hers. It was not that he was devoid of gratitude. Some of his letters to her are rich in gratitude, but it was to be a private, an epistolary gratitude. We shall return to this later.

Meanwhile Berenson's urgent desire was to become a resident student at America's most distinguished university, rather than a day student at Boston's fine city university. At last, possibly with the financial aid of Mrs Gardner, it could be satisfied. Six miles up the wide and then unembanked River Charles lay what was then the small town of Cambridge, seat of the oldest university in the New World, founded in 1636. In 1638 it was named after a young Cambridge graduate, John Harvard, who died within a year of landing in the Colony and left his three hundred books to what was then called Newtown College.[2]

For over two hundred years Harvard had existed to provide New England parishes with educated parsons. For a long time the parish and its meeting-house was the civic centre of New England life. Then, as civil law courts began to be established, the old power of the parish began to wane. Strange things had happened in the early nineteenth century. Emerson, a New England parson, had announced one day in 1831 that he could no longer subscribe to the whole of the Creed, nor in all conscience administer the Lord's Supper in his Concord Church; his parishioners begged him to stay nevertheless,

[1] Even in the mid-twentieth century some three million Americans make a pilgrimage to New England every year (engaging at the same time in plenty of fishing, sailing and swimming off the north shore) to see where the Pilgrim Fathers landed in 1620, and where 150 years later George Washington's 'underground' had its first clashes with George III's redcoats on Lexington Common, Concord Bridge and Bunkers Hill. (*National Geographic Magazine*, Washington, D.C., Vol. CVII, No. 6, p. 733, June 1955.)

[2] John Harvard was a graduate of Emmanuel College, Cambridge. His little library consisted almost entirely of the works of the early Church Fathers, of Apostates, of Reformers, as well as Greek, Latin and a few English classics.

and from Concord his essays and lay sermons rang out to provide New Englanders, and among them Bernard Berenson, with a native ethical lore, filled with optimism, with love of nature and love of man, with desire for experience and, above all, with a passion for individual private honesty and the courage of one's opinion.[1]

Emerson died at Concord in 1882, when Berenson was seventeen. Harvard was at this moment ethically Emersonian if religiously Unitarian,[2] and in that diluted form Berenson imbibed his first dose of German transcendentalism—for Emerson, like his English friend Carlyle, had been immensely stimulated by Kant, Fichte, Schelling and the new German excursions into the unexplored territories of human perception and human consciousness.

Berenson remained (and one might add, mercifully for his career) free of an all-absorbing concern with German or any other philosophy. He took his brief and early dose of it in Boston, and only read a little of the German giants much later in his life, when his ideas had already been formed, and then the Germans had a mainly archaeological interest. The English philosophers, except Berkeley, he never seriously read, nor the French. Only one man at Harvard, George Santayana, penetrated the Emersonian, William Jamesian and Roycian philosophic thickets with a pretty sharp sickle, hacking mercilessly until he cut a path through it all in his *Character and Opinion in the United States*.[3] It was a brilliant analysis, but not a popular one (in the United States of America). George Santayana, a contemporary at Harvard, and a lifelong acquaintance of B.B.'s, had emigrated with his Spanish parents to Boston a year before the Berensons arrived there. He was two years older than Bernard. Santayana had run the full course at Boston Latin School, winning 'many prizes especially in declamation and reading before the whole school'.[4] He edited the college's little literary magazine, the *Harvard Monthly*, just before Berenson became its editor, and Santayana stayed on and became Professor of Philosophy at Harvard from

[1] Ralph Waldo Emerson's address to the Phi Beta Kappa Society in Harvard on August 13, 1837, entitled *The American Scholar*, is still a bedside book in many American homes. Its inspiration is evident in the document with which Chapter III opens.

[2] Harvard had already ceased to be the main purveyor of New England parsons. [3] Published by Constable in 1924.

[4] Mr John J. Doyle, Headmaster of Boston Latin School, in letter of August 22, 1956.

1889 to 1912. But the Spaniard never became an American citizen, and indeed never returned to the States after 1912.[1]

Santayana would say that philosophical opinion in America had been rooted in 'genteel tradition'; that it was inspired by religious faith, or else artificially created in the larger universities and that its practitioners, the young professors of it, had the 'type of mind of a doctor, an engineer or a social reformer'.[2]

Among the Harvard professors, teaching on the fringes of philosophy, was the friend of Carlyle, Ruskin, Burne Jones and Matthew Arnold: Charles Eliot Norton, who held the Chair of History of Fine Art from 1873 to 1898.

Berenson would, one imagines, have come directly under the influence of Professor Norton, whom Santayana describes as that 'most urbane, learned and exquisite spirit . . . descended from a long line of New England divines',[3] but there was not much love lost between the Fine Arts Professor and the student of the Renaissance. One day in Harvard Yard, Professor Norton found young Bernard immersed in a book and asked him what it was that he was so intently reading. It was Walter Pater's *Studies in the History of the Renaissance*. Professor Norton that day borrowed Pater's *Renaissance* from Bernard. A few days later he returned it, 'laid his hand in a friendly way on his pupil's shoulder, saying, "My dear boy. It won't do. I don't like the book. It's a book you can only read in your bathroom." '[4]

---

[1] George Santayana, *Character and Opinion in the United States*, p. v, footnote, Constable, London, 1924.

[2] *Ibid.*, p. 142.   [3] *Ibid.*, p. 144.   [4] U.L., II, I.

CHAPTER III

Pater and Winckelmann

What he saw was like the vision of a new world,
by the opening of some unsuspected window in a
familiar dwelling-place.

WALTER PATER: *Marius the Epicurean*

THE slender volume which Professor Norton had borrowed
from Bernard and had returned so scornfully, first appeared
in 1873. Walter Pater, its author, a young Fellow of Brasenose who had taken a Second in the Greek and Latin humanities,
had astonished his colleagues and his students in Oxford by his
inclusion in the *Renaissance* of a far wider range of subjects than
classical dons were wont to tackle in their first works. Moreover,
tradition demanded a literary method, not imaginative excursions.
Here was something quite new in the English language. The book
was detached, pagan and broadly catholic, written in a kind of
pre-Cromwellian language, and dangerously communicative. People
like Winckelmann and Goethe, Saint Beuve and Madame de Staël
and a number of others had penetrated these fields before him, but
no English writer, as yet.

Other young men had travelled abroad to Germany, France and
Italy, but none quite in Pater's way. He seemed to enter with a
peculiar zest into the works of art he visited, and into the poetry
and prose he read on the Continent and to come home determined
to communicate his enjoyment of them with those who cared for
these things. Dr Jowett, the powerful Master of Balliol, is said to
have been so annoyed by the essays that he prevented Walter Pater
becoming Junior Proctor, or indeed from ever holding a higher post
in the university than that of tutor and lecturer at Brasenose. Jowett
felt that Pater's kind of writing threatened accepted religion possibly
far more than the passion for causality of the scientists and the early
historical materialists.

'. . . cautiously as he [Pater] had phrased his views, this book was

43

instantly assailed with that hostility which greets all who run counter to accepted prejudices, particularly those few who in an English-speaking country are bold enough to claim an importance for the arts and the intellectual life above mere pastime and idling',[1] wrote Richard Aldington in a biographical sketch of Pater even as late as 1948[2]—just before the flood of art books, amply illustrated, was let loose in England.

It was not a little unfortunate that one of Pater's pupils, and that one Oscar Wilde, should have launched, as an undergraduate at Oxford, what he believed to be an aesthetic cult. Wilde travestied Pater's ever-recurring theme of a fine moderation in all things, and rendered the very word Aesthetic (which in Greek simply means perception) notorious. That was the last thing Pater wanted. When the guying began each new jab hurt him, and he gave up his Oxford house in 1885 in the hope of finding the larger atmosphere of London more congenial. But he held to his Fellowship, for he was never a rich man and he had to provide for himself and his sisters. Pater's hopes and dreams were those of a poor scholar, whose circumstances never allowed of more than a minimum expenditure on carefully chosen household objects and on books.

A pupil and admirer of Jowett's, William Hurrell Mallock, in a thinly disguised satire *The New Republic*, published in 1877, put Pater in a country house week-end party in the person of Mr Rose the Pre-Raphaelite, 'a pale creature with large moustaches' who always spoke softly about only two subjects—'self-indulgence and art'.

Mr Rose's utterances in Mallock's amusing book are about as different from Pater's gospel as chalk is from cheese, but had not Dr Jowett let it be known that in his view art *was* self-indulgence? And Dr Jowett's *dicta* were the height of fashion.

By 1881 the term 'aesthetic'[3] was being bandied about in London

[1] *Walter Pater*, p. 7. Selected Works, edited by Richard Aldington, with an introduction, William Heinemann, London, 1948.

[2] In 1860 when Dr Jowett was teaching Pater Greek he said: 'I think you have a mind which will come to great eminence', but he was 'incensed' by some remarks in the *Renaissance* in 1874, especially by the treatment of Winckelmann's *ad hoc* conversion to Rome.

[3] The term 'aesthetic' was linked with the adjective 'transcendental' because that was how English students of philosophy met with it in their set books of the works of Immanuel Kant. 'The science of all the principles of sensibility *a priori*, I call Transcendental Aesthetic.' Immanuel Kant, *The Critique of Pure Reason*, p. 42, Everyman's edition. Gilbert was educated at King's College, London.

to describe almost any man who dressed with taste or spoke well. Gilbert seized upon it, and picked on Rossetti,[1] whom he caricatured that year as Bunthorne in *Patience*:

> If you're anxious for to shine
> In the high aesthetic line
> As a man of culture rare,
> You must get up all the germs
> Of the transcendental terms
> And plant them everywhere.
> You must lie upon the daisies
> And discourse in novel phrases
> Of your complicated state of mind.
> The meaning doesn't matter
> If it's only idle chatter
> Of a transcendental kind, etc. . . .

Gilbert admirably caught the little sneer of Caliban, with:

> If that's not good enough for him
> Which is good enough for me,
> Why, what a very cultivated kind of youth
> This kind of youth must be.

Sullivan's tune was, of course, delicious, and the song was on everyone's lips, and indeed still is, long after the immediate circumstances of its composition have been forgotten.

Doubtless, if Bernard Berenson had remained in either New or Old England, he would, as a very young man, have received his share of the shafts which the Press and the publishers, college heads and clergy began to aim at those who believed that aesthetics might be a serious study, involving time and trouble, as well as uncommon reward. For Pater's *Renaissance* came to Berenson as a revelation, and *Marius the Epicurean*, when it came out in 1885, was read and re-read by him with delight. He knew whole passages of both by

---

[1] Sir Max Beerbohm remembered that Edmund Gosse had invited Gilbert to lunch with Dante Gabriel Rossetti at the former's request, and that the meeting had been a failure. 'Gilbert took a dislike to Rossetti, found him stout and inarticulate and almost immediately guyed him as Bunthorne in Patience.' [To the author in Rapallo, November 23, 1955.] But the general public who knew less of Rossetti, thought Bunthorne was Oscar Wilde.

heart. To no single writer does Berenson acknowledge such gratitude and appreciation as to Pater. Many years later, during the isolation of the Second World War, when writing his *Study for a Self-Portrait*, he says of Pater:

'It was he who encouraged me to extract from the chaotic succession of events in the common day what was wholesome and sweet, what fed and sustained the spirit, what could soar and take Pisgah sights of promised lands and yet be happy to return to the kindred points of heaven and home. The genius who revealed to me what from childhood I had been instinctively tending toward was Walter Pater in his *Marius*, his *Imaginary Portraits*, his *Emerald Uthwart*, his *Demeter*. It is for that I have loved him since youth and shall be grateful to him even to the House of Hades, where, in the words of Nausicaa to Odysseus, I shall hail him as a god.'[1]

Most young Anglo-Saxon readers of *Marius* during the last fifty years confess to having 'got stuck' after a very few chapters. Hardly any women since Pater's day have read *Marius*, yet those who have seriously tried, and Pater has to be read slowly and in small doses, have discovered in his work the kind of wide and quickly moving sensibility to people, scenery, colour, sculpture, architecture and situations, which is usually called feminine and is associated with one of the essential gifts of women: curiosity. Such sensibility and curiosity had certainly never been found among Englishmen writing on art before Pater. He works on a different plane from Ruskin. Ruskin at his best draws your attention to a hundred details you might have missed: he asks you to 'note' this and that, both about the painting and the painter. Ruskin's facts (where Italian art is concerned) are all or nearly all taken from an excellent source, Giorgio Vasari's *Lives of the Most Eminent Painters, Sculptors and Architects* (1550). Ruskin likes anecdotage; also he is happiest

[1] *S.S.P.*, p. 129. No one except A. C. Benson in Pater's day and Berenson and Richard Aldington in our day has recaptured the spell of Pater. Sir Max Beerbohm paid an ethereal tribute to Pater in a broadcast talk on Christmas Day, 1955. To the author, shortly after writing it, he said, 'I found Pater's cadences were always dying. I never felt he had really enjoyed what he saw, and then, you know, I really felt he was a bit above my head' (at Rapallo, November 23, 1955).

Lord David Cecil, who gave the Rede Lecture at Cambridge in 1955 on *The Scholar-Artist, Pater*, was also fairly complaining.

when the painter is a good man, and omits any adverse facts about him if he is not.[1]

For Ruskin, art is an escape into the beautiful, the good and the true. If artists do not achieve all three ideals they cannot be named among the great artists. The trouble with this point of view is lack of agreement about the good, the true and the beautiful. Endless psychological explanations have been given for Ruskin's 'escapism' in latter-day studies of his unhappy life. The fact remains that his point of view coloured English art history for a generation, and cast the Victorian student, the tourist and the amateur into a sort of moral (and gothic) trance, not always helpful to the understanding and enjoyment of pictures and buildings in England or abroad.

John Addington Symonds, whose writing on Italian art so easily became diffuse and rhetorical, was an inspiration to many, a safe guide to none. He passionately pursued historical settings, the tracing of influence and schools, and the deeds of the 'great', of whom he found more examples in the Italian Renaissance than in any other period.[2]

What was it in Pater's *Renaissance* in the 'seventies and in *Marius* in 1885 which so fed and sustained the spirit of young Berenson, that Pater became a lifelong inspiration? Berenson re-read *Marius* for the eighth time during the Second World War. Without some knowledge of its quality the procedures of Berenson himself cannot be appreciated.

*   *   *

Marius is a Roman boy living in a declining old country house, half farm, half villa, near Porto Venere, on the coast of Tuscany, in the reign of Marcus Aurelius at the turn of the second century A.D.,

[1] Ruskin often legislates. Once he defined four conditions necessary to 'great' art. They are:
  (1) Wrought in entirely consistent and permanent materials.
  (2) Faultless workmanship and perfect serenity.
  (3) You are compelled to think of the 'spirit of the creature, and therefore of its face more than its body'.
  (4) 'In the face you shall be led to see only beauty and joy, never illness and pain.'
  (John Ruskin, *Relation between Michelangelo and Tintoretto.*)
[2] J. A. Symonds took eleven years to write the *Renaissance in Italy*, and the final volume appeared in 1881. For an interesting study of J. A. Symonds, see *England and the Italian Renaissance*, by J. R. Hale, Faber and Faber, London, 1954.

at the moment when the early Christian Church occasionally ventured above ground out of its subterranean catacomb life, into a brief period of respite from persecution, but before the Aurelian persecution of A.D. 176 and a century or more before the final recognition and legislation of the Emperor Constantine, which made the church into the imperial successor of Rome and the Roman Pontifex Maximus into the Christian Pope.

Inevitably the moment is one of religious, political and artistic intensity and expectation for any boy of education and careful upbringing. Marius, when we meet him, 'was acquiring what it is chiefly the function of all higher education to impart, the art, namely, of so reliving the ideal or poetic traits, the elements of distinction in our everyday life . . . that the unadorned remainder of it, the mere drift and debris of our days, comes to be as though it were not'.

This immediately became Berenson's view. His own words were '. . . to extract from the chaotic succession of events in the common day what was wholesome and sweet. . . .'

It is, of course, much easier to become absorbed or bogged down in the business of the day, in its gains and losses, or its ambitions and material pleasures, than to dwell on its 'elements of distinction'. Berenson very early saw the process as a habit, which could be cultivated, and he cultivated it, every day, almost as a ritual. Once formed, the habit became an important part, possibly the most important, of his writing and his correspondence.

Marius reads a great deal and tests all he reads by his immediate personal experience of it. He never skims. He uses his 'intuition', refining it by constant exercise in whatever tasks he has to perform whether they be religious ceremonies, which involve some beautiful, some merely bestial forms of sacrifice to the Latin gods, or duties on the farm as a boy with the flocks or in the vineyards and olive groves. Pater grants that Marius is a fortunate youth, '. . . farm life in Italy, including the culture of the olive and the vine has a grace and dignity of its own and might well contribute to the production of an ideal dignity of character, like that of nature itself in this gifted region'.

It might well contribute—and in the case of Marius it did, and eventually also in Berenson's case. One day in early manhood Marius sets out for Rome with letters of introduction. He is trim and fresh in the morning of his life, and as he climbs the first hill after Pisa, a

48

small boy, a complete stranger, takes his hand and paces along with
him to a point where the road descends into the valley, and there
leaves him. No words are exchanged. This kind of occasion was
simply called 'IT', by Berenson, in his later terminology. 'ITNESS'
like 'life-enhancing', he coined. Such first-hand moments had
to be described, so he coined words to describe them. Pictures,
sculptures, buildings, as well as human beings, might give him this
sensation of enhancing and enriching life.

Generally speaking, Marius finds that life 'came fullest in morning hours in new places'. So did Berenson.

In Rome Marius is introduced to the Imperial palaces and notices
the 'high connoisseurship of the Stoic emperor'—in the statues and
furnishings on the Palatine. In the amphitheatre Marius suddenly
realizes that its horrors are intended to stimulate the sluggish
imagination of the masses. The amphitheatre leaves him 'weary,
indignant and isolated'. He has to pay this price for trusting his eye
and never falsifying his impressions. He holds fast to his belief in
temperance and moderation in all things, after a period of storm and
stress (the *Sturm und Drang* of Goethe's *Wilhelm Meister*) which is
neatly described as 'that ardent apprehension of half-truths'.

There is a discussion between Marius and Marcus Aurelius in
which Marius defines himself as composed in equal parts of physical
instincts and slowly accumulated intellectual judgments. He owns to
a 'void place' which may be filled either by 'chance or providence'.
There is throughout a kind of suspended judgment, for youth is a
'precious, treacherous and critical' time. The boy's Epicurean upbringing has had its disciplines. In Rome he encounters the Stoic
philosophy and then through the friendship of Cornelius he sees the
inside of a Christian household and becomes aware of 'a strange new
heroism'. He has moments of immense despair, but safety lies in his
relentless pursuit of first-hand experience and his determination 'to
take flight in time from any too disturbing passion, from any sort of
affection likely to kindle his pulses beyond the point at which the
quiet work of life was practicable'. This, too, Berenson adopted in
youth. Marius admires the 'wonderful mansuetude and calm of the
aged Antoninus Pius'. For Marius the Epicurean at all times,
sacred places, sites of disused temples, shrines and altars have
an irresistible attraction. Wherever humanity had once worshipped,
Marius lingers a little, for piety's sake. So does the young Berenson,
as soon as he can cross the Atlantic to reach such places.

Marius returns home at a moment of renewed persecution of 'heretics', including Christians, and in the confusion of an earthquake he is accidentally arrested with some Christians in Tuscany and marched back to the capital. After five days' marching many collapse, including Marius, who is abandoned in a small farm where the peasants watch over his last hours in the firm belief that he is a Christian martyr, and he receives a Christian burial.

Pater says that Marius had always set greater store upon *seeing*, rather than upon the having, or even the doing of anything. 'For such vision, if received with due attitude on his part, was, in reality, the *being* something—and how goodly had the vision been! one long unfolding of the beauty and energy in things, upon the closing of which he might gratefully utter his "Vixi".' No sentence could more accurately define the spirit in which the young Berenson at Harvard now began to long for Europe.

For Marius 'life was not a means to some end, but . . . from dying hour to dying hour, an end in itself', in which the disciplines were various and constant. Marius kept a diary, as 'no idle self-indulgence' but 'as a necessity of his intellectual life', to put down his daily observations upon what he was thinking, upon what was going on round him, upon people seen and situations that arose. So did Berenson, writing in it briefly, on waking. Marius rejected the futile aestheticism personified in wayward Lucius Verus who 'had come to love his delicacies best out of season and would have gilded the very flowers'; who had a 'capacity for misusing the adornments of life', and 'a following, of course, among the wealthy youth of Rome, who concentrated no inconsiderable force of shrewdness and tact upon minute detail of attire and manner. . . .' One of the best passages in the book is the Emperor's Stoic speech in the Forum upon the passing vanity of all things, during which Marius suddenly perceives the Forum grass-grown, the broken columns and the gorgeous palaces of the Palatine humbled in poor men's dwellings. But of notable passages there are many. At times, and most of all in the Christian scenes, the intensely chiselled prose palls, only to flare up again in vigorous epithets devoted to the main theme, which remains the aesthetic of Pater: that by *seeing* well, by penetrating the experience which is yours, you will become somebody quite different and altogether richer from yourself if you neglect of this capacity, leaving it untrained or rarely using it. No one can 'see' for you. You must 'see' in this sense for yourself or not at all. For Pater an 'aesthetic'

is simply someone who tries to see into and through (to perceive)[1]
the experience of his senses throughout his life, and in that context
of course the word has a very serious meaning.

Clearly this kind of 'seeing' is not wholly dependent on the eye.
A blind person who can read Braille and hear music would not be
excluded from Pater's world, in that other arts besides the visual
would be open to him, as certain arts would be accessible to a deaf
person who could see. This is 'seeing' in the Platonic sense. Pater
describes it in his essays on Plato: 'The Platonic Socrates in fact does
not propose to teach anything: is but willing "along with you", and
if you concur, "to consider, to seek out what the thing may be. Per-
chance, using our eyes in common, rubbing away, we might cause
Justice, for instance, to glint forth, as from the firesticks".'[2]

By reading Pater, Berenson greatly enriched his vocabulary but
his style formed itself in simple and far less chiselled sentences. Some
native genius in Berenson led him to shun purple passages in the
contributions he was soon to make to the *Harvard Monthly*.

To Pater's *Renaissance* Berenson owed his introduction, as most
English readers of Pater at the time owed theirs, to early Florentine
and Venetian art, to Botticelli, Leonardo, Luca della Robbia and
Giorgione, to French mediaeval and early Renaissance literature and
to the great German Hellenist, Johann Joachim Winckelmann
(1717–68), who first developed a German consciousness about the
beauty of Greek art.

Ruskin and Norton, the Eastlakes and of course Morelli and
Cavalcaselle had written much about the early Florentines and
something about the Venetians. Pater's prose fired the old and the
young tourist from England to Italy in the 'eighties to slip the slim
volume of his *Renaissance* into their pockets along with Murray's
guide.

Winckelmann was almost unknown in England, and still is.
Pater's essay on Winckelmann is a small masterpiece. If Victorian
readers of Pater recited his famous passage about the Mona Lisa in
front of Leonardo's painting in the Louvre, German tourists to the
Vatican did likewise with Winckelmann's interpretation of Laocoon,

---

[1] αἴσθησις — 'to perceive or apprehend by the senses, and therefore
sometimes *to feel*, sometimes *to see*, sometimes *to hear* and *learn*' (Liddell and
Scott).

[2] Walter Pater, *Plato and Platonism*, pp. 162–3, Macmillan, London and
New York, 1893.

'a creature in the greatest distress . . . who is trying to gather all the known forces of the spirit against it. . . . His own suffering is less alarming to him than the pain of his children who look to their father and cry for help'.[1]

Winckelmann examined every detail of ancient Greek sculpture he could find in Rome and explained (in his *History of Ancient Art*) the rules of proportion which governed the Greek statuary known to him, as well as the details of execution—the size of the eyes, the faintness of eyebrows, the high collar bones, the importance of the feet, balance, grace (memorable pages about this). Among the limited objects he examined and collected (he never got to Greece) he discourses with a fine and exciting observation.

Pater was especially fascinated by Winckelmann's early passion for Greek art, when but the poor son of a small tradesman in Saxony, and determined at whatever cost to get to Rome.[2] Conversion to Rome was part of the cost, so was night study which reduced his hours of sleep to four. A. C. Benson, who wrote his life of Walter Pater in 1906, says: 'It is plain in the *Winckelmann* that the writer has been hitherto occupied in somewhat experimental researches; but here he seems to have found his own point of view in a moment, and to have suddenly apprehended his attitude to the world. . . . Pater saw in Winckelmann a type of himself, of his own intellectual struggles, of his own conversion to the influence of art.'[3] So did the young Berenson. The success of Winckelmann spelt hope for the young Harvard youth who had 'no money', whose parents 'could not provide it', whose 'thought is, and for some time has been occupied with aesthetic problems which I must solve for myself and which I cannot begin to solve until I have the necessary first hand acquaintance with art'.[4] Europe was essential in this plan, and to reach Europe from Boston was a far bigger proposition for a penniless student than to reach Rome from Saxony.

[1] '*Laokoon ist eine Natur im höchsten Schmerze, . . . der die bewusste Stärke des Geistes gegen denselben zu sammeln sucht. . . . Sein eigenes Leiden aber scheint ihn weniger zu beängstigen als die Pein seiner Kinder, die ihr Angesicht zu ihrem Vater wenden, und um Hilfe schreien.*' J. J. Winckelmann, *Ausgewählte Schriften und Briefe*, p. 179, edited by Walther Rehm, Dietrichsche Verlags Buchhandlung, Wiesbaden, 1948.

[2] Goethe said of Winckelmann that one learned nothing from him, but one became something.

[3] A. C. Benson, *Walter Pater*, pp. 28-9, Macmillan & Co., 2nd edition, 1907.

[4] See following chapter.

Berenson was to be more fortunate than Winckelmann. He reached Paris at the age of twenty-three and Rome just before he was twenty-four. Winckelmann only reached Rome when he was thirty-eight and, after twelve years under the patronage of Cardinal Albani, during which every visitor of note to Rome would call on Winckelmann, his life was taken by a vulgar thief in Trieste, on a journey home, when Winckelmann was only fifty-one.

*   *   *

Late Victorian prosperity and industrial success made it fashionable among the young Victorians to decry the ignorance and superstition of unscientific studies. Pater upheld the values and aims of Plato's dream as the inescapably true desire of mankind, however great the new volume of knowledge might be. He even ventured to define the task of the modern artist 'in the service of culture', as 'so to arrange the details of modern life as to reflect it, that it may satisfy the modern spirit'.

To fulfil the desire for blitheness and repose, generality and breadth[1] was, according to Pater, the aim of the ancient Greeks, and he never doubted that the man who sets out to provide such fare for his fellows or to enjoy such fare for its own sake and not for any immediate gain it might bring him, would need fairly severe disciplines. Marius divided his day regularly into the mornings 'for creation', the afternoons for revision and correction ('the perfecting labours of the file') and the evening for friends and newcomers ('the reception of matter from without, of other men's thoughts and words'). The routine of Berenson's day gradually took this form also. Unlike Ruskin, Pater never concerned himself with those whose labours are vital to the community and who could hardly hope to have 'the mornings for creation', but Pater would probably have said that if the gifts to engage in such activities were outstanding, the factory or field worker would doubtless achieve the disciplines required (Winckelmann, the little trader's son had done it); but, like Plato, Pater is mainly concerned with the people who are destined to inspire thought and taste in the State. From them he expects an 'indifference which lies beyond all that is relative and partial' and a 'well-rounded unity of life despite a thousand distractions'. They

[1] Winckelmann's *Heiterkeit*, which Pater translates as 'blitheness or repose' and *Allgemeinheit* as 'generality or breadth'.

must never pander to or adopt the tastes of persons less fortunate than themselves.

Robert Ross found *Marius* 'a shrine in literature, but not a lighthouse'. He compared it to Shorthouse's *John Inglesant* unfavourably, and found 'the background (in *Marius*) merely a backcloth for mental *poses plastiques*'.[1] A. C. Benson, whose life of Pater appeared in the English Men of Letters Series, says 'to deal with a book that is so sacred a document in the spirit of finding fault with it for not being other than it is, is wholly out of place. . . . It is a passionate protest not only against materialism but against the intellectual ideal too; it is a no less passionate pronouncement of the demand of the individual to be satisfied and convinced, within his brief span of life, of the truth that he desires and needs.'[2] Benson (son of the Archbishop of Canterbury) finds Pater's insight into Christianity deficient and regrets the introduction of too many 'alien episodes and actual documents into the imaginary fabric', yet he is on the whole delighted with it: '. . . it stands as one of the great works of art of which it may be said that the execution comes very near the intention—the style of it is absolutely distinctive and new—a revelation of the possibilities of poetical prose which the English language contains. . . . Before the advent of Pater, English prose could display . . . lucidity, force, vigour, stately rhetoric and even glowing ornament, but it had never before exhibited the characteristic of seductive grace', and he ends, 'The triumph of his [Pater's] art is to be metrical without metre, rhythmical without monotony. There will, of course, always be those whom this honeyed, laboured cadence will affect painfully . . . but to such as can apprehend, feel, enjoy, there is the pleasure of perfected art . . . with a supreme felicity of the intention of the writer.'[3]

Neither Robert Ross nor Benson wished Pater to introduce a new school of writing.

'Though he is the greatest master of style the nineteenth century produced, he can never be regarded as part of the structure of English

---

[1] Robert Ross, *Masques and Phases*, p. 130, Arthur L. Humphreys, 1909. Robert Ross was the part owner of the Carfax Gallery in Ryder Street which dealt in old masters and in contemporaries. He was also a Treasury valuer of works of art for probate, and a contributor to the *Cornhill* and other journals, and is remembered as a fine conversationalist and a friend to many artists of his day. (He was my husband's cousin and step-uncle.)

[2] A. C. Benson, *Walter Pater*, pp. 110–11.

[3] *Idem.*, pp. 113, 115, 214–15.

prose. He is rather one of the ornaments. His place will be shifted as fashions change . . . it is not merely the ritualistic cadence of his harmonies which make his works imperishable, but the ideas which they invoke.'[1]

'Above all,' Robert Ross says, 'as Fuseli said of Blake, he is damned good to steal from.'[2] And steal from him Berenson did with both hands and much delight. Berenson did more than steal: he modelled himself on Marius. Marius swept him into a new world, and since that world was the world of Greece and Rome, Berenson became impatient to get there. Moreover, Berenson certainly received from Pater the gift of translating an almost feminine sensibility into vivid prose. This gift makes Pater particularly accessible to women readers: so it was to make Berenson likewise easily appreciated by intelligent and sensitive women, which is a merit. There was, as far as one knows, no love of women in Pater's life, although Vernon Lee recorded that she once found him surrounded by twenty-four ladies at tea in London. There was to be an unending succession of devoted women friends and loves in Berenson's life, as well as a small but growing number of young male disciples.

But for Oscar Wilde's flagrant homosexuality, his trial and sentence to two years' imprisonment in 1895, it is unlikely that Pater would have suffered such a lengthy eclipse. Robert Ross, who befriended Wilde to the end of his life, thought it necessary to record that Wilde was 'pathetically inaccurate' when he claimed that Pater was the only contemporary to influence him.[3]

Ruskin, Poynter, Symonds, Eastlake and certainly Sir Joshua Reynolds before them, hoped that one could lay down, however inadequately, certain rules of beauty. Pater asked something quite different from the art historian. He expected his art critics to search within themselves. 'What is this song or picture, this engaging personality in life or in a book to me? How is my nature modified by its presence and under its influence?' Pater asks, and 'the answers to these questions are the original facts with which the aesthetic critic has to do: and as in the study of light, of morals, of number, one must realize such primary data for oneself, or not at all'.

Universal formulas for 'beauty' Pater discouraged.

'To define beauty not in the most abstract, but in the most concrete terms possible, not to find a universal formula for it, but the

---

[1] Robert Ross, *op. cit.*, p. 132. [2] *Ibid.*, p. 132. [3] *Ibid.*, p. 131.

formula which expresses this or that special manifestation of it, is the aim of the true student of aesthetics. . . . For art comes to you frankly proposing to give nothing but the highest quality to your moments as they pass, and simply for those moments' sake.'

It is true that Pater asked such a student to burn 'with a hard gem-like flame', and wrote that 'to maintain this ecstasy is success in life. Failure is to form habits. . . . Not to discriminate every moment some passionate attitude in those about us . . . is to sleep before evening. Of such wisdom the love of art for its own sake has most.'

The gem-like flame, the art for art's sake (so different, be it noted, from Pater's 'love of art for its own sake') were a boon to the satirist; yet in England itself there was really little to satirize. Across the Channel a tremendous exposition of sensuality had just appeared—a famous book by J. K. Huysmans. In *A Rebours* Huysmans drew a kind of composite portrait of the poor mad Ludwig of Bavaria, Baudelaire, Edmond de Goncourt, Robert de Montes-quiou-Fezensac and himself, all potted into the character of des Esseintes. The 'dandyism' of the 'eighties and 'nineties is but a passing phase among des Esseintes' innumerable phases, *l'art pour l'art* is another, the indulgence of every kind of rarefied taste in drugs, perfumes and clothes, another. But this book was written by a man on the threshold of conversion. It is far removed in design and tendency from *Marius*. For our purposes, the link between the two lies in young Berenson. One of the first books that inevitably fell into his hands when he finally reached Paris, was Huysmans' *A Rebours*, three years after its publication in 1884. One is glad that he had read his Pater first.

But we must return to what Berenson called in one of his *Harvard Monthly* contributions, 'the muddy little village of Cambridge', with its horse-drawn trams rattling down Mount Auburn Street, where Berenson lodged at No. 64, with Pater's *Marius* as one of his most treasured possessions.

CHAPTER IV

Harvard 1884—1887

And what we mean, we say, and what we would,
we know.
A man becomes aware of his life's flow,
And hears its winding murmur; and he sees
The meadows where it glides, the sun, the breeze.

MATTHEW ARNOLD: *The Buried Life*

WHEN the three years at Harvard were drawing to a close,
Bernard's future seemed completely dark. The little household in Minot Street had not been able to finance Bernard
at Harvard, nor to let him go, as many undergraduates went, on a
first trip to Europe in the long vacation. The slender gains from
Albert's work or from his mother's varied labours could not suffice
for any travel after Harvard. So Bernard put in for the Parker
Travelling Fellowship, and he wrote his application in a regular,
sloping, very small and neat hand on a score of small sheets. There
it still lies today in his Harvard Record, and there I saw it by his
permission and the kindness of Mr Sargent Kennedy, the Keeper of
the Records.

It is given here almost in full, because it summarizes his whole
young career up to 1887. He himself suggested that he had to stress
the desire to enter the field of literature, because this travelling
fellowship was after all a literary one. The reader will see how
gradually the word art canters up. The race is a close one, and the
jockeys (for several young Berensons compose this little curri-
culum) are not quite sure of their style either. Prepositions are (and
ever remained) nasty fences, and Germanisms creep in here and
there.

The application is dated March 30, 1887, three months before
Bernard's twenty-second birthday. It begins by announcing that the
writer is intending to devote himself 'to the study of belles lettres',
and to fit himself 'as a critic or historian of literature'.

'My native language was German, but I used to hear Russian, Polish, Lithuanian spoken about me, and this sound of many languages about me fostered within me what I afterwards found to be the comparative or historic method of study.

'At eight I could read German, Russian, Hebrew and could make myself understood in Polish and Lithuanian a little. Already I was comparing words and speculating about their relation.

'At eleven I came to America and the comparative spirit already fostered in me found enough on which to exercise itself in the United States. I saw life in the U.S. with pleasure and wonder. I went to the public (State) school immediately and learned a lot from those teachers who personally appealed to me and nothing at all from mere pedagogues.

'But my great school has been the Public Library at Boston. I began to use it on arrival and ever since I have been a pest there. I drew so many books which they could not believe I read. I used to read many hours each day, even during school hours, with the permission of the wise teachers. Reading and thinking naturally urged me to write.

'At fourteen I was trying to write for publication. At first I read everything—especially popular science, then Oriental history and antiquities, books of travel and all books about Russia. Then more and more I read literature only. . . . I have endeavoured to augment my capacity to observe, to understand, to be able to convey to others what has been done in literature . . . as an expression of human life.

'I have resisted two temptations: to strike for academic honours; to abandon study and earn. I have seen the toil to which my father has subjected himself in order to earn even the necessaries of life for himself and his five children of whom I am the eldest and I have never been anything but miserable at the thought of the burden I have been to him from the expenses of my apparently unremunerative education. . . .

'I spent my Freshman year at Boston University. It was quite natural, however, that I should find Boston University insufficient for my needs and I came here in 1884.

'In my first year I took a number of courses, getting from each as much as I could, in Greek especially.

In Hebrew I took 85 per cent.

In English 85 per cent.

In Professor James' course 80 per cent. I coached a senior in the James Class who knew nothing at all about the course and who got 92 per cent.

In required physics and chemistry of that year I got no more glory than I intended to gain.

In Mediaeval German Literature and Art I got 98 per cent.

'In the second year I took first courses in Arabic, Assyrian and Sanskrit and the second course in Hebrew. Only Arabic was profitable. It was well I took the others, otherwise I should have been haunted all my life with the thought that there were treasures of literature in Sanskrit and Assyrian of which I knew not. It was well to take them, and to find out by taking hold of them I was biting on trunks of trees the fruits of which I already had enjoyed. Still I carried off 90 per cent in Sanskrit and 75 per cent in Assyrian, 75 per cent in Hebrew and 85 per cent in Arabic.

'From the first in Arabic my heart shut itself against all that was not belles lettres or art. This year (1886–7), aside from Arabic I did nothing but write and prepare for writing. I took English Course V under Professor Hill, and English Course I under Professor Child, but with less profit than if I had given it my whole-hearted attention. I took Arabic with Professor Toy and in future I intend to devote a good portion of my time to Arabic literature.

'I feel what few have realized that Arabic literature has a tangibility, a virility and a sanity of passion . . . a revelation to the Occident where Arabic literature has been little appreciated.

'I am not intending to hunt for new treasures or to edit new editions. I want to increase my appreciation of Arabic and perhaps tempt others into it by my writings. All this I owe to Professor Toy who understands me.

'This is a fair summary of my college work which never, in reality, meant anything to me compared with the reading I was doing. For many years it has been my reading first, my school work afterwards, and whatever I am now, I owe to this.

'I have not been idle. I sleep very little. Few men sleep less and devote themselves to their true interests more than I do.

'It is because I have the idea of fitting myself to speak to any age that I have pursued the course I have described. I feel some power as a critic already. In time, if my growth cease not, I may be able to address my generation in the most direct way, through the novel and the story.

'I shall be graduating in July this year [1887] if at all. What I

59

shall do afterwards depends largely on your decision. I have no money. I cannot ask my parents even to "keep me" another year. I should be obliged therefore to take what I could by which to earn my livelihood, although come what may, I mean to devote every spare minute to literature.

'This is the most decisive moment in my life. I feel the next three years are vital. I feel that if I stay here longer I shall stagnate and lose my savor. And it is because I love this my adopted country so well, and have such hopes for its future, that I long to be able to prepare myself to serve it, in as far as literature and art can serve it.

'I plan, if I get the Parker Travelling Fellowship, to go to Paris in mid-July and visit its buildings, galleries and cathedrals. In September I would go to Berlin University and spend the winter there studying practical art problems and Arabic. Then I would go to Italy in April and stay there until the end of the year in the study of art and of Italian literature.

'Art prevails in this programme because it is there I feel myself weakest. One can study literature after a fashion here but art not at all. And if I am to do what I want to do I must at least have a fair familiarity with art.

'My thought moreover, is, and for some time has been occupied with aesthetic problems which I must solve for myself and which I cannot begin to solve until I have the necessary first-hand acquaintance with art.

'In a sojourn abroad I would extend my plans to the study of literature which had its origin in the place in which I happened to sojourn, and I would continue with Arabic, Hebrew and Persian. In Paris I would be listening to Renan and going to the theatre and I would hope to have short stays in England and in Russia.

'I should be able to let things dye me through and through instead of having to swallow them. I should be able to acquire that indispensable thing for the critic: familiarity with the atmosphere of the writers of whom he is to speak. . . .

'I should employ every minute of my time in fitting myself by reading, study, observation and susceptibility to all cultivating influences, to enable me to do the work I feel I may do.

'Your obedient servant,

March 30th, 1887.   'Bernhard Berenson.'[1]

---

[1] The 'h' in Bernard was not dropped until early in the following century, during the First World War.

This solemn, self-assured, and, as it turned out, truly prophetic document failed to achieve its purpose. The Parker Travelling Fellowship was awarded not to Berenson, but to another graduate who was never heard of more.

One of the striking things about it is the variety of subjects an undergraduate could read at Harvard in the 'eighties. Such a range of choices was an innovation due to the President, Professor Charles William Eliot, President from 1869 to 1909, a chemist by training, an educationalist by disposition. He introduced gas and running water into Harvard, an ugly third storey to Boyleston Hall, steel stacks (metal bookshelves) into Gore Hall, which he then pulled down as unsafe and not proof against fire, and in his last year he presided over the opening of Harvard's newest faculty, the Graduate School of Business Administration, where thousands of America's 'executives' have been trained.

He found Harvard the little divinity college we have described and introduced the 'elective system' by which undergraduates could henceforward choose almost any five or six unconnected subjects they desired to study. He abolished Latin and Greek as qualifications for entry and removed religious conformity as a restriction on entrants.

Such liberty might degenerate into smatterings of knowledge. Already in 1886, in Bernard's second year,[1] James Russell Lowell, the Cambridge (Massachusetts) poet and Professor of Modern Languages and Literature at Harvard (and United States Minister in London from 1880 to 1885, and sometime Editor of the *Atlantic Monthly*), voiced the anxiety of a number of Harvard teachers about the elective system. Speaking at the two hundred and fiftieth anniversary of Harvard's foundation in that year, Lowell said the elective system might be pushed too fast and too far. He declared boldly that Harvard was still a college, and had not yet 'reached the full manhood of a university, so that we speak with that ambiguous voice, half-bass, half-treble . . . proper to a certain stage of adolescence . . . we still mainly occupy the position of a German *Gymnasium*'. What America needed, he said, was a great increase in cultivated men, and Harvard needed 'post-graduate courses and research for the chosen, and then the voluntary system may bear fruit.'[2]

[1] It counted as his third, owing to his first year at Boston University. The 'course' at Harvard was four years, and Berenson belonged to the 1887 'class'.

[2] *A Record of the Commemoration*, John Wilson and Son, University Press, Cambridge, Massachusetts, 1887.

After President Eliot's death his elective system had to be revised, and President A. Laurence Lowell in 1914 limited the undergraduates' choice to four faculties. Later, President Conant introduced other innovations and increased the places where Harvard final examinations could be taken to 147, all over the American world.

Then, as now, the harvest of a Harvard degree is only occasionally intellectual. For Bernard Berenson, Harvard offered infinitely more than the academic distinctions he won there in his day. He passed out with a *cum laude* Bachelor of Arts. There was one better, *Magna cum laude*—achieved by one member of his 1887 class. What Harvard meant to him does not appear in his unsuccessful application for the travelling fellowship, for he does not mention two of his activities there, which endeared the place to him beyond all other institutions.

In his second year at Harvard he began contributing to the *Harvard Monthly*.

The *Harvard Monthly*, of which Berenson was to become editor in March 1886, began its brief life under the editorship of A. B. Houghton with Santayana, T. P. Sandborn, W. M. Fullerton and G. R. Carpenter on the Editorial Board. Santayana, then aged twenty-one, is 'the poet' of the little review and a fearfully gloomy one, in a kind of Rousseau mood, constantly bewailing the now lost innocence man allegedly enjoyed in his unhoused, uneducated, unclad days. When not thus engaged, he would lament 'I would I might forget that I am I' and write '. . . Would that my thought might live and I might die' a wish which has been fulfilled, for Santayana died in 1953 and his books are likely to be read for many a year.

The little magazine aimed high. An unsigned editorial (presumably by Santayana) in the first number announced that it was to contain 'the best literary work done here at Harvard, and to represent the strongest and soberest undergraduate thought'. The editor and his four assistants maintain that 'the real life of the college has been misunderstood' and that 'around this new Oxford of ours there has grown up a love and desire for truth', akin to the same passion in 'that old Oxford across the seas'. In the days before the great scientific advances at Cambridge (England) and Cambridge (Massachusetts), which turned into close and friendly collaboration in the two world wars, Oxford was certainly the more popular university both at Harvard and at Yale. Perusal of the magazine leaves the impression that of the undergraduates' contributions, Berenson's have most merit. From time to time a Professor would contribute. Berenson's main contribution was critical, in the sense in which he, like Pater, conceived criticism, not as detraction but as appreciation. Hardly ever did detraction entice this positive young man. Life was too short, experience too rich, to waste time on running down an author or a work. With one exception he did not review what did not fully engage his appreciation.

Bernard's first contribution[1] reviewed Gogol's play *The Revisor*, which was being acted about then at Harvard. He retold the whole grotesque story of the visit by a Russian Government inspector to a remote Russian town, and introduced the reader to the Russian setting with which (on its fringes in the Pale of Settlement) the Berensons were familiar, and about which as we know, Bernard had also read a great deal in the Boston Public Library. He had already come to certain conclusions. He discussed how very slowly and how much later than elsewhere Russian literature awoke. 'When the awakening did begin in the second decade of this century . . . was it an awakening to a wonderfully glorious and beautiful past as in Italy, to a consciousness of boundless power and joyousness, and delight in living as in England; to a profound insight into the world of thought and to a tender, inspiring sympathy with the mystic and enchanting that is discovered within itself, as in Germany?'

The twenty-year-old Berenson answered his own question with no mercy towards the Russians; 'they awoke in the midst of the profound and unlovely sleep of Slavo-Tartarism', he wrote. 'They' are Tolstoi, Dostoevski, Turgenev, Gogol.

Later in life he believed the unlovely sleep to have enveloped Russia again with Lenin's 1917 Revolution, possibly 'for ten to fifteen centuries' (he would say gloomily), 'the time it took from the birth of Christianity to produce any community which could bear comparison with the civilization of Rome'.

It is almost impossible to avoid tracing the pattern of later ideas, opinions, and criticisms in these first writings. They are like the plankton of Berenson's aquarium, embryos of the ideas to come.

Reviewing Lotze's *Outline of Aesthetics*, he likes Lotze's 'distinction between our individual impressions and accepted canons of criticism'. Like most young writers, he is much less sure when not reviewing. There is an essay entitled 'Was Mohamet an Impostor?'

[1] *The Harvard Monthly*, March 1886, Vol. II, No. 1.

(April 1886), a doubt which was raised and in part dismissed by
Gibbon himself in the *Decline and Fall*. Berenson had been reading
Gibbon that winter, as well as many of Gibbon's sources and some
of his critics.

In the July (1886) number he reviewed Vernon Lee's latest book,
Baldwin: being Dialogues on Views and Aspirations, which had just
been published in Boston. She was soon to play an important part
in his life.

Vernon Lee, or Violet Paget, was in 1886 a young author of
thirty with a number of travel and art appreciation books to her name.
Her father was the son of a French *emigré* called De Fragnier, who
fled the 1789 Revolution to open a college for nobles in St Petersburg.
His son Henry, Violet's father, chose the names Ferguson Paget,[1]
and after becoming involved in the Polish risings in the 1840's,
earned his living as a tutor. As such he met a well-to-do Welsh
widow, Mrs Lee Hamilton, in Dresden, and became tutor to her son
Eugene and eventually married the lady. They had a child—Violet
Paget—who wandered all over Europe with them and her half-
brother. In her 'teens Violet educated herself wherever they went,
seeing pictures, reading, listening to music, always trying to distract
her morose brother. She contributed regularly to the *Westminster
Gazette*, and her *Studies in the Eighteenth Century in Italy*, published
at the age of twenty-four, were greeted as a classic study of the
music of a then almost unknown period. She was a true pioneer in
this. Berenson reviewed all her books with great attention, and liked
the way she tried to give an accurate description of works of art.
But he was relentless about her capacity for getting lost in meta-
physics. When they did meet he found that she had become engrossed
in the psychology of art.

Bernard's verses in the *Harvard Monthly* were few and not successful. There was a stilted one in the October number (1886) about
'the god, who wraps the field and wood in fur of snow', and another
in the November number, two months later, when Berenson had
been co-opted on to the editorial board. It is autumnal doggerel,
full of inversions:

<blockquote>
The leaves fast fall
The skies with pall
</blockquote>

---

[1] *Vernon Lee's Letters*, privately printed, London, 1937; preface by her
executor, Irene Cooper-Willis, pp. vi–vii, quoted with Miss Cooper-Willis's
kind permission.

The memorial to Professor Charles Eliot Norton in the courtyard of the Fogg Museum, Cambridge, Mass. Photographed for the author

PLATE IV 'The whole was covered with an immense glass roof, enabling the courtyard beneath to be filled with flowers all the year round' (p. 121). Fenway Court, Boston, Mass. (By courtesy of the Director)

PLATE V Mrs Isabella Stewart Gardner, as painted by Sargent in 1888 (by permission of the Isabella Stewart Gardner Museum, Fenway Court, Boston, Massachusetts)

Of heartless gray are covered
Loud roars the blast
To earth are cast
The latest leaves that hovered
On topmost bough
Where whistle now
The raging winds of autumn.

The second verse describes how he does not mind the chilling finger
of winter . . .

We stay behind
And here do find
Great joys despite the winter.

Even May　　　　might stay away
Until the day
When we of love are weary.

The reading of poetry was until the age of eighty a great solace
to Berenson. After that age he used to say that its eternities were
too familiar. His own poetry lay in his looking, his observation, his
prose, and his conversation, and not in verse or metre. Insufficient
command of grammar in all his languages may account for this.

Love, or rather marriage, is the subject of a short story by Bernard
in the *Harvard Monthly*, called 'The Third Category'. The hero
'Christie' (clearly a self-portrait) puts his women friends into three
categories, and only the girl who enters the third is to be eligible
as a wife.

The story describes three women in Christie's life, one ethereal,
'with ocean-deep blue eyes and rich golden hair' whom he could
look at 'with unending pleasure as at some drooping poppy-saturated
Pre-Raphaelite sketch' (Burne-Jones and William Morris had just
designed their windows in Boston's new Trinity Church, begun in
1877), 'or at a drawing of the divine Sandro Botticelli'.[1]

The second lady in young Bernard's story is a spontaneous creature
'with a touch of the Bohemian' and a dramatic toss of her hair, to
whom he read the old French poets, after which she would 'bend

[1] In these days, forty years before colour photography, the best reproductions
were prints of etchings and chromolithographs made by the Arundel Society,
which Ruskin, Layard and Samuel Rogers founded in 1848; black and white
photography was only just beginning to be used for recording single works of
art. Photographs of details were quite unknown. It was Berenson who proposed
them, much later.

over her guitar and improvise'. Lastly there was another beauty given to playing Wagner on the piano. She was a lady even more responsive to Christie's most usual mood: 'a mood disenchanted, disillusioned, without faith in the future, full of sadness yet full of the gladness that comes from a spirit of utter autonomy, of Titanism almost, coupled with a keen joyance at the beauty and magnificence of Nature'. All these ladies affected Christie 'in a way he deemed marvellously curious'. Christie could burn with passion, but only very briefly. 'It was no woman he loved, as he readily saw, but loving itself. . . . How could he love, as long as it was impossible to forget himself?' How indeed? The great adventure, however, was not more than three years, if 3,000 miles, away, and destined to occur in a small village on the slopes of the Hog's Back in southern England.

The eligible one in Bernard's story lacks religious experience, so Christie introduces her to a famous Boston church, in which she becomes so absorbed that she disqualifies herself for the third category. As chance would have it, at the very moment he wrote this story, his future wife, Mary Pearsall Smith, was there in Cambridge unbeknown to the young Bernard; also, her brother Logan was at Harvard, and Logan and Bernard did occasionally meet.

*   *   *

Mary, Alys and Logan were the three handsome children of two Philadelphia Quakers, 'a handsome florid father and a beautiful straightforward Quaker mother',[1] whose religious vicissitudes are quite as stormy as those of Mary herself, and almost as varied as those of Bernard. For their age is not to be understood except with religious imagination and sympathy. A century later political and pseudo-scientific 'isms' had largely taken the place of these religious adventures, at least temporarily. The psychologists are quick to label, but do not get us very far in the one case or the other. Friend Robert Pearsall Smith when he married Friend Hannah Whittall in 1851 married into glass, as well as marrying the daughter of a long line of prosperous New Jersey Quaker settlers. Hannah's family continually crossed to England to visit the Quaker Gurneys at Ham House, or dine at Stoke Park with Friend Granville Penn, a descendant of the founder of Pennsylvania.

Logan says in his memoirs that Eliza Gurney on her visits to

[1] Logan Pearsall Smith, *Unforgotten Years*, Constable, 1938.

Philadelphia reigned as a kind of Quaker queen 'with many courtiers to listen to her holy boastings'. Logan says the Revivalists went much further in physical ecstasy in the Philadelphia Meetings than they did in England.

Into the flood of revivalism which poured over America in the 'seventies the Pearsall Smith parents were swept. Both became preachers and wrote tracts.[1] In Logan's eyes they lived in constant expectation of the Day of Judgment. Mr Pearsall Smith stopped travelling in glass, though the income from the Whittall factory continued. He was at one time, but briefly, interested in the Harrisites and their strange cult. There was one stay in England in 1873 when a certain confusion (in the mind of a young lady disciple) about the practice at Mr Pearsall Smith's meetings of saluting 'one another with an holy kiss',[2] caused a sudden cessation of his mission and he then lost his faith. The family went back to the United States, to return to England later, where the father died in 1898. Mary (who was born in 1864) was sent to Smith College and Logan to Haverford College in Philadelphia and then to Harvard. A little band of pioneers from Smith College, among them Mary and Gertrude Stein, had gone to Cambridge in 1886 to claim the privileges of the exclusive male Harvard education for women also, and they called themselves the Harvard Annex. They attended lectures, when the professor was willing. Later Harvard Annex developed into the present-day Cambridge women's college called Radcliffe.

In Cambridge the beautiful Mary began to soar, 'followed by an unusual train of male admirers . . . and it was into the higher realms of poetry and culture that she winged her flight'.[3]

But her heart was already given to an Irish barrister, a Roman Catholic, twelve years older than herself, who had come over from London and stayed with the Pearsall Smiths, to write a survey of the American law schools. He was electioneering as a Liberal to get into the London County Council for East St Pancras, and she was entranced by his 'ideals of service to humanity'.[4] She became engaged to him by cable from Cambridge. Meanwhile she was attending Elihu Vedder's lectures on Omar Khayyám, and one day, when Edmund Gosse was invited over from England to give the Lowell lecture, 'when he mentioned the sacred word "Botticelli",' she

---

[1] Hannah Whittall Smith's tract, *The Christian's Secret of a Happy Life*, sold over a million copies (*Vernon Lee's Letters*, privately printed, London, 1937).
[2] Romans xvi. 16.   [3] *Unforgotten Years, op. cit.*, p. 73.   [4] U.L., I. 8.

remembers looking at her brother 'with eyes brimming with emotion and excitement', and saying, 'O Logan, we are at the very centre of things'.[1] With one accord brother and sister became Pre-Raphaelites and hung reproductions of Rossetti's pictures in their rooms.

The direct translation of high emotion into action, the immediate contact between religion and life, flourished among these Quakers as it flourished among the Jews. Mary battled for a decade in true Anglo-Saxon fashion to rationalize it all. Berenson was never inclined on such a course.

In 1885 Mary went to a concert at Harvard, and there, in another row, sat the small, handsome Berenson, with his long auburn curls. He was pointed out to her as 'the most brilliant member of the Harvard class of 1887'.[2] A glimpse—nothing more. They were not to meet for three years, and by then she was married to Mr Costelloe and already had two daughters by him.

*　　*　　*

Harvard had a great many Greek-letter societies (excluding Phi Beta Kappa, which was nation wide and literary) with lifelong membership by election. Initiation was often a painful and bullying process. The Faculty had clamped down on these societies some time in the 'fifties on account of serious misadventures at the initiations, and a society with the curious letters O.K. whose motto was *Ars Celare Artem* (the motto we have met before) had been founded in 1859 as a direct reaction to the Greek Letter Societies.

This society renewed its charter in 1860, and became a most exclusive New Englanders' literary institution with a limited membership of sixteen 'life members'. Its founders' objects, according to the statutes, were 'the practice of declamation and everything connected with public speaking'. Six declaimers spoke and a different 'Editor' presided at each meeting. The 'Editor' also read a paper of criticism of the previous meeting. Bernard Berenson was elected to the Society in 1885. Santayana was elected in 1884. It failed completely to equip Bernard as a *public* speaker. Judge Learned Hand, a lifelong friend of Berenson's, and one of America's great judges, was elected to it in 1892. It was the only Harvard Society Berenson belonged to. Its motto alone would have attracted him. Each member paid seventy-five cents to belong. It met in the old station on Holmes Place, later pulled down to make way for the new Law School, and

[1] U.L., I. 8.　　　　　　　　　　　　[2] U.L., I. 7.

then met vagrantly in members' rooms and occasionally became pastoral, meeting in various country inns until its demise just before the turn of the century.

The O.K. Society possessed a fine seal, notepaper and envelopes, and by 1861 the declaiming was replaced by debate and the meetings became convivial and fortnightly. A certain roughness had crept in by 1870 with the neophyte's duty to give an account of his past life, dressed in a nightgown, and to sing a song.

One secretary wrote in 1870:

> I as Scratch must here record
> The business of the meeting,
> With shame I say 'twas given up
> Entirely to eating.

A resolution was passed soon after this saying: 'In case of a hitch in literary proceedings, let the Society feed.'

By 1880 it had reached gastronomic fame and was endowed with good silver. By Berenson's time initiation was limited to the neophyte's paper on what he thought the letters O.K. signified (if anything), and dinner meetings were usually accompanied by champagne.

Members were all distinguished: Phillips G. Wendell, John Fiske the historian, Theodore Roosevelt, all the Adams, the Coolidges— all the scions of the old Boston families belonged—as well as three who were not at all Bostonians, Santayana and Berenson, both editors of the *Harvard Monthly*, and Charles Loeser, their friend. About the time when old Boston began to fade from the national scene, the Society died.

To the end of his life Berenson recalled this society with affection, and so did Santayana.[1] It was a great place for conversation. At Mrs Gardner's there had always been conversation and music. But this society was the first scene of really congenial male talk which Berenson met in Boston. In it Boston's brightest sons claimed him. He belonged. It sealed his 'Harvard-ness', and gave him a most convivial setting for his gift of words.

One or two rare contemporaries of Berenson, still surviving in the mid-'fifties of our century, were not members of the 'O.K.' When asked to recall the young Berenson at Harvard one of them said, 'You

[1] George Santayana, *Persons and Places*, p. 206, Constable, London, 1944.

know he kept much to himself and few people knew him. I only came to appreciate him much later.'[1] Few people knew him . . . that was true always, despite the vast concourse of acquaintances that were to throng round him in later years. At Harvard three or four professors and a dozen of so fellow-members of the little society were enough to grapple the place to his heart with cords of lifelong gratitude. How best to thank his old University became one of his earliest concerns, immediately after the concern about his impoverished, struggling parents.

*   *   *

Berenson and Santayana were the two most brilliant men of those three years at Harvard. Berenson is appreciative of Santayana, while Santayana compares Berenson with Charles Loeser (another contemporary and friend of both men, who later supported Berenson for a year's travelling in Europe) and to Berenson's disadvantage.[2] Santayana confesses to using Loeser as his Maecenas all his life.[3]

Santayana had a country—Spain—to which he returned for the first time as a young man of twenty, and was so pleased with it that he never gave up his Spanish nationality. In Berenson's case the Pale was no country, and one never returned to it. This privation was serious. He was therefore busy adopting, and being adopted by America at Harvard. Santayana was a Catholic born and bred. Berenson was a Jew born and bred, with an Episcopalian baptism behind him.[4]

[1] Mark Anthony de Wolfe Howe, to the author in Louisberg Square, Boston, July 1955.   [2] *Persons and Places, ed. cit.*, p. 232.

[3] *Ibid.* I find here a possible cause for estrangement between Santayana and Berenson. When Santayana stayed in Florence, he stayed with Loeser, and sometimes with Berenson. And a long coolness had sprung up between Loeser and Berenson, the rights and wrongs of which I will not venture to describe. The radical differences between Loeser's and Berenson's temperaments might explain much. Harold Acton, who was a Florentine neighbour of both most of his life, recalled 'Charles Loeser's fantastic disquisitions—the catherine wheels and bengal lights—he let off before any painting that excited his attention— from Coppo di Marcovaldo to Cézanne'. (Harold Acton's B.B.C. broadcast of his memories of Berenson in 1955 on November 9th.) Loeser spellbound the young Acton, but 'B.B. never lectured, speechified or thrust himself physically to the fore . . . a suggestive and ever-helpful supervisor of studies, a gentle guide and dropper of fertilizing hints, his teaching was quiet and individual'.

[4] No Jews are in fact listed in the 1887 class.

Each of these two men was to enrich the world with quite different contributions. Santayana was from the first held by philosophy. A disciple of Spinoza, he became a philosophic critic of a very high order. Berenson was not, as a youth, interested in philosophy. His gift and his achievement lay elsewhere.

The economic circumstances of the two men at Harvard were vastly different. Santayana calls his father's house at Avila 'a working-man's house', although it had four bedrooms, sitting-rooms, a walled garden and a 'wing' for the kitchen and more rooms which formed another complete dwelling. No comparison is possible here with either the small wood houses inhabited by three generations in the country ghettos of the Pale, or with the hard-pressed little Berenson household in Minot Street, Boston, with no Avila overseas to repair to. Santayana had an undying love for England, but very few English friends. Berenson had a critical love of England, a large number of English acquaintances, and some lifelong English friends. Yet it is the way of a man with his circumstances, how he sets and achieves his aim, that holds us in both cases. Both found the *Harvard Monthly* and their membership of the O.K. Society to be among their happiest activities on the threshold of life. In the end Santayana seems to turn sour about Berenson, mainly, I think, because the visual arts ceased to move Santayana, and he began to think that anyone's need for visual beauty was an affectation.[1]

Bernard's last contribution to the *Harvard Monthly* was a short essay on Matthew Arnold in the November number of 1887. He wrote it abroad, for by then, with the assistance of a little fund raised by his professors, he was in Europe, and Mark Antony de Wolfe Howe was the new editor. In that essay he says he read Matthew Arnold 'every day for two years before coming to Harvard'. He had discovered Arnold's poetry in his last year at school, and confesses that 'after living alone with one's thoughts and anguish and despair for ten years . . . it made me feel that after all there was hope in life

---

[1] *Letters of George Santayana*, ed. Cory, Constable & Co. Ltd., 1955. London, 1956. Letter to Mrs Toy from the Danieli Hotel, Venice, October 10, 1939. After regretting that 'the flame of art' is no longer alive in himself, Santayana writes, 'It is lucky for B.B. in one sense that he keeps the old flame alive, but I can't help feeling that it was lighted and is kept going by forced draft, by social and intellectual ambition, and by professional pedantry. If he were a real poet, would he turn away from the evening sky to see by electric light how Veronese painted?' See also *The Times Literary Supplement*, June 29, 1956, p. 386, column 4.

. . . my social life began with him, it was caused by him'. He names each of his favourite Arnold poems. '*Sohrab and Rustum* carried me bodily to the banks of the Oxus, the land of my dreams . . . the *Prayer of Stagirius* I read with fierce intensity. . . . In *Empedocles* I read the songs of Callicles day after day, but now, at times, I think that *Empedocles* was to me as the fatal pool of Narcissus. . . . *Obermann* became wholly mine . . . the poems are perfect in form, austere and chaste in expression, solemn and cooling—*Marmorschön.*'

One does not doubt that Matthew Arnold caused 'a feeling of satisfied sympathy' to rush through Bernard's soul, as he says. One only wonders that *Culture and Anarchy* and Arnold's other essays should be deemed unworthy to find a place in the little essay. Bernard's future was not to lie in the field of pure literature. He was already writing about poems as though they were pictures, and poems are not pictures. He never wrote about pictures as though they were literary works, although his fiercest enemies never tired of belabouring his books with that stick.

*   *   *

In his Harvard record are the recommendations of several professors which accompanied his application for the travelling fellowship in this last year at the university. '. . . He is at home in several languages, has a wide knowledge of literature, has ideas of his own and can express them in language usually effective and sometimes striking. It is not often that Harvard has so good an opportunity to lend a helping hand to a young man whose tastes and talents so strongly urge and so well fit him to pursue a literary career.' This was written by the Boylston Professor of Rhetoric, Mr A. S. Hill.

Bernard's favourite tutor, the Professor of Arabic C. H. Toy, wrote: 'His natural gifts and his attainments appear to me uncommonly excellent, and I should hope for some very good result from his study abroad. . . . His reading is enormous without being superficial. He combines in a very unusual way acquaintance with Eastern and Western literatures.' Yet another, Professor D. G. Lyon, wrote: 'Bernhard Berenson is still very young. I regard him as a man of unusual ability and of brilliant promise. $83\frac{1}{2}$ measures his work largely philologically, whereas his heart is in work of a different kind.'

These generous words were not empty. The professors who wrote them and a few friends subscribed several hundred dollars for Bernard, and he set off immediately after taking his degree in June

1887.[1] He called on Mrs Gardner before leaving and promised to write often. It was a real farewell. He was never to return to America except for rare visits of a month or two. It was the second great break in his young life.

Like Arnold's scholar-gipsy he was seeking some work that might yield heaven-sent moments, but he did not quite know what. Would he seek cathedrals like Henry Adams? Mediaeval texts like Charles Norton? To this pilgrim to Europe the names of Winckelmann, Lessing, Ruskin, Pater, Cavalcaselle, Burckhardt and now suddenly most stimulating of all, Giovanni Morelli, author of a little book which had appeared only in German so far, called *Italian Painters in the Galleries of Munich and Dresden*, were already intimate. His professors were vaguely aware that he was likely to achieve distinction in some field, but it is probable that only Mrs Gardner knew of the passionate visual appetite his latest reading had stirred in him, and even she dreamed of a literary career for him. 'My thought moreover is, and for some time has been occupied with aesthetic problems which I must solve for myself, and which I cannot begin to solve until I have the necessary first-hand acquaintance with art.'[2]

A time had come when books must be laid aside.

[1] See plate III.   [2] See p. 60 above.

CHAPTER V

To Europe 1887—1888

I have leave to go
And play out my fancy's fullest games;
I may fancy all day—and it shall be so——

ROBERT BROWNING: *Pippa Passes*

THE Continent of Europe. Paris. To be there alone—for the first time at the age of twenty-two—not penniless, is and always will be, high adventure. Words seldom catch the excitement, the promise and the despair of it, because the young are too busy living it to write it down. The secret of the adventure by which (as Henry James has it) 'things but simmer and brew in the silver cup of initiation, safe to clarify later in the less brimming, if more precious vessel of acquired wisdom',[1] the secret is to be alone, or often alone. That is probably why dictatorial governments hesitate to let their citizens travel abroad alone.

Poor Ruskin, travelling for the first time abroad just forty-seven years before Berenson's first journey, at almost the same age, went everywhere with his parents. Ruskin sulked. He developed a hatred for the Italians and then a hatred for 'all sacred art'.[2] The palaces of Florence seemed prisons to him. It was a negative start for a great expositor of the arts. In 1845, when Ruskin came again to Florence, he came alone (with a manservant) and sightsaw for two months. Then the vision came. Yet those early prejudices bobbed up from time to time, later on, as early prejudices will.

Abroad, alone, early in life, all that has been studied and argued with contemporaries at school or university suddenly receives a setting and a testing. Berenson was in a tumult. He wrote to Mrs Gardner that he had a temperature, that he was laid up in rooms that were depressing (although the address is 54 Rue de Vaugirard),

[1] Henry James, *William Wetmore Storey and his Friends*, p. 191, Houghton Mifflin, Boston, 1903.
[2] John Ruskin, *Praeterita*, Vol. II, p. 48, George Allen, 1886.

that it poured, and that those first August weeks in Paris in 1887 were 'a time of horrible solitude'. The youthful despair of ever achieving anything was upon him. Mere historical sites, he wrote, could not enthrall him, unless they had beauty as well. What should he do? He felt he had no right to live. 'All I have thought has been thought before.' He found he 'talked a language all his own. Others talked their way'. There was 'a clash' and all he could do was 'to get out of the way, for understanding and reconciliation seem hopeless'. The futility of hot argument he discovered early.

He tells of a 'metaphysical discussion' walking in the Bois de Boulogne with a *'French Bostonian'*, possibly Bourget, who had been to Boston. 'I hate such discussions, but I take great pleasure in the *nuance* in which it is carried on. Finally I told him he talked as a man who sees a vision talks to a man who does not see it.' The other man was deeply offended, and thought Berenson was making fun of him, whereupon Berenson comments: 'What is there in me that impresses so many people that I am sarcastic or something of that sort, when I am not so, not at all. I cannot accuse myself of flippancy, yet I seemed doomed to be suspected by so many. . . . So often you say something earnestly which your friend misunderstands. You realize it and that it is hopeless to explain.' For some people, this false impression of Berenson was all they ever received, even far into the next century.

He was being introduced everywhere as a Russian 'which I protest I am not, being a thorough Lithuanian'. The privation of a convincing nationality was playing tricks again. Try as one will, one cannot perceive anything Lithuanian about the Jews of the Pale of Settlement. He goes often to the play, and finds that one of Sardou's, in which Sarah Bernhardt was acting was altogether 'too cruel', so that he 'quivered in every nerve', an experience which no Boston theatre at that time could provide. Art offered no escape to the extreme sensibility of youth. He found that the pictures he saw at the Louvre reflected 'the utter irremediable misery which is all about us'. Art was 'full of tenderness for the little helpless things and full of longing for a better something in which we neither believe nor hope'. He found especial comfort in the paintings of Botticelli: in re-reading Matthew Arnold and William Morris, in some contemporary Russian writers.[1] The latter were young Russian Jewish writers

[1] Berenson-Gardner Correspondence at Fenway Court, Boston, whence come all the quotations in this chapter, unless otherwise annotated.

whom he scanned fairly thoroughly all that winter, and they yielded a long article from his pen which appeared the following year in a religious monthly, 'at home in Massachusetts', called the *Andover Review*, edited by five professors at the Andover Theological Seminary.

Harvard had done its work all too well. In this article Bernard now dissociates himself from the Jewish race and from Lithuania. He complains of the ignorant and ill-informed character of recent writing about the Jews which appeared 'a few years ago when the riots and persecutions directed against the Jews made us aware of the existence of a large number of them in Russia'. He invites more study of Jewish institutions and literature so that 'we shall begin to understand the puzzling character of the Jews; begin to understand, I say, for comprehend them we never shall. Their character and their interests are too vitally opposed to ours to permit the existence of that intelligent sympathy between us and them which is necessary for comprehension.' He calls himself 'one of their forced admirers'.[1]

'Us' and 'them'. One never again meets this unwarranted dissociation. In the course of the article itself such intimate knowledge of the condition of Jewish communities in Russia is revealed that almost any reader becomes aware that the writer has something like first-hand experience of it. The absurd pose of racial critic quickly becomes untenable. He throws himself into a sympathetic examination of the works of Abraham Mapu's *Love Tale of Zion*, *Fall of Samaria* and *Painted Birds* as 'great weapons against Rabbinism', which 'should be read before the age of fifteen to be enjoyed like *Paul et Virginie*'. Mapu has not 'a particle of historical perspective; it is just a fancy' but these works stirred the young Jews of the times 'to picture their past life and glory'.

Berenson finds the poems of Halevi, al Charisi, ibn Gabirol and ibn Ezra 'so many odes to the spirit of the nation, so many battle hymns, so many songs of encouragement and hope for the restoration of the glory of David'. Then he examines the novels of Smolenskin in Yiddish *Astray in the Paths of Life*, *The Dark Young Man*, Shaikevitsch's *Felon*, *Two Cats in a Bag*, *Pious Assassin*, *Gloomy World* ('in which it seems almost incredible the amount of chastisement that a Jewish public will bear from one of its own writers').

[1] Bernard Berenson, *Contemporary Jewish Fiction*; article in *The Andover Review*, December 1888.

He runs through other contemporary young Jewish writers writing for Jews, Rabbinowitch of Odessa, Shatzke (*Passover Eve*), Benedict Buchbinder (*Sins of the Kahal*), and a very young writer calling himself Spector whose 'sarcastic sharpness' in his story *Rabbi Treitel* tempts Berenson to translate a page of the work. Berenson finds that most of this writing is a weapon of propaganda reflecting the new awakening among the isolated Jewish communities in Russia. He thought these writers would soon begin writing in Russian, and if they did they would 'add a wealth of novelty and to some extent modify the flavour of that wonderful literature'. But these writers were soon to be on the move westward, fleeing from ever-increasing Russian massacres and pogroms, and their work to this day remains almost unknown. The point of the article for us is that it marks the last of Berenson's published ventures into literary criticism until after the Second World War. From now on, any notes he makes, and all that he memorizes, concern painting. There will be one or two other attempts to 'place' a tale or an essay—none successful. The stress and strain of the nationality question was to find its own solution— and not a literary one.

Berenson's letters to Mrs Gardner in these first eighteen months in Europe, before he purchased a single picture for her, furnish a restless, unaffected, but unsatisfied account of his fresh experiences. He thanks her again and again for the happiness her letters gave him. 'You ask me whether I am going on. I think I am—I am forgetting a good deal. But I am learning many things.' He said he was reading, but he felt he should use every moment 'for observing, looking at pictures, going to the theatre, talking, and above all loafing miscellaneously'. He knew no better way of letting things 'dye him through and through' as he had put it in the unsuccessful application for the Parker Fellowship. The fashionable hostess in Boston believed in the boy and was encouraging him to 'write'. The others, the Harvard contributors, were on his mind. He wrote to her that they would expect him to return 'a paragon of learning' and they would be sadly disappointed. Often he mentions them, wondering 'what the donors of my bursary will say, at home in Boston? They may get so disgusted with me, they will pull the plank from under me. Then I will return to the city I love so well, and as of old drift in to 11 Minot Street, until I drift into something.' But he can hardly have believed in the sentence himself.

In Boston he had seen engravings of Paris, but they 'lacked

beauty', he wrote, 'after one has seen it in almost all the moods of his own soul, under all the lights and shadows and times of day and night'. The mood, light, shadow; these are ingredients of all visual experience, as necessary to the traveller as light and water to a rainbow. Yet there is no appreciation of the gardens, the *Places*, the river, the great houses of Paris—not this time.

He was often in and out of the Louvre. Like most of Pater's readers in the 'eighties, Berenson knew the passage on the Mona Lisa in the *Renaissance* by heart. In the Louvre he stood observing the half-smiling Gioconda and murmuring:

'. . . The presence that thus so strangely rose beside the waters is expressive of what in the ways of a thousand years man had come to desire. Hers is the head upon which all "the ends of the world are come" and the eyelids are a little weary. It is a beauty wrought from within upon the flesh, the deposit, little cell by cell, of strange thoughts and fantastic reveries and exquisite passions. Set it for a moment beside one of those white Greek goddesses or beautiful women of antiquity, and how would they be troubled by this beauty, into which the soul with all its maladies has passed?'

On and on to '. . . the animalism of Greece, the lust of Rome, the reverie of the middle age with its spiritual ambition and imaginative loves; the return of the Pagan World; the sins of the Borgias'.[1] He stopped. The words had lost the spell they had once woven, far away in Boston. Here, in front of the Mona Lisa herself, Berenson found 'a woman beyond the reach of my sympathies, or the ken of my interests . . . watchful, sly, secure, with a smile of anticipated satisfaction and a pervading air of hostile superiority.'[2]

Years later Berenson wrote that Pater had wasted his famous chant upon the Mona Lisa, and when the picture was mysteriously stolen in 1912, the news was first brought to him as a rumour in the High Alps, where he was on holiday. He was told that it might have been cut out of its frame, and records that he found himself murmuring ungrievingly under his breath 'if only it were true', and that when the rumour proved to be true he heaved a sigh of relief.[3]

[1] Walter Pater, *Studies in the History of the Renaissance*, p. 118, Macmillan, London, 1873.
[2] B.B., *The Study and Criticism of Italian Art*, p. 12, Third Series, 1916.
[3] *Ibid.*

To Europe 1887–1888

Within a few months of these first days at the Louvre, Berenson cast his boyish eyes on Leonardo's *Last Supper* (or what was left of it) in Milan, and there, too, felt a repulsion. He found 'the faces uncanny, too big and too many'.[1] Leonardo as a painter never won Berenson. He had been too experimental; his paint had not lasted. Many a so-called 'Leonardo' was to be submitted to him for his *expertise* in the years to come, and every one of them he had to turn down, except the '*Benois*' *Madonna*, which he disliked and found 'a young woman with a bald forehead, a puffed cheek, a toothless smile, blear eyes and furrowed throat . . . a child who looks like a hollow mask on inflated body and limbs'.[2]

Nevertheless he found it was a Leonardo. The subject a painter might choose for a portrait was always of importance to him. Leonardo's women certainly appalled him.

Mrs Gardner's letters arrived with a seal upon them, which he deciphered as three Arabic words, *Man Sabar Safar*, meaning 'he who waits will attain'. She was delighted about this.

On Christmas Day, 1887, still in Paris, he wrote to Mrs Gardner that it was 'the loveliest day of the year, for it celebrates the dawn of the most glorious dream we ever have dreamt and that many of us dream even after waking up'—a memorable definition, certainly.

Immediately after Christmas he crossed the Channel for his first taste of England. London was tidying itself up after the protracted jubilations of a fifty-year reign. Berenson hardly notices the life of the city, the men's grey frock coats, the apotheosis of the ladies' sailor hats at right angles to their severe coats and skirts: all this in one part of the town with its carriages, hansoms and horse 'buses. For the rest, London was mightily full of the poor, the lame and the halt, begging and stealing. Minot Street by comparison was respectability itself. But the poor never notice the poor. He makes straight for the National Gallery after finding 'little of architectural interest, the Abbey, the Temple Church. . . .' He misses the more ancient churches out altogether, and he would, like all Americans, expect to find the graces of Beacon Hill repeated in the squares of London and perhaps be rather disappointed, for Beacon Hill was (and still is) a small early nineteenth-century oasis. London has many such, but they need finding, and are seldom near major places of interest.

[1] B.B., *The Study and Criticism of Italian Art*, p. 12, Third Series, 1916.
[2] *Ibid.* The '*Benois*' *Madonna* is now in the Hermitage, Leningrad.

Once inside the Gallery he writes, 'The pictures! I hardly fancied there were so many in the whole world, almost a bewildering mixture'. There were in fact just over a thousand pictures displayed in 1888.[1] The National Gallery had just issued a new guide to the many new acquisitions which, as John Ruskin said in the Preface, made the Gallery 'without question now the most important collection of paintings in Europe for the general student'.[2]

In the previous forty years the Gallery had increased its treasures tenfold. Ruskin sees no reason for pride in the extraordinary growth of the Gallery 'by the sale of former possessions of our nobles'. For Ruskin the parks and castles of England had been 'its pride and beauty and political strength'. They were 'now doomed by the progress of democracy', and one must be 'thankful that the funds placed by the Government at the disposal of the Trustees of the National Gallery have permitted them to save so much from the wreck of English mansions and Italian monasteries'.[3]

The young visitor from Boston absorbed and shared these views. He never met Ruskin, although he once saw him in Venice, and just watched him. Like others, he found Ruskin's later works 'too fantastical'. 'The wreck of Italian monasteries' was a reality. One of the first acts of the new United Kingdom of Italy in 1866 had been to abolish the corporate personality of the religious orders and to hand over many of their schools and hospitals to civilian administrators. Hundreds of nuns and monks were pensioned and sent home to their families. A very few elderly members of the dispossessed Orders were sometimes allowed to stay in residence, but not to wear the habit.

In 1888, twenty-two years after the Religious Orders Bill, the poverty of the monks, the neglect of the works of art and the venality of many isolated and impoverished priests made Italy for the time being once again a tremendously fruitful hunting-ground for such collectors and connoisseurs who might be prepared to go off the beaten track. There had been many such periods before in Italian history (even in the mid-century when Sir Charles Eastlake was buying for the National Gallery and J. J. Jarves was collecting his

[1] In the mid-twentieth century the National Gallery owned over 6,000 and displayed just over 2,500.
[2] *A Popular Handbook to the National Gallery*, including, by special permission, Notes collected from the Works of Mr Ruskin, compiled by Edward T. Cook, Macmillan, London, 1888.　　　　[3] *Idem.*, Preface.

Senator Giovanni Morelli; self-portrait, 1889. (Photo by courtesy of Direzione Belle Arte, Palazzo Venezia, Rome)

PLATE VI

Left: The portrait of Giovanni Battista Cavalcaselle put up by his friends and admirers in his native town of Legnago in the Polesine, a decade after his death. The sculptor is Policronio Carletti. He worked from a photograph. The legend reads: To G. B. Cavalcaselle, Historian of Italian Painting. His admirers, 1911

PLATE VII   'A large, somewhat forbidding and very remote Benedictine Monastery.' Monte Oliveto Maggiore near Siena. (Photo, local postcard)

Mr and Mrs Albert Berenson in 1895 at 65, Fort Avenue, Roxbury, near Boston, Mass., the house provided by their son Bernard. (Snapshot lent by Miss Elizabeth Berenson to the author)

Bernard Berenson in one of the 'resplendent chairs covered in mossy green' at 5, Via Camerata, Florence, in 1899 (p. 152). (Photo from 'I Tatti' lent by Miss Mariano)

Primitives, now at Yale), and this was but the latest one. As a period, it plays a major part in this story.

*   *   *

The 1888 *Guide to the National Gallery* is informative, amusing, enlightening. The young Berenson found it rich in ideas. Every picture is listed with its price, its time of purchase, and its former owner. The editor, Mr (later Sir) Edward Cook, who was to become a friend of Berenson's, modestly claims that it is a guide for the amateur or lover of the arts, and suggests that one day a *painter's* guide to the Gallery should be written. Certainly the amateurs of the 'eighties in England were well-read folk, glad of an apt quotation in verse or prose to enrich their acquaintance with a favourite painter. Cook does not claim that the Gallery is complete. It is smaller than Dresden, Berlin or the Louvre but 'more wisely weeded'. It has, as yet, no Masaccio, no Palma Vecchio, no Fra Bartolommeo. The pictures were hung then, as now, according to their different countries and schools. *Tempera* and *Fresco* painting is defined. Ruskin gives his views about periods of rise and of decline in high art, a subject which began to interest Berenson from that instant and for the better part of his life. Ruskin takes delight in the 'painted preaching' of the thirteenth- and fourteenth-century Italian artists, and in the way (as he puts it) 'the early Florentines kindled the dream of the Byzantine with the fire of charity'. All this made Berenson's desire to reach Siena all the keener.

Inevitably the guide was based largely on Vasari, whose *Lives of the Italian Painters* had received their first full English translation in 1850, by Mrs Foster, published in Bohn's Library. A certain objectivity about Vasari was hardly to be expected. He was taken neat.

Ruskin's view that 'the Sixteenth Century closed, like a grave, over the great art of the world', and that 'those who came after trained themselves under masters of exaggeration' was also Berenson's view. Exaggeration never held any fascination for him. In all these matters Berenson owed much to Ruskin. Also now, at twenty-three, he was guided by his private reading in Burckhardt's *Cicerone*, with its marvellous economy of expression and self-imposed condensation in order to cover the whole Renaissance inside Italy, in architecture, sculpture and painting; in the writings of Giovanni Morelli (to which we shall return), in Cavalcaselle's descriptions

81

and lists of Italian schools of painting,[1] not forgetting Walter Pater and Vernon Lee and desultory excursions into the writings of J. J. Jarves,[2] of Lotze and some of the German and Swiss aesthetic theorists.

This National Gallery guide of 1888 culled the flowers from the art essays of Sir Henry Layard (of Nineveh fame, and the friend of Morelli); Mrs Jameson (Sacred and Legendary Art), Sydney Colvin and Cook, and the cream of Ruskin. Berenson went to its sources and read them whole. The essay in the guide on what is and is not English in English art, on the 'warped power' of painters like Barry, Haydon and Blake, bears re-reading today, as well as the introductory essays on Dutch and French art. Berenson could hardly have had better or keener lights to guide him on his adventure. Yet none gave him the masterly brief touch he was to provide himself, in the end.

With the knowledge of what is to come, we have concentrated on Italian art. But why did he? A number of circumstances combined to render Italian Renaissance painting immensely popular and fashionable in England from the middle of the nineteenth century. The arrival of the Neapolitan refugee Gabriele Rossetti and the contributions to poetry and painting and criticism of his gifted son Dante Gabriel, his friends, Holman Hunt and Millais, and later of his brother William, all founders of the Pre-Raphaelite movement; the political interest in the Italian desire for unity and the visits of the two Risorgimento leaders Mazzini and Garibaldi; the revival of Dante studies and translations, and (as Ruskin noted) the break-up of some of the great collections, all these things accelerated the passion for things Italian. Scholars of repute engaged in Italian studies, and the Grand Tour, which had been the privilege of eighteenth-century noblemen's sons, became an oft-repeated Italian pilgrimage for hundreds of English amateurs of painting and literature. That pilgrimage brought undreamed-of private aesthetic

[1] J. A. Crowe and G. B. Cavalcaselle, *A New History of Painting in Italy from the Second to the Sixteenth Century*, John Murray, 1866.

[2] 'I have had a cult for him, as the first American who wrote discriminatingly about Italian painting of the early Renaissance, indeed as well as any European, British or Continental. Then there is his collection (at Yale), which again does him great honour. Few Europeans in his day would have done better.' Letter from Bernard Berenson to Francis Steegmuller, quoted in the latter's *The Two Lives of James Jackson Jarves*, p. 265, New Haven, Yale University Press, 1951.

pleasures. You read, you visited, you read again. The enjoyment of beauty was within your reach.

Bernard Berenson in 1888 would at least set out on the Grand Tour rather better read for it than most. Mrs Gardner was still encouraging him to enter literature.

But he writes to his 48-year-old benefactress in Boston, 'I am too wise now to have plans and ambitions . . . where I finally find myself would be a matter of indifference, were I self-dependent'. He wrote that if ever he had a boy, he would have him avoid Nihilism. 'A Nihilist is worse than Saturn.' Orgies of Nihilism are, no doubt, far worse than Saturnalia. Shades of his father flit across this letter.

He is off to Oxford for the Lent Term. He takes rooms at 31 Holywell. He asks Walter Pater if he may attend his lectures. The answer was a polite No. Pater, shyest of men, kept his classes small. So Berenson never met Pater, but he never ceased reading him. He wrote to Mrs Gardner: 'Many a midnight, in coming home, I took up the *Renaissance* and read it from cover to cover.' He must explain to her that Pater's style was not the point: 'his greatness lies in his epithets, in their accuracy and rarity'.

Oxford fulfils the dream of it. 'It had been my dream before I went to college at all to go to Oxford and spend my life there. I was almost used with longing for it, and I never quite got over it, although in five years I have travelled far from the aspirations I had then. Now I find that I should have been happy had I been able to come here, that I should have found a place at last almost perfectly beautiful, all the books I wanted, and the most congenial people possible! At any rate I find all these things at Oxford now. I cannot get over my surprise at the English whom I admire beyond measure. Poor Harvard and its men; it is not fair to compare it and them, especially them to Oxford men. These are all—in as far as I can see—very clever, brilliant, serious even, although without too much gravity, and well-taught; just the men whom I admire and even adore. There is something so crude and vulgar and stupid about many if not most Harvard men.' Looking back a little later, he was to be just as critical about Englishmen, about London, about life in England.

He began to revise his New England gods and heroes. Thoreau, he complained, reached his results too easily and was not free from cant, even if there is 'great similarity' between his philosophy and Tolstoi's—'Tolstoi speaks from a lifetime of profoundly lived experience'. American literature suffered from smartness and amateurishness. Emerson was an amateur in 'life philosophy', Long-fellow was an amateur in poetry, Hawthorne an amateur in romance. All this he wrote to Mrs Gardner. He finds something professional in the very air of Oxford. He finds 'among Oxford men: their learning is likely to be found in strata. One knew Theocritus literally by heart, but not Aristotle's dates'. Another 'called Milton a poor follower of Marlowe'. Another 'said that Oxford hitherto had been quite free of human interests and he hated to see them introduced! He could not bear philanthropy. I am quite with him'.

He liked the detached way the young barbarians exercised their wits. Also he was delighted (as many an American still is) to land in so definitely a man's world. He writes that he got to know 'more men in England, during my three months, than in all the ten years in Boston'. He recalls that he had left Boston 'quite the compound of vanity, affectation, and intensity to write things the public loves well, nonsense'. Now he feels he has cut with the past. Each day is a new dawn. If there is one gift all these early letters reveal, it is a rich capacity for living in the present—for living, in short.

Oxford seems to have given him a glimpse into the lone fields of literary scholarship where the tussle is long and arduous, but something inside him drove him on to forge his own instruments in his own field, not however without a pang of regret. On February 25, 1888, he writes that he had 'a funny dream' on the previous night. He saw Browning running up and down Pall Mall 'trying to make people parley with him'. He liked the dream. He had been reading much Browning, also Bridges, also 'the poet who is quite the rage called Michael Field'. This was a pseudonym for two maiden ladies, an aunt and a niece, Katharine Bradley and Edith Cooper, whose first poem *Calirrhoe* had received high praise from the seventy-seven-year-old Browning. Yet 'book after book appeared and, save by a few, remained unnoticed'.[1] Sturge Moore attributes 'the coldness of the literary world'[2] to the discovery that the name Michael Field stood for two maiden ladies (and one might add, to the discovery that when they sang of love, it was of love for each other). Victorian England would not take them seriously. In their little house in Richmond, Miss Bradley and Miss Cooper gave fairly exquisite

[1] William Rothenstein, *Men and Memories* 1872–1900, p. 202, Faber and Faber, London, 1931.

[2] 'Works and Days', from the *Journal of Michael Field*, edited T. and D. C. Sturge Moore, p. xvi, John Murray, London, 1933.

tea-parties, which Logan Pearsall Smith judged harshly, saying that they resolved themselves into a kind of seance in which they would assume the airs of disinherited princesses, tragic muses or priestesses of Apollo. It is not easy to recapture these two little ladies who left many letters and papers which were to be published some fifty years after their death. They died one in 1913 and the other in 1914, but their executor, Sturge Moore, died before the task was completed. They play a considerable part in the early years of Berenson's life. One reason was that they liked writing poems about works of art, without however Browning's gift for that.

All seem to agree that there were no limits to their imagination. They wrote no less than twenty-eight verse dramas. Perhaps they were the nearest thing to English female d'Annunzios. Their own opinions of people (most of whom seem to come into the category of what they vividly called 'the hiss of the world') are curious. George Moore they described as a tree of silver sallows by the streams of Innisfree, Max Beerbohm's face (in the early 'nineties) seems to them an angel sheep turned into a kid's, and grey in its baby old age. Yeats, Robert Trevelyan and Zangwill, whom they see at a party, they describe as 'curious devilkins', and the only figure they seem to appreciate is that of George Bernard Shaw.[1] Logan Pearsall Smith describes Miss Bradley as 'a slight ruddy, vivacious grey-haired lady, full of small talk and mild gossip', Miss Cooper as 'a rather shy gentle spinster in fragile health and one felt at first as though one might be taking tea at Cranford with little conversation. . . . Gradually the sybilline aunt would be roused from her dreamy lethargy, and their voices rose and mingled in a kind of chant, and the two quietly attired ladies would seem to undergo the most extraordinary transformations'. George Santayana visiting them about this time recalled that 'the aunt stood at the door, serene

---

[1] Works and Days, *op. cit.*, pp. 249–50. Some of the later letters, especially to Mary and Bernard, are sheer ejaculation. Some remind one of Gerard Manley Hopkins, especially this one written in 1894: 'We went to the Bodley Head to purchase a copy of *The Yellow Book*. As we came to the shop [in Vigo Street] we found the whole frontage a hot-ground of orange colour . . . the infamous window mocked and mowed a fiz gigged saffron and pitchy, till one's eyes were arrested like Virgil's before the wind of flame.' A silence of thirteen years fell on this correspondence when poems about their beloved dog failed to win any response from the Berensons. 'All is not lost, though Fiesole condemn', they then wrote. Mary restored relations, but to little avail. At the end of their lives they joined the Roman Church.

but intense, dressed in rich black lace: I noticed a preciously bound small volume in her hand and pink roses in her bosom. The niece kept somewhat in the shadow . . . on the tea table there were red and green apples in a golden basket . . .'[1] and they had a dog, of such importance that he prevented them from travelling during his lifetime.

Like the later Roman emperors they had a liking for all human 'curiosities', fauns, mermaids, centaurs. The faun in their poem Calirrhoe (Berenson wrote) 'would have delighted Hawthorne'. The poem itself he calls 'amusing, so very crude, so very earnest, so ignorant and full of the most exquisite poetry'. The Michael Fields called him The Faun, after meeting him. Miss Cooper and Miss Bradley clearly felt themselves to be vestal virgins serving the flame of inspiration. Not a few artists called on them and found respite there from 'the hiss of the world'. A modest legacy from Miss Bradley's father (a Birmingham business man in coal) enabled them to keep open house in the afternoons for Oscar Wilde, Ricketts and Shannon, William Rothenstein and a few other callers.

Another English woman who assumed a man's name for authorship in those pre-emancipation days was Charles Kingsley's eldest daughter, 'Lucas Malet', whose novels Berenson was reading. He describes her as 'a very narrow, typically English woman'. The limitations of Englishwomen disturb him. He writes to Mrs Gardner, 'It seems to me the most difficult thing in the world to know what women think or feel. One's own experiences count for so little, and women almost invariably, when they write, either would have one believe they are men, and so tell you very little about women, or they are so little creative, so merely imitative of men novelists that they write merely conventional things.' He exempts Elizabeth Browning with a touch of irony, because 'she can tell us about women's half-masculine, half-hysterical aspirations'. He tells Mrs Gardner that he is still looking for his 'Third Category' (of his *Harvard Monthly* tale). Love is still a theoretical affair. Meanwhile England 'delightful, lovely England', was a port, but only a port of call. The plan he had outlined in his application for the Parker Travelling Fellowship would still be the blueprint for using this private bursary given by his well-wishers. And Burckhardt and Morelli would be his guides. The Kaiser Friedrich Museum in Berlin would be his next destination, with a call at the chief Dutch and Belgian museums on the way. Thereafter he would like to make 'a

[1] George Santayana, *The Middle Span*, p. 46, Constable, London, 1947.

June rush' into Russia, though he felt he 'must resist that temptation'. 'It would be quite inconvenient to have to spend several years there, and the young friend from Harvard', who is to travel with him, protests 'he will not go all the way . . . to get me out of prison'.

Berenson's parents, like most of the Pale emigrants, probably left Russia without a passport, a fact which might be awkward if discovered. One could travel everywhere in Europe except to Russia and Turkey until 1914 without a passport. Jews in the former, and Christians in the latter, were constantly used as scapegoats and massacred. One way and another it would be best to avoid both.

This last letter from England reveals that the break with Oxford after such a brief acquaintance was painful. 'I have never drifted so in all my life', he wrote to Mrs Gardner. 'Not that I am doing less or acquiring less, only that it all seems aimless. I have cut with scholarship. I am as yet *far* from being a writer and farther still am I from having the means or the spirit to be what on the whole I might best be—a man of the world. But you see that is not a profession anywhere—least of all in America.' He could hardly have been more at sea; a poor wandering scholar who enjoyed good talk and toyed with the idea of a literary career. He wrote that he wanted to translate Baudelaire's poems; could Mrs Gardner suggest an American publisher who might be interested? 'I feel at times that I am falling to pieces, which is not a bad thing, if I only knew what new self would be reconstructed out of the pieces.' He ends more hopefully, 'Some day I will get to a kind of jumping-off place', and with that he takes a ship to Antwerp. In Belgium and Holland he is chasing 'matchless Rembrandt', Rubens, Van Eyck, Memling and, of course, reading the appropriate Fromentin. None of these letters to Mrs Gardner takes us very far. He says that before going to Belgium, 'I had wondered why Rubens was so much admired. Since then, though unable to join in the admiration, I have been able to understand it.' One marvels at his discrimination.

Mrs Gardner was on her way to Europe. He says he will 'write out in full' all he wants her to see in the Paris museums when she comes over. The list is not in the correspondence. Perhaps she took it with her and lost it.

Berlin looms on the horizon. 'I can so well remember when the word Deutschland made me sing, when Moritz Arndt was among my favourite poets, and now I go to Berlin with a shiver.' On May 23, 1888, the shiver vanishes during an expedition to the

Spreewald, south-east of Berlin. There he finds the 'Slavonic Wends'. 'It was almost like getting back to my old home, except that they use boats for everything instead of wagons, exactly like the peasants I knew at home. I felt a newness of relationship to the people, almost sentimentality. . . . Most of the Wendish have Botticelli faces even to their very eyes.' In Berlin he sits through four and a half hours of Goethe's *Faust* 'bored to death . . . it is *not* a play, whatever else it is'. He listens to Glinka's *Life of the Tsar* and 'some of the choruses were familiar to me as harvest songs I used to hear'. The Spreewald and Glinka are as near as he will ever get to woods of Lithuania on this or any other journey. He attended the Jewish synagogue in Berlin to hear some 'beautiful singing' and found the building 'one of the finest in Berlin'. He is reading Fromentin every night and finds him 'the only writer on pictures worth his salt, though I do not always agree with him'. Mrs Gardner has arrived in Venice. He envies her and boldly declares, without ever having been in Italy, and with the Louvre, the National Gallery, the Kaiser Friedrich Museum and the Amsterdam and Brussels museums as his only sources: 'after all, the Venetians are the only great artists of modern times'. If ever a young traveller knew where he was heading, Berenson now knew it. Still he dallies with literary efforts. He sends Mrs Gardner a copy of *Aucassin and Nicolette* in 'Provençal', and translates two of the strophes. Very soon after this she receives a heady enthusiastic letter about the painter Veronese, full of passionate appreciation, much of which he later revised. The letter comes from Dresden, where there were twelve Veroneses in the Zwinger, and opens with the news that *Lippincott's* (a Boston magazine) had rejected a short story he had sent them. 'I sometimes fancy I'll die without having anything published', he writes; but it is the last time that plaint appears in the Berenson–Gardner letters.

Now he was heading south, towards the Mediterranean. There was a semi-final halt in Vienna where he finds the galleries badly lit and too many of the paintings restored by clumsy hands. Also he runs across some Boston acquaintances who wonder a little at his changed appearance. At first they complain that he has grown very thin, and then they discover that he has shorn his locks—those ritual locks which he had worn since earliest boyhood in Butremanz, through school and university in Boston, and even in London.[1] As though to make up for their loss, he very soon grew a beard, auburn,

[1] See Plates VI and VII.

short and trimmed, which enhanced the already striking dignity of his static regular features. Whatever went on inside that head rarely altered the features of the face. Only a pair of remarkable grey-green eyes, pools of reflection, caught every detail of what he saw, what he felt and what he heard.

There is a final stop in Geneva, where Berenson climbs the table mountain behind the little city one June afternoon to arrive in time for a superb sunset, 'the best ever', during which the whole *massif* of Mont Blanc glows in the last lights of day.

With that farewell to the North, he crosses the Alps into the land of his heart's desire.

CHAPTER VI

From Appreciation to Connoisseurship

THAT first descent into Italy is recorded in the Berenson–Gardner correspondence of 1888, but it is clear that these Berenson letters, though informative and sometimes overflowing with the first joy of Italy, bear no comparison with Berenson's letters from Europe, written two years later to a very different correspondent, and one with whom he was deeply in love. Mrs Gardner, among her many talents, lacked the talent for writing letters. Had she possessed it, there is no telling how her correspondence with Berenson might have developed, for he certainly enjoyed letter writing all his life.

His letters to her never take wing. They serve, for this early period, as a record of places seen, people met, and above all for the glimpses they give us of how the child of Pater gradually becomes an adult disciple of Giovanni Morelli, and thereby begins to engage in the professional pleasure of identifying painters and schools of painting. This is a step which many European amateurs take, somewhat vaguely, so that after a time they are at least able, despite various errors, to identify Dutch, French, German and Italian classical schools of painting. In any case the museums of the world do this for the amateurs. Travel, attention and habit endorse the arrangements of the museums, and in time the amateur who looks at the walls of a room at all (and how few people do!) is able to recognize there the originals or the reproductions of groups and periods of painting with which he is familiar. And because drawing and painting are the most ancient and the most constant records of humanity everywhere from prehistoric to post-atomic ages, the amateur who reaches this stage in the visual arts often finds himself on the threshold of new worlds and new experiences denied to those whose eyes never stray upwards from the immediate business in hand.

In the autumn of 1888 at the very moment in Berenson's life when appreciation alone was no longer an adequate activity and the identification of masterpieces began to exercise the mind, he met the man whom he was to acknowledge as his master, whose book on the Italian paintings in the Dresden Gallery he had read in Boston, and whose studies in connoisseurship had already won him international fame. Senator Giovanni Morelli[1] was seventy-two in 1888, and his friend and one-time secretary, Giovanni Battista Cavalcaselle,[2] whom Berenson also met that year, was sixty-eight and occupying the position of National Inspector of Fine Arts in Italy. Undoubtedly these two men gave Berenson the first notion that one might become professionally equipped for connoisseurship. Mary Berenson, looking back on this moment of his life, records that this meeting with them in Rome turned Bernard 'from a passionate amateur into a young professional'.

Sir Henry Layard, the discoverer of Nineveh (in 1845), a man of many parts, scholar, archaeologist, diplomatist and M.P. for South-wark, has left us a vivid portrait of Giovanni Morelli. They were friends for nearly forty years. They met some time in the late 1850s in the house of Sir James Hudson the British Minister in Turin, where the British Legation had become a meeting-place for Cavour and his friends, among them Morelli, of whom Layard says:

'. . . he had no taste for politics which in Italy at that time, and perhaps necessarily comprised intrigues and conspiracies repugnant to a man of his upright and honourable character. He turned to art as a solace and a source of inspiration to divert his thoughts from the sufferings of his native land under the cruel rule of the stranger. He devoted himself to its study with the earnestness and thorough-ness of the German, and the acuteness and imagination of the Italian.'[3]

Morelli had studied medicine in Berlin as a young man, excelling in comparative anatomy classes held by the then Rector, Professor Bollinger. Morelli came from a Venetian Protestant family which had fled the counter-reformation and settled in France. Early in the nineteenth century Morelli's father returned to Venetia and settled in Verona, where he married a Protestant lady from Bergamo. In that twin city, half hill half valley town, Giovanni Morelli was brought up and later settled. Today his collection of paintings which

---

[1] See Plate VI.   [2] See Plate VI. (Portrait of Cavalcaselle.)

[3] *Italian Painters*, by Giovanni Morelli, translated by C. J. Foulkes. John Murray, London 1892–3; Preface by Sir Henry Layard.

he left to Bergamo is one of the glories of the little place. His six years in Berlin made him bilingual, and all his books were written and published first in German. In Berlin he used sometimes to pose for German sculptors. One of his many friends was Goethe's late passion, Bettina von Arnim. Morelli even had a link with Harvard, for some time in the 1840's he accompanied the Swiss-born naturalist, Jean-Louis Agassiz, on some of his expeditions on the Swiss alpine glaciers, and Agassiz was later to emigrate with his brother to Boston and to found there the great Natural History Museum at Harvard which still bears their name, and the faculty of Natural Sciences of which Jean-Louis held the first chair.

Morelli took a vigorous part in the Italian Liberation struggle of 1848. He raised a corps of volunteers in Bergamo to help expel the Austrians from Lombardy. At their head he stormed one of Milan's city gates and was immediately chosen by the Liberation Committee of the day to represent Milan in negotiations with the Austrians. Off he went to the Diet in Frankfurt, where in between negotiations he wrote and circulated a wonderfully modern little pamphlet called *Worte eines Lombarden an die Deutschen*. In it he recalled the days when the wars of religion divided the peoples of Europe, 'though Raphael remained in friendly correspondence with Dürer, and Galileo with Keppler'. And he predicted what we in our equally harshly divided world may yet find, that though savage instincts divide peoples, art, science and commerce will eventually unite them.

Shortly after Layard first met Morelli war again broke out against Austria, and again (in 1865) Morelli was in the ranks of the Italian Volunteer Army, fighting hard in the Valtellina Valley, where Layard joined him, much as English volunteers seventy years later were to be found in the trenches round besieged republican Madrid.

There is something attractive in the vigorous participation of these studious archaeologists and art historians in the living history of their day. That other great pioneer in the study of Italian painting, also a citizen of Venetia, Giovanni Battista Cavalcaselle,[1] was of the same fibre. Nor was he brought up for a career in art matters. He was trained as an engineer. He was twenty-eight when the Venetian patriot Daniel Manin rallied the Venetians in 1849 to throw the Austrians out of their lagoons and their mainland. He too fought that day. The struggle lasted four months and ended in temporary defeat. Cavalcaselle was captured by the Austrians in

[1] Plate VI.

Piacenza and sentenced to death with four others. When three had already been shot a band of Italian patriots arrived and rescued Cavalcaselle. He then joined up with Garibaldi, was again captured and taken to Paris, where an Englishman, Joseph Archer Crowe, whom he had first met on a German tour two years before, came upon him in conditions of great poverty. Crowe was the son of an English journalist in Paris, and made a little income that way himself. Like Ruskin, Crowe had developed a talent for copying (Flemish) paintings in line drawings before the days of photography, and he travelled for the pleasure of visiting pictures. Crowe took Cavalcaselle to London in 1850. They worked in one room in Silver Street off Piccadilly. They visited the National Gallery and private collections, they read in libraries, argued and debated acrimoniously about the authorship of Flemish and Italian paintings until one or other yielded—usually it was Crowe—and then Crowe wrote down their conclusions. Although they hardly knew it, they were engaged on giving the world a new Vasari, checked and counterchecked in the light of subsequent knowledge, inevitably with a good deal less liveliness than the passionately partisan Tuscan had employed. None had yet made reliable lists of the Flemish schools.

Their room contained a large round table and three chairs, two candles and no fire. They would sit heavily wrapped in winter, occasionally visited by Sir Charles Eastlake, then President of the Royal Academy, and after 1855 Director of the National Gallery. There was an evening, a year after Crowe and Cavalcaselle had set up their joint household, when everything gave out: no tea, no bread, no food indeed since supper the night before. They went to bed hungry and woke up very early. They went into Kensington Gardens and a beggar joined them, complaining that he had had no breakfast, and they all laughed together.

Their work has many references in it to Morelli (as his works have to their volumes), for Cavalcaselle and Morelli had this in common, they both were amazed at the false and mistaken attributions of Italian and other pictures in Europe. Faked pictures went under the titles of Raphaels and Leonardos; Botticelli went unrecognized; most of the famous Venetians which are household names today (the Bellinis, Giorgione, Lotto, Pordenone, Bonifazio) were not even identified. Many of the pictures were dirty. Many were shockingly restored. When Morelli had finished his studies in the Dresden Gallery and published his first book on his findings, the

Director of that Gallery accepted forty-eight out of Morelli's fifty new attributions. His method carried conviction. He had the brilliant idea of using his anatomical studies at Berlin University. He describes his method in detail accompanied by his own drawings. He takes some anatomical or some drapery or some landscape feature in the authenticated picture of a master; in the case of Botticelli, for example, 'the hand, with bony fingers . . . the nails, square, with black outline; the nose with dilated nostrils'; or in the case of Sebastiano del Piombo (the contemporary of Raphael and the protégé of Michelangelo, whose works present the connoisseur, even today, with occasional problems of attribution), the ear, which Morelli sketches in all its unanatomical simplicity,[1] or he draws the ball of Titian's thumbs as another and a very useful point of reference when dealing with a doubtful Titian. How the folds of drapery fall, how haloes are set, how landscape is used by different painters: these and many other details Morelli used and memorized as data to help him in attributing and in identifying the proper authorship of masterpieces.

Morelli rarely accepted the signatures on Italian Renaissance paintings. He had found that 'many signatures were inscribed on paintings even centuries ago with intent to deceive'.[2]

Even documentary evidence from the archives of Europe he found at best could only apply to large paintings ordered by the Church or by princes, and still he quotes many instances in which such ancient documents had been wrongly interpreted or forged.

Morelli was a well-to-do man. He never needed to earn a living. He engaged in his researches and published his books for the sheer love of the thing, to get at the truth. He did of course buy and occasionally sell pictures. So rare is sound knowledge of painting and so active the market in pictures, that a good reputation once formed is constantly in demand. The connoisseur also has other talents, else there would be many more connoisseurs than there are. Cavalcaselle, for instance, never moved in the kind of drawing-rooms or auction rooms in which classical pictures change hands. One imagines Cavalcaselle (from a fine statue of him in the little town of Legnago in Venetia whence he came) as the Martha rather than the Mary of art, the erudite art historian faithfully concerned with the subject of a picture; the painter's age and patrons; by whom the painter was influenced and whom he in turn influenced—the whole study to be

[1] *Italian Painters, ed. cit.*, p. 44.   [2] *Idem.*, p. 45.

as well documented as possible, preferably from contemporary sources. Cavalcaselle left London in 1857 with a travel allowance from John Murray the publisher, who was so delighted with the volume on the Early Flemish Painters that he asked Cavalcaselle to bring out a new and annotated edition of Vasari. The allowance ceased in 1863 and Cavalcaselle then had no other visible means of support. He became Morelli's secretary on a Fine Arts Commission, set up by the very young and very new Italian Government, to list outstanding works of art in Italian galleries, collections and churches. Together they travelled all over the Abruzzi and the Marches and elsewhere, discovering paintings and frescoes which had not been visited for centuries.

Then Cavalcaselle was appointed Chief Inspector of Fine Arts in Italy, and devoted himself to tidying up some of the galleries and recommending the hanging of pictures in schools as he had seen them hung in London. He died in harness almost unnoticed. Years later, in 1911, when a statue was put up in his honour, Adolfo Venturi, the great Italian art historian, recalled that he had been a lone mourner at Cavalcaselle's funeral. Today no student of Italian painting can embark on his studies without consulting 'Crowe and Cavalcaselle'. It should be 'Cavalcaselle and Crowe', for Crowe neither had the talents nor the time to devote his life to these studies. He joined *The Times* with a recommendation from Thackeray, and reported the Crimean War in 1852–4. Then he went to Bombay for *The Times* and also taught in an art school there which had been opened by the Bombay philanthropist Sir Jamsetjee Jeejeebhoy. Crowe was back in Europe at the Battle of Solferino, still reporting for *The Times*, after which he married a well-to-do German lady, was knighted and ended up as Consul-General in Leipzig and then as Commercial Attaché for the whole of Central Europe, until his death in 1896. In his leisure hours he remained the faithful translator of Cavalcaselle, to whom the credit for the enormous labour of research and the many journeys to visit remote pictures must be given. Their three-volume work, *The New History of Painting in Italy from the Second to the Sixteenth Century*, grew in size under successive editors (Arthur Strong, Langton Douglas, Tancred Borenius). Of course it is dull, heavy reading. It was meant to be a reference book, and so it still is.

*   *   *

It was necessary to dwell on these two giants of Italian art history.

Of the gay, popular, sociable Morelli, Berenson used to say that connoisseurship owed him a method but that he lacked a 'psychology' in that method and therefore made a good few mistakes which too strict adherence to a method usually brings in its train. When Berenson began regularly consulting Crowe and Cavalcaselle's *New History* he was suddenly amazed at how much of the ground he had covered had already been travelled over by the Italian Inspector of Fine Arts, and with the same results in new attributions.

In Rome that autumn and winter of 1888 Berenson's funds were low and no more were likely to arrive from the donors of his bursary. Berenson often lunched off a few chestnuts, 'which I not only appreciated for the nourishment they brought but because they warmed my hands'.[1] In the remote unmotorized small Rome of 1888 living was cheap; a halfpenny would buy a cup of coffee. For a few pence Bernard rented a trestle bed in a painter's studio.[2]

He walked the city from end to end every day, looking inside most of its four hundred churches, and all its galleries and museums. In the evenings he joined a group of young Scandinavian students in a famous old courtyard tavern which still exists in the Via della Croce, the *Concordia*. There, too, was an Englishman by the name of Davis with whom he explored the Campagna on foot. They walked whole days and very fast, as was Berenson's habit.

He read the Goncourts' *Journal*, the first volume of which was just out, and he was excited by what he called their rediscovery of the French eighteenth century, and even more by the way they recorded their discovery of the 'gold-background' panels, the Italian primitives and the fifteenth-century frescoes, at a moment when the primitives could hardly have been more unfashionable.

England is such a literary country that the Goncourts are usually put into a niche labelled 'Precursors of the Realist Novel' and their *Journals* are forgotten. But these brothers had devoted their earliest writings (mainly in articles in *Eclair* and in *Paris*) to the cathedrals and mediaeval buildings of France, to Flemish and then to Italian primitives. In Florence churches and galleries they liked 'contemplating those women, their long necks, their foreheads rounded with innocence . . . the ardent copper of the hair streaked by the brush with gold light, those pale complexions which have blossomed in the shade, . . . those fluted suffering hands where wax-light plays'. After

[1] *Corriere della Sera*, 'Diario Romano', 1953, article by Bernard Berenson.
[2] *Ibid.*

reading that in the *Journals*, Frenchmen went to look again and so did Berenson. One has to see the Goncourts as pioneers in a world still governed by the pseudo-classical taste of the Napoleonic age, revived and reinstated for the Second Empire.

The important thing is to be spurred to new artistic enjoyments by a book or an article. The Goncourts gave the spur with their *Journals*. One looked at Giotto, Orcagna, Pietro Lorenzetti, Fra Angelico and Masaccio with a new eye after reading them. There was no better road towards yet further discoveries which Berenson himself was to add to those periods of Italian painting.

In England even more than in France the period was scorned. Ruskin as early as 1843 had recommended the purchase of several Italian primitives to the Director of the National Gallery, and the Director consulted the then First Lord of the Treasury, Sir Robert Peel, who remarked 'I think we should not collect curiosities'. But the Prince Consort quietly collected them.

In Florence, in the middle of the century, Walter Savage Landor had purchased a few primitives, not because he particularly liked them but from an artist's fellow-feeling for a work of art: he had found Italian carpenters hacking them into tables and boxes. The American J. J. Jarves bought some from Landor and others wherever he could find them, and tried to sell them to Harvard, but he met with fierce opposition from Charles Eliot Norton. The unpublished correspondence of Norton and Jarves on this subject is in the archives of the Athenaeum Library in Boston. The Jarves collection went to Yale, where it is one of the glories of that university.

*   *   *

That year and the next Berenson covered the Italian peninsula from north to south, writing every few weeks to Mrs Gardner. Financial help seems to have come from Charles Loeser with whom he began to travel to Spain and to Germany again and back to Italy. Mrs Gardner wrote back encouragingly. Her letters, he writes, gave him a new assurance. One is sure that they did. But the true assurance came from knowledge and from the inspiration of his meetings with Morelli and Cavalcaselle. Within a year of that meeting he was back in Bergamo, this time with a young friend he had picked up the year before in Florence, 'half Peruvian, half Genoese, with a slim long face . . . fine black eyes, black hair too and of course a dark complexion' called Enrico Costa. In Morelli's home town the two young men sit down at a small café table and Berenson says:

'You see, Enrico, nobody before us has dedicated his entire activity, his entire life, to connoisseurship. Others have taken to it as a relief from politics, as in the case of Morelli and Minghetti, others still because they were museum officials, still others because they were teaching art history. We are the first to have no idea before us, no ambition, no expectation, no thought of reward. We shall give ourselves up to learning, to distinguish between the authentic works of an Italian painter of the fifteenth or sixteenth century, and those commonly ascribed to him. Here at Bergamo, and in all the fragrant and romantic valleys that branch out northward, we must not stop till we are sure that every Lotto is a Lotto, every Cariani a Cariani; every Previtali a Previtali, every Santa Croce a Santa Croce; and that we know to whom of the several Santa Croce's a picture is to be attributed, etc. etc.'[1]

This was precisely what Morelli had hoped to achieve in his visits to the Dresden gallery and to the Borghese collection in Rome. The young Harvard Morellian was in 1889 outmastering the master in his ambitions, and is quick (in recollection) to say so. 'Luckily', writes Berenson, 'one's daimon, one's will to grow to achieve, to serve, knew better, and before long I was writing the *Venetian Painters*, my *Lorenzo Lotto*, and earlier than either, an essay on *Rudiments of Connoisseurship*'. Undoubtedly the reading of Morelli and then the meeting with him in 1888 inspired Berenson's essay on *Connoisseurship*, his first original work.

It appeared in 1902 as the ninth essay in Berenson's *Study and Criticism of Italian Art* (Second Series). It should be read after reading Morelli's two volumes of *Critical Studies of Italian Painters*. There is its source and its inspiration. There, too, the frequent use of a painter's drawings, as an aid to identification. Morelli used drawings long before Berenson finally embarked upon the *Drawings of the Florentine Painters*, which was to turn him into 'an expert'.

In 1890 Berenson returned to London. Already connoisseurship was claiming a big share of his spontaneous enjoyment of art.

[1] *S.S.P.*, p. 51.

CHAPTER VII

Love, Conversion and an Income

> I have remarked how, in the process of our brain-
> building, as the house of thought in which we live
> gets itself together like some airy bird's nest of
> floating thistle-down and chance straws, compact
> at last, little accidents have their consequence; and
> thus it happened that, as he walked one evening,
> a garden gate, usually closed, stood open; and lo!
> within a great red hawthorn in full flower . . .
>
> WALTER PATER, *The Child in the House*

IN the spring of 1890, in London, Berenson posted a letter of
introduction to no less a lady than 'H. W. S.', author of *The
Christian's Secret to the Happy Life*, a pamphlet which had sold
over a million copies. When her son, Logan Pearsall Smith, composed
a brief introduction to some of his mother's remarkable letters in the
1930s, he wrote of her pamphlet that 'thousands of copies were still
being printed every year'. The Pearsall Smiths had returned to
England after the rather precipitate retreat in 1873[1] with no other
purpose than to be near their grandchildren and to provide a home
for their son Logan, who vastly preferred living in England, and
their daughter Alys, who attended lectures at Oxford. The parents'
Mission days were over. The income from the glass factory in
Philadelphia continued. They had bought a pretty house called
'Friday's Hill' at Fernhurst near Haslemere, and their daughter
Mary, the wife of Frank Costelloe, was often down at week-ends
with her baby daughters Ray and Karen.[2] To 'Friday's Hill' Berenson
was invited for the Easter week-end, 1890, and it was as English as
only Americans of English descent knew how to make it. The tall,
handsome and forthright Philadelphia Quaker mother had confessed
to a passion for the English aristocracy. In England she visited

[1] See above, p. 67.
[2] Ray married Oliver Strachey and Karen married Adrian Stephen, Virginia
Woolf's brother.

99

Lady Pembroke, Lady Lothian and Lady Brownlow, and in a letter to American friends in 1886 she wrote, 'I frankly confess if I *lived* in England, I should want to belong to the aristocracy'.[1] When, very soon after, she came to settle in Sussex, the most important local friends and guests were writers and artists. Apart from the Quaker aristocracy the only member of the English aristocracy who regularly frequented the house was Bertrand Russell, who was to become her son-in-law when he married Alys Pearsall Smith.

One old neighbour whom Mrs Pearsall Smith visited was Lord Tennyson the poet. She had visited him earlier in the Isle of Wight with an introduction from Walt Whitman. On the road to Fernhurst a very quiet trio of artists, Beardsley, Conder and Henley the poet shared a cottage. To acquire ferocity they called themselves the Hellfire Club and sometimes visited at 'Friday's Hill' at week-ends. Another visitor was Vernon Lee.[2] Her books and essays had won her some fame and she herself was the centre of a large circle of friends and acquaintants, historians, literary people, art critics, with whom she corresponded (as was the custom of the day) by telegraph. Nevertheless she would sometimes refer impatiently to them (in letters to her mother) as 'a boring little clique' or 'rather seedy art-critical people', even though they included Gosse, D. S. MacColl, Garnett, the Humphry Wards, Millais, Leighton, Allan Monkhouse, Leslie Stephen, Burne-Jones, the Rossettis, Henry James, who 'fathered' her for some years, the 'Michael Fields', the Tennants, Eugenie Sellars, who married Arthur Strong and herself became the famous Roman archaeologist, Librarian and Assistant Director of the British School in Rome, the Quaker Gurneys and the Quaker Pearsall Smiths. Vernon Lee's friends and often her hosts in London in the 'eighties were Walter Pater and his sisters. But she did not introduce Berenson to them. Time and again she complained that her London

---

[1] Logan Pearsall Smith, *A Religious Rebel*, p. 87, Nisbet, 1949. In one of her books (*The Unselfishness of God*) Mary's mother recorded that as a girl she read a book called *The Earl's Daughter*, by Grace Aguilar, and 'to my young American and Quaker mind an Earl was more like an archangel than a man, and to be an Earl's daughter was almost akin to being a daughter of heaven. And to this day, in spite of all the disillusions that life has brought me about earls and their daughters, the old sense of grandeur that filled my soul with awe . . . so long ago, never fails to come back for at least a moment when earls and countesses are mentioned in my presence.' It was an attitude shared in part by her daughter Mary, and by Bernard. Royalty especially exercised his curiosity greatly.   [2] See p. 64, above.

days were rushed. Her circle was large, her curiosity great, and her interest quaintly psychological, sometimes heartless. Everyone she met abroad was a friend of friends. In those days of limited travel Vernon Lee, the most travelled of them all and an indefatigable talker herself, found 'a frowsty British world' in London, but not at the Pearsall Smith's house at Fernhurst.

At week-ends there she found

'Life is much more home-like than in any house I have been in. The family consists of Mrs Costelloe's father, mother, brother, young sister Alys and, at present, the future brother-in-law, a young grandson of Lord John Russell. They are very well off but live in extremely modest style, quite without show or luxuries. Mr Pearsall Smith and his wife, who is a delightful woman, have both been famous lay preachers, and he founded a sort of sect which claims that Christ redeemed the world not from hell but from the necessity of sin, which seems to have taken an incredible load off ever so many people's souls. He used to preach to thousands of people; and in Berlin the old Emperor lent him a large church where he preached through an interpreter! He is now old and exhausted. But his wife is full of zeal for every sort of good work, and of humour, cheerfulness and shrewdness which appear so often to have characterized the great saints. Indeed she is most fully aware of the absurdities and dangers of mysticism, while being a mystic herself.'[1]

At Fernhurst Vernon Lee said she found a complete absence of that 'English discrimination', by which she probably meant snobbishness, which had made her 'shudder'. The letter goes on:

'These people are absolutely tolerant, all their children being atheists quite openly; and indeed they profess to care only for the essence of religion, which they say is the same in all. . . . I never saw so united independent and cheerful a family.'

*   *   *

Philanthropy rather than philosophy ruled the prosperous household at 'Friday's Hill' and kept its women folk busy. Mary's marriage had brought her into the philanthropic world of the London of the 'nineties, peopled with the very poor, with sweated child and adult

[1] From a letter dated July 30, 1894, in *Vernon Lee's Letters*, privately printed by Irene Cooper-Willis, and reproduced by her permission.

labour, and consequently full of crime. Frank Costelloe, who had once appeared to Mary-in-love as a 'brilliant Irish barrister', partly because he had 'shared an exhibition with Asquith at Balliol', had somehow lost his glow for her. He had failed to win election to the London County Council, and he had tried to turn her into a convinced Roman Catholic and failed also. She thereupon felt 'relegated to the limbo of the invincibly ignorant'. It seems that he got bored with her doubts and she, for her part, felt he was living by formulae. One of their climaxes was reached over the question of Hell. Mary refused to believe in Hell. Costelloe insisted that a Catholic must believe in Hell, even though it might possibly be empty. There was time in those days, perhaps too much of it.

Like many of the well-to-do young women in London Mary worked a little at Toynbee Hall, the new settlement in Whitechapel which was to bring knowledge, recreation and the arts to an overcrowded district under the inspiration of Canon and Mrs Barnett. Once Mrs Barnett asked Mary to talk with a prostitute in the Chapel, to convince her of the wrongness of her ways. The eager young American Quaker listened to the whole story and found that the sinner had three children to support and 'no other means of livelihood but her good looks'. The talk ended by Mary wishing her, when they parted, 'a successful evening'. Another evening Mrs Barnett had asked Mary, who was herself tall and handsome and gay, to give away the boxing and wrestling prizes at Toynbee Hall. Mary found the fights so cruel and sanguinary that she fainted and had to be carried out like the loser. For the too busy all around her she formed a 'Sloth Society' whose emblem was a tortoise.

Now, in earnest preparation for the guest of this Easter week-end, she thought she would read George Moore's *Confessions of a Young Man* and wear her new pink satin dress for dinner. Mary was twenty-six, Bernard twenty-five. That first encounter is best described by herself:

'I had often stolen round to the National Gallery and had even organized pitiful little Art Classes in my own drawing-room. I felt somehow wicked although uplifted in doing this, in a world so full of ignorance and misery and so desperately in need of betterment. Art and music and literature seemed to me at the most ornamental excrescences upon "real" life.

'Therefore when this beautiful and mysterious youth appeared,

102

for whom nothing in the world existed except a few lines of poetry which he held to be perfect, and the pictures and music he held to be beautiful I felt like a dry sponge that was put into water. Instinctively I recognized that those were the real values for me, however wicked and self-indulgent they might be. He was a brilliant, eloquent talker, and not only I but the whole family listened to him with astonishment and delight during the whole of that Bank Holiday week-end he spent at our house. He unrolled before us a great panorama of human history and achievement, in course of which man had reached a few—but how few—really high points of perfection. Greek poetry and sculpture he mentioned but did not dwell upon; for Arab and Provençal poetry he showed enthusiasm; for the music of Wagner he was fire and flame, and he rapidly sketched the course of European painting from Giotto to Velasquez, and on—truth compels me to say —to the last and greatest achievement of art, the painting of Bonnat.'[1]

It is no slight on Mary to remember that all his life Berenson was to have this kind of exhilarating effect on most of the women he met, and on not a few young men. He could kindle, whenever he wanted to. He was certainly a unique guest at 'Friday's Hill', the like of which these Americans, avid for culture, had not yet encountered. Mary notes how Bernard 'exhaled an enticing if frightening atmosphere of foreign culture'. In one respect she thought he was not at all exotic. He quoted easily from the Old Testament, a familiar book in that Quaker household, and she felt the Jewish sense of being the Chosen People was not far removed from the sense the Quakers had of a like destiny. Every word of his found an echo, real or imagined. For Mary it was love at first sight. The whole family was a little breathless. She says that they had grown up (like many an American family) 'practically unaware of the existence of anything earlier than the discovery of America', and politics were for them 'eternally summed up in the American Constitution'.

At dinner Mary determined to play her trump card. She turned the conversation to George Moore's *Confessions of a Young Man*. To her discomfiture Bernard replied, 'Oh, that rotten book'. Much later she learned that he thought her conversation very silly, her pink satin dress enchanting, and she adds modestly, 'I suppose he must have felt in me a spirit that reached out towards the things he cared for'.

A fellow guest she remembers was indignant that Bernard (whom

[1] U.L., whence come all the quotations in this chapter unless otherwise annotated.

he called 'the young whipper-snapper') should have announced that
the moon looked more beautiful through the branches of the trees
than sailing across a clear sky.

At week-ends the young people often camped in the woods at the
end of the garden, the youths in one tent, the young women in
another. So they did this memorable week-end. Mary and Bernard,
within talking distance, talked all night. Then the week-end was over.
The young Pearsall Smiths immediately ordered reproductions of
Giorgione and of Botticelli, an edition of Provençal poetry, a translation of the Greek Anthology and a number of Russian novels.
They all became regular pilgrims to the National Gallery. At home
in Sussex Mary looked at the moon through the trees and waited.
For a week Bernard was silent. Then he wrote and told her what
was in his heart. He wrote from Cambridge that he wanted to give
his whole life to her except for that part of it which belonged to his
work on Italian painting, in which he hoped she would join him.

Passion and compassion are rarely bedfellows. One is not allowed
to wonder about Frank Costelloe. One just knows that Mary
Costelloe's marriage had been a Roman Catholic one, that there could
be no divorce, and that the course of her new love could hardly be
smooth. Yet she and Bernard were to negotiate every obstacle (and
some were high and difficult ones) for fifty-five years, until her death
in 1945. 'H.W.S.' was of course furious. Children to her were a
sacred trust, and to abandon them as Mary began to abandon Ray
and Karen for many months of the year in order to live near Berenson
in Florence and travel with him, estranged Mary from her mother
even if it gave Mrs Whittall Smith a new and vital interest in her
grandchildren. To be nearer them Mrs. Whittall Smith bought a
house near the Costelloe house in what is now Millbank and used to
be Grosvenor Road. Logan makes heroic efforts to preserve the
conventions in a note in his collected letters of H.W.S.:

'Early in 1890 H.W.S.'s daughter, Mrs Costelloe, went to
Florence to study Italian Art under the tutorship of Mr Bernard
Berenson, whom she married (1900) a year after the death of her
husband B. F. C. Costelloe. In the intervening period she stayed in
Florence, with only occasional visits home, while her two young
daughters lived with their father at 41 Grosvenor Road, only three
doors off from the home of H.W.S. at No. 44.'[1]

[1] *A Religious Rebel*, ed. Logan Pearsall Smith. Nisbet & Co., Ltd., 1949,
p. 106, footnote.

One is meant to forget that the pupil was twenty-six[1] and the teacher twenty-five. Logan's memory was never very accurate. His sister's first journey to Italy was made in the early autumn of 1891. In the summer of 1890 Mr and Mrs Costelloe *and* Bernard Berenson set out together for Paris, and relations between Frank and Bernard seem to have been close enough for the Irishman to provide Bernard with a detailed exposition of the Mass. 'How much I owe Frank for having first opened my eyes to what the Mass really meant', Bernard was to write to Mary within a few months from the mountain fast-ness of the Monastery of Monte Oliveto Maggiore near Siena. Here was a church and a service which seemed to gather grandeur and glory into its bosom. For the next few months the church seemed the very epitome of all the beauties he had been seeing.

Bernard left the Costelloes in Paris and journeyed down the Loire and then eastwards to Berlin, Budapest, Vienna and back to Venice. Frank or no Frank, he writes every day to Mary in very great detail about every picture and school of Italian painting in the national and private galleries of these cities. She was, for him, quite clearly his first pupil: not only a contemporary correspondent wholly after his heart and affection, but a woman most anxious to learn all she could from him, and if possible to see through his eyes. Hitherto his only correspondent had been a benefactress, older than himself.

Were ever stranger love letters written?

Mary hoped to write a life of her husband out of these letters. She strung the first hundred or so together enthusiastically and then gave up. She had begun the task too late in life. Looking back she writes that she enjoyed every word of those letters partly because they were written 'in a handwriting I had come to love and partly because it made me feel I was taking part in the kind of life I longed for—free, devoted to beauty, fortified by study and leading to endless spiritual and aesthetic adventures'. For Mary he was the passionate pilgrim; for Mrs Gardner in this decade of 1890–1900, he was to become, unbeknown to Mary, the cool and assured pur-chaser of masterpieces.

To Mary he sent lots of homework: pictures to look up in the National Gallery. She sent him Fabian pamphlets, including one by Bernard Shaw, which he struggled with but rejected with 'Mr Shaw's attempt to rise to moral heights is perfectly ludicrous'. She sent him others by Sidney Webb and Graham Wallas, both of whom

---

[1] *A Religious Rebel, op. cit.*, p. xv. Mary was born in 1864.

often came to 'Friday's Hill'. Bernard said that unless the pamphlets were better written he could not read them; he would 'as soon drink the Thames'. There was, however, one by Sidney Webb on Sweated Labour which he found 'unpretentious and sincere', and he singled out a sentence in it:

'If we desire to hand on to the afterworld our direct influence, and not merely the memory of our excellence, we must take even more care to improve the social organism of which we form part, than to perfect our individual development.'

The whole pamphlet gave him a twinge. Its effect in England was cumulative. It led to an intense interest in the whole question of twelve- and fourteen-hour days for children and others in dark, unhealthy workshops, and finally to an Exhibition in London in 1906 of articles produced by sweated labour, and a general boycott of these articles.

Was Mary trying to make a Socialist of him? He wrote apologetically that his whole inspiration from boyhood had been to regard culture as a religion and it would be a cruel thing to have to give up that view 'for something as directly opposed to it as socialism, even in Mr Webb's meaning'. He said he had been worrying about his right to all the culture he could get. What made Italy so wonderful, he wrote, was that he could forget such problems there. In England one had 'a horrible fit of the blues' because on the very skies of England was writ that 'culture could not be the aim of true, noble life, while socialism was'. Mary being away in England for much of the year, England frequently comes in for some nasty knocks.

These young students of the arts were not alone in their quandaries. A few years earlier, in 1887, Vernon Lee in her *Juvenilia*, describing her affection for Pater's *Marius the Epicurean* and the desire it gave her to live 'only for and with the beautiful serenities of art', adds that in so doing 'we are passively abetting, leaving unfought, untouched, the dreadful, messy, irritating loathsomeness of life'. She was happier before she discovered that, 'but while we were happy other folk were wretched; and this convenient division of property and class cannot be kept up for good'.[1] Vernon Lee decided that 'in order that the great mass of mankind which has

[1] Vernon Lee, *Juvenilia*, Second Series of Essays on sundry aesthetical questions, Vol. I, p. 11, Fisher Unwin, London, 1887.

neither peace nor dignity, nor beauty of life, should obtain a small allowance of any such qualities, it becomes necessary that we, who happen to possess thereof, should deprive ourselves of a portion for their benefit'.[1] In this she was prophetic, at least about England.

Berenson did not take this view, and the moment of decision not to take it occurred in that autumn of 1890 when he wrote to Mary (the italics are his own):

'It will be so hard, so nearly impossible, for me to give up culture —not the Boston thing, but the real selfish passion for training oneself *to have enjoyment of one exquisite and beautiful thing lead on to the enjoyment of one even more beautiful.* I suspect you do not realize how impossible it is to drive the two, culture and socialism, as a team. Perhaps you even think that is what I might do. Even now what makes me hate writing is to a great extent the fact that it takes time. The article on Sweating made a lump rise in my throat. It is too terrible. I am afraid you will end by making me feel it is my duty to give up everything that I have cherished hitherto. I don't want this to happen.'

B.B.

It did not happen. There was too the awful example of Ruskin, obsessed and overwhelmed by the contemporary conditions in England. Mary gave up trying, and Bernard in turn began, in his letters, to wean her from the Fabian sense of social responsibility and from her not very successful activities at Toynbee Hall towards a more Mediterranean contemplation of life and art. And time was of the essence of the matter. He felt they must hurry; there was much to do. He told her she could hardly know how much work needed to be done on Italian Renaissance painting and how chaotic existing attributions were. To the passionate pilgrim revealed in these letters we shall return in Chapter VIII.

*　　*　　*

Monte Oliveto Maggiore is a large, somewhat forbidding and very remote Benedictine monastery, far from the railway. It lies among steeply eroded grey and treeless hills about thirty miles south-east of Siena. Those hills often appear in fourteenth- and fifteenth-century panels of the Sienese school of painting, especially

[1] Vernon Lee, *Juvenilia*, p. 12.

in Sassetta, and they always give an impression of utter desolation. The earth has crumbled away through deforestation into awful canyons where no foot holds, leaving ghostly Gothic spires of grey earth: on other nearby hills the trees have bound the land and preserved it for generations of peasants to cultivate. A road conducive to mysticism winds up to this far place from Asciano. Alternating visions of hell and paradise meet the eye on every side. Then on the final plateau of pine and cypress and gentler trees stands the huge red brick monastery with its towered gateway and vast stables and buttresses, like some mediaeval fortress. Once it entertained Charles V and 2,500 of his troops; Popes stayed there and learned men called to read in its great library which was five centuries a-building.[1] In its cloisters are among the finest frescoes Signorelli painted —the story of St Benedict. In the Napoleonic wars many of its treasures were dispersed. After the establishment of Rome as the capital of Italy in 1870 its Benedictine monks were disbanded and its lands divided among the people. For the next seventy-five years only an abbot and two monks were allowed to live there as caretakers. In 1945, a Catholic Party being once more in office, the monasteries regained some of their land (and much new land) by purchase. Today about a hundred white-robed 'Olivetani' chant their way out of the refectory shortly after noon, and among them (in 1956) was still an old monk over eighty, Padre Patrizi, who had been one of the two servers to the famous Don Gaetano di Negro, Abbot of Monte Oliveto in 1890, the year that Bernard Berenson first stayed at the monastery.[2]

In the monastery refectory there is a chalk drawing of Don Gaetano. It is brought out for those who especially wish to see it. He has a long, intelligent, lively face. He is dressed as a secular priest, for the wearing of the habit had also been prohibited to the caretakers of 1890. The Abbot was then seventy. He was the son of a Genoa marquis who claimed collateral descent from St Catherine of Genoa (not Siena). He was a highly educated man and a delightful talker. He had taken his doctorate of philosophy at the Gregorian University in Rome. In 1856 he was Chancellor of the Benedictine Order, and he had been a Prior in France before coming to Monte Oliveto. When he died in 1897 Paul Bourget, who had spent several

[1] See Plate No. VII.
[2] Padre Patrizi claimed to have a vivid memory of those days and recalled them to the writer.

weeks as his guest in 1890, wrote of him as a *saint vieillard* and *vrai patriarque*, and recorded (with his usual apostrophes):

'Avec quelle bonté paternelle il reçut et hébergea les voyageurs! Avec quelle cordialité empressée il leur fit visiter l'antique monument! De par délégation de l'État italien qui s'en était emparé, il en était le gardien officiel, singulière et navrante situation!'

Many were the old Abbot's distinguished visitors and corre-spondents, for he was a great stamp collector and received gifts from all over the world. There is a memorial tablet to him signed by many famous names in the Refectory today. The Abbot's humour, his artistic sensibility, his innumerable Latin quotations and Tuscan proverbs were the subject of enthusiastic letters from Berenson to Mary. The young American enjoyed the Abbot's confused geography (he could never be sure where the Cape of Good Hope was) after American competence in such matters. 'The American is choked with information, is he not? Just as comfort is his only notion of blessedness, so information is his only idea of education', wrote Berenson from Monte Oliveto at the end of November 1890. He liked the Abbot's good husbandry, his new terraces and arboretums. He loved the old man's reminiscences. Don Gaetano remembered the Joseph Pennells[1] arriving on tricycles to the amazement of the peasants who had never seen such vehicles. And the old and the young man had many debates about whether or not Rome should have become the capital of Italy. The Abbot thought not. He believed in the temporal power of the Papacy and deemed that United Italy, having left San Marino alone, might have left Rome to the Popes. Berenson argues the other way in a manner which shows he was acquainted with the history of Rome from the days of Cola di Rienzo to those of Gioberti and Rosmini and their idea of a Papal Presidency of Italy. The Abbot was also knowledgeable about wines, and one evening he composed a Latin antiphon of contempt for all teetotallers.

'I so admire his perfect simplicity, his contentment, the utter lack so far as I can see, of stirring or high-flown spirituality. He is still the kindly prelate of old days—one of the last' . . .

[1] The friend and biographer of Whistler.

wrote Berenson, and shortly after, Mary says, 'such was the friend who received Bernard Berenson into the Church'. Writing this many years later, she felt that 'the vaccination, if I may so express it, did not "take"'. She defines the conversion as the culmination of Bernard's European experiences and of his great love for Italy itself, of his longing to escape from the sordidness of ordinary existence and finally 'of his feeling that, in being members of the same Church, he and I were drawn together'. Neither of these two was born for lasting conversions, but rather for a great variety of religious, artistic and literary experiences.

During these winter months of 1890–1 affectionate letters from the Abbot would reach Bernard on his wanderings in eastern Tuscany, inviting him to return whenever he pleased. He writes to Mary that he was now attending Mass very often. He says he feels suddenly at home with the poor worshipping in every church he enters. Mary sends him Latin hymns which have been translated by members of the Oxford Movement. One evening he watches a moonrise 'finer than any picture'. A friend warns him that he had been 'simply crammed' with pictures portraying Catholic sentiment and Catholic ideas, and that he was getting very one-sided. But (he writes to 'Friday's Hill') he would glory in being one-sided. He did not want to become one of those whom Dante described as rejected both by heaven and by hell,[1] and anyway his friend was 'vague and boozy'.

And then he went back for the third time to Monte Oliveto in January 1891 and Mary recounts that he was received into the Church, adding her penetrating comment, 'He was really being received into Italy.' After these events Bernard went to confession regularly for a few weeks.

No record at all remains of Bernard's entry into the Church, either at Monte Oliveto or elsewhere. Suddenly in 1944, after the German Nazi Jew-baiters had occupied Florence, it became a matter of supreme importance for a baptized Jew to give documentary evidence of the event, on the chance of enjoying the local Bishop's

---

[1] *Questo misero modo*
Tengon l'anime triste di coloro
Che visser senza infamia e senza lodo
. . . Cacciarli i Ciel per non esser men belli:
Nè lo profondo inferno gli riceve,
                    Inferno, III, 34–41.

protection.[1] There were, according to Padre Patrizi, several urgent telephone calls from Florence to the monastery asking for confirmation of Bernard Berenson's entry into the Church. A thorough search was made, without avail. What Padre Patrizi remembered best about the several sojourns of the twenty-five-year-old Berenson were the long evenings of talk with the old Abbot, that old saint's delight in his young transatlantic visitor and then the frequent dawn departures of Bernard, riding out on a small horse to visit the villages in the neighbouring hillsides and in the valleys between, and his return 'at sunset with one or two small fourteenth- or fifteenth-century Sienese panels in his saddle-bag, purchased for a song from some indigent priest or some impoverished sacristan'. Padre Patrizi described this vividly. He also maintained that on one occasion Paul Bourget stayed at Monte Oliveto at the same time as Berenson, and thereafter wrote a short story called *The Saint*, in which the famous old Abbot is the chief character.[2]

Mary-in-love became a devoted and apt pupil. She already possessed a vivid memory for poetry, and recited whole poems all her life. Now she cultivated that essential quality of all art students—a visual memory—the capacity as it were to learn pictures, buildings and sculpture by heart, and to recall them in detail and *in situ* when wanted for comparison. Few mental disciplines yield as much pleasure as this one. Hitherto the chief English art scholars, men like Reynolds, Ruskin and the Eastlakes assisted their memories with their draughtsmanship. Bernard (and Mary) began their labours in

[1] Many Italian priests were so horrified in 1944–5 at the German Jew-hunting in Italy that they offered baptism to save life. In Rome several hundred Jews were baptized. Not all even of these survived. Thousands were taken away to concentration camps and then to extermination camps in Germany.

[2] After reading the tale up at the Monastery (it is very brief), I asked Padre Patrizi whether he identified the Abbot's English visitor in the story with Berenson, for I wondered why he wanted me to read it, there and then. He blandly replied, 'No'. This is one of Bourget's sentimental conversion tales. A young visitor from abroad studies the Abbot's collection of *medals*. That evening a precious medal is missing. The Abbot does not lock away his collection. A fellow guest notices that a medal is missing. Next morning the medal is back. The first visitor is observed to be closeted for a long time with the Abbot and leaves shortly afterwards, having taken the road to repentance. In another tale, *La Dame a perdu son peintre*, Paul Bourget may have had Berenson and Mrs Gardner in mind. If he had, he may have been envious of their collaboration.

attribution just at the moment when the photograph (preceded by the etching and the chromolithograph) was beginning to assist the art scholar. Snapshots were all the rage in the 'nineties, after George Eastman had introduced the first daylight loading film in 1891: pictures were not being photographed yet for the general public. Neither of them could draw a line, or were so foolish as to try, any more than for instance their contemporary Eugénie Sellars (later Mrs Strong) who was to become one of the finest authorities on Roman sculpture, tried herself to become a sculptor or a draughts-woman. The line drawings which had been essential before the arrival of photography—if art historians were to illustrate their books—could now be dispensed with. Yet visual memory was still of vital importance. What would be the use of owning many photographs of works of art if you could not visually recall the one you needed to consult, what city and what gallery it was in? The photograph in itself was to prove an immensely valuable aid to the art scholar. Morelli was the first to appreciate the photograph in his work.[1]

Just now the young couple possessed very few photographs. These were expensive and mostly taken to order.[2] It became all the more necessary to remember. Whenever Mary toured galleries with Bernard she made notes of his comments on the Italian pictures. He deplored the habit. He wanted her whole attention. She says that later on he was more than grateful for the notes. Together in 1891 they catalogued the Italian pictures at Hampton Court. He wanted her to have the credit and to make her first excursion into print with it. He coined a combination of her own and her brother's name for her: Mary Logan. This early Hampton Court catalogue, a little brochure, sold for 2d. in 1894. She kept the pseudonym for a number of years.

During most of the 'nineties Bernard and Mary toured hundreds of churches and galleries in Northern and Central Italy. Her first

[1] Morelli remarks that colour frequently misled him when he was trying to attribute a picture. Once he possessed a photograph, he could study the form only. See Giovanni Morelli, *Italian Painting, op. cit.*, p. 54.

[2] Vernon Lee remembered her first meeting in London with Bernard Berenson in July 1893 when 'he was so poor that he asked me if I had any photographs of Italian paintings, and was delighted when I gave him some—as he could not afford to buy them.' (Recalled by Vernon Lee's executor, Miss Irene Cooper-Willis to the author in London in 1954.)

view of Italy in the early autumn of 1891 was from a railway window:

'Hot sunshine, blue hills, vine orchards with swags of ripening grapes, and then to my surprise and delight, churches churches everywhere. No hill was too high not to be crowned by a church, no clump of trees too dense to hide the Campanile, no village too tiny not to cluster around a church—scarcely a villa too humble not to have its chapel. Already I knew that many a work of art lurked in consecrated buildings, that every altar had its picture, and that many of them might turn out to be even a masterpiece.'

It was a passion with them both in those days to try to put the name of a school or even a painter to any significant painting. 'We used to wonder', she notes, 'if Adam had half as much fun naming the animals, as we were having renaming those ancient paintings.' They were a diligent pair, leaving some modest *pensione* at eight every morning for a cup of coffee in the piazza and then setting forth. 'We attack church after church in a slow, systematic way, leaving nothing to our purpose unseen.' In the afternoon they would go to the gallery or set out to hunt for altar pieces in outlying villages. They came full of 'precise information from Crowe and Cavalcaselle', but 'blinded to the excellence of their work, by our hot partisanship of our adored Morelli. In a way we consulted Crowe and Cavalcaselle much as we did Baedeker to find out where there were things to be seen, so that we were almost unaware of our debt to them, until later years and the library habit caused us to find in their pages many of our own "discoveries".' Burckhardt's *Cicerone* they also had with them, and it led them 'to endless excursions and was the cause of endless delight'.

Of course they made mistakes and developed enthusiasms which had to be reconsidered, and they argued together for hours about certain painters, especially Veronese. Mary, like any intelligent amateur, had her strong prejudices. 'Bernard', she writes, 'never lets *anything* stand in his way of appreciating a work of art, if it has any qualities whatever.' Their lovers' quarrels, like their love letters, were about pictures. She says that when she first met him (after his two and a half years' pilgrimage in Europe) 'Italian art was already with him a subject almost too professional for drawing-room conversation'.

At this time Mary was given an idea of Bernard by Bernard

himself which is only half the truth. Until the very end of the century
Mrs Gardner is never mentioned, nor is Mary mentioned to Mrs
Gardner. Mary concludes 'there we were: two young people extraordinarily different in origin, although both in our own homes
saturated with the Old Testament, caught by chance in the waning
tide of Transcendentalism, and both of us formed to some extent by
the same outstanding personalities of New England—by Emerson,
William James and Browning, who was at that time a New England
hero'.

It was nearly two decades since Bernard's home had been
'saturated' with the Old Testament. Vernon Lee had found all the
Pearsall Smiths 'atheists'. Transcendentalism, in the form in which
Emerson imbibed it from the German philosophers, was for some
time an important prop for Mary, but Bernard had long since been
reading and enjoying quite different writers, French and Italian and
Latin, and was profoundly bored by philosophy.

Matters came to a head one day in Paris, some time about 1893.
Perhaps it was just after a flying visit they both paid to the British
Embassy in Paris where Bertrand Russell was an honorary attaché,
an early and short-lived experiment in diplomacy. As Lord Russell
recalled it over half a century later:[1]

'The runaway couple were desperately short of money. Mary
rushed in with Bernard. It was the first real meeting I had had with
Bernard. I was delighted with him. My beautiful and gay "sister-
in-law" asked for £100. It was forthcoming there and then. I
remembered too how Mary had become quite estranged from the
family after she had run off with B.B.; I think perhaps I was instru-
mental in healing the breach.'

Mary recalls how she and Bernard sat down in the then famous
Duval restaurant, 'a luxury we rarely permitted ourselves', and how
she had once again expounded her views 'that the purpose of life was
to know God, to help our fellow men, and that the only way for an
intelligent person to obtain knowledge of God, was through
philosophy'. This fine meal was suddenly spoilt. Mary records an
outburst by the young Bernard, which ran, 'In Heaven's name, Mary,
do drop all that transcendental nonsense. Philosophy is a pursuit
for pretentious muddle-headed fools: it leads nowhere, and it is sheer

[1] To the author, at Richmond, in May 1954.

waste of time to bother your head with it. Study the human mind if you will, but don't pretend to understand the mind of God.'

The effect on Mary was that she felt 'as the Italians say, *fatta di gesso*', best translated as 'struck all of a heap'. But she was more than converted to the study of the human mind. In later years she became an ardent devotee of psycho-analysis and much encouraged an interest for it in both her daughters. The younger one became a consulting psycho-analyst, to the distress of her step-father, who thought it would not bring her any sense of fulfilment.[1]

Meanwhile, Mary's chief ambition was to make Bernard take up his pen. Her visits to galleries with him, her notes on his comments, wholly convinced her that he had something to give the world in print. There was also the ever-recurrent need for money. Unless he published, unless he began printing articles, where would an income come from? She was contributing to much of their travel. She did not then know that his knowledge was already lucrative in other ways. She had arranged a course of paid lectures for him at the National Gallery on the Venetians. Miss Bradley and Miss Cooper, the 'Michael Field' aunt and niece, went and noted in their diary that he looked very handsome and again made them think of a faun. Lecturing he disliked: he never gave another lecture in his life. His voice would not carry, being a silver voice, quiet and even. Without the give and take of conversation, talking lost its vitality. Lecturing is an art, but it would not be his art. Much later, all attempts to magnify and record his voice were firmly rejected. From both sides of the Atlantic men and women called with the paraphernalia of the screen and the recording tape, but in vain.

He possessed a capacity for caricature. He could mimic almost anyone, especially the solemn and the fanatical, by a modicum of alteration in the tempo of his speech—fast or slow, by the lift of an eyebrow, or by a mere suggestion of a stare or an over-keen glance, normally quite alien to his composed features. It was an accomplishment he shared with the late Sir Max Beerbohm. He too could convey worlds in the lift of an eyebrow, a pause, an intonation.

*   *   *

[1] When a little controversy arose three years later with Bertrand Russell over the MSS. of Berenson's *Florentine Painters*, Bernard wrote to Mary: '. . . Botticelli . . . keys up, fortifies my capacity for *life*. Whether the latter statement is psycho- or bio-logical is to me utterly indifferent, biology being after all nothing but psychology in a packed down form'.

The pace of these years—of the 1890–1900 decade—is fast and furious. Travel between Italy and England is continuous, but the base is in Florence once his first earnings begin to come in. The operative date is 1894. Until that year Mary was undoubtedly contributing financially to their joint travels and purchasing essential photographs out of her personal allowance of a few hundred pounds a year. She firmly believes (in her unfinished memoir) that he decided to stay in Europe on her account, but there is no other evidence for this view. On one trip to Naples he made acquaintance and formed a friendship with the man who first popularized those exotic fish tanks, since then the hobby of hundreds of homes. Anton Dohrn, the founder of the famous Naples Aquarium in 1872, a German zoologist of international fame, arranged his crustaceans and his fish in such attractive tanks that visitors flocked to see them. He rented research space on the first floor to various learned societies abroad, and so financed his great venture, which with various international grants has survived two world wars. Bernard spent hours in the aquarium in the company of a German zoology scholar, whom he then took to see pictures in Naples. The exchange was typical of many of his later friendships. Each gave of his best, incited by the other. And the exchange belonged to his view, expressed in a letter to 'Michael Field', that 'the perfect critic cannot have too broad a range'.

Between 1891–6 Bernard and Mary set out on what must always be perilous assignments for the art historian—the tours of the more famous private collections of paintings in England and Scotland. Together they visited Robert Benson's collection, Mr Salting's, Lord Brownlow's, Mr Brinsley Marley's (since bequeathed to Cambridge), Alfred Mond's, Captain Holford's Collection at Dorchester House. They went to see Sir Herbert Cook's pictures in Doughty House on Richmond Hill, to Panshanger, to Petworth, Chatsworth and Windsor. Everywhere they made notes. Everywhere they met with some chilliness. Attributions matter enormously to State Galleries, to ancient families and to new collectors alike, for they represent capital. To question an attribution is to question the very patrimony which the owner of masterpieces hopes to realize himself or to bequeath to his heirs. In England, as elsewhere, attributions of Italian Renaissance paintings were in a state of some confusion in the last century. Moreover, England had for generations sent its wealthy sons abroad on the Grand Tour. Some had gone abroad again in later years, and had adopted the practice of centuries, of having a favourite masterpiece copied by a highly skilled hand. Copies therefore abounded in English collections, even fairly early ones, made in the seventeenth and eighteenth centuries. Undoubtedly Bernard's small, elegant, bearded figure must have made a strangely authoritative impression on the well-known owners. 'The fact of standing in front of a great picture for a period in which your vital energies became enhanced was something new in aesthetic theory.'[1] So wrote one of Bernard's chief pupils many years later in describing a slim volume to which Bernard had now put his hand, *The Venetian Painters of the Renaissance*, as a result of what was generally recognized as Mary's continual urging him to publish.

The tours of English collections certainly tested Mary and Bernard's friendship fiercely. She was very ambitious for him. She would have faced anything at that time to assist his career. But even she, with her lifelong sense of humour, must have found the account of an experience in one Scottish country house a little daunting. At Lord Wemyss's castle, Gosford House, a thunderstorm began during the afternoon. There was an immense number of pictures to see, candles were brought, and a general gloom seems to have descended as the young Herbert Cook and Bernard failed to stand for very long in front of some of the paintings. Suddenly a direct question about a 'Leonardo' (Mary says) failing to bring the expected confirmation the noble Lord flew into a rage and put them both out at the front door into the storm. Bernard's version of the event (to Mrs Gardner) was that the noble Lord thought he had as many brace of Leonardos and Titians in his house as of grouse on his moors.

If acquaintances and even friendships were ruptured over attributions, others were soldered over unexpected discoveries. Mary tells of the great discovery of Bellini's *Feast of the Gods* at the Duke of Northumberland's at Alnwick (later in the Widener Collection and bequeathed to the National Gallery in Washington), although at the time Herbert Cook and Bernard thought it a Basaiti. The same error of judgment (calling a Bellini a Basaiti) occurred on a visit to Robert Benson's pictures and 'Mr Benson carried his enmity so far as to blackball my husband's name when he was proposed for membership to the Burlington Club'. But a few decades later, when

---

[1] Sir Kenneth Clark on Berenson's *Venetian Painters of the Renaissance* in the Italian Encyclopaedia (published by Trecani).

Bernard wrote an essay on a notable but unrecognized Antonello da Messina in the Benson collection,[1] the enmity was forgotten and 'Mr Benson became one of our best friends, often staying with us in his later years, in Florence'.[2] Other important discoveries were made on these exhaustive visits, a Castagno at Locko Park (in Philadelphia now), a Masaccio Madonna (now in the National Gallery) and a host of minor attributions or re-attributions.

Every profession has its testing times, when nothing but skill helps. The connoisseur is always hoping to attribute pictures to their proper authors, but he faces the constant possibility that no such correct attribution can be achieved, and he must recognize that an attribution may only be a temporary one, and that even a positive attribution may, after lengthy consideration and new knowledge, demand a re-appraisal and even a new attribution. Berenson was long in deciding and revised some of his attributions even twenty, thirty and fifty years later.

In a letter to Mary from Germany in the early 'nineties, Bernard had written that he could not console himself with the 'aesthetic excellence' of a given picture. 'To me it does make all the difference in the world in the mere enjoyment whether it is or is not a Botticelli.'

Thirty years later, at a particularly difficult and very prosperous moment in his life, he was to write in the preface of a second edition to the Second Series of his *Study and Criticism of Italian Art* (1920):

'I see now how fruitless an interest is the history of art and how worthless an undertaking is that of determining who painted or carved or built whatsoever it be. I see now how valueless all such matters are in the life of the spirit.'

He wrote that the 'parasitic growth of petty documentation' was 'a stupid inheritance, continued out of bad habit'. And he bid the layman shun all this 'if his purpose be what it should be—to enjoy the kernel of the work of art, shelled of all the husks of historical, literary and personal consideration'.

Fifty years later he was to write with equal disillusionment: 'In truth I possess no technique of any sort except the one that has led to the kind of success that I regard as a merely financial and worldly

[1] Bernard Berenson, *The Study and Criticism of Italian Art*, Third Series, 1916. (Fourth Essay on *A Madonna by Antonello da Messina*.)
[2] As with all the quotations in this chapter unless otherwise specified, U.L.

118

one, not at all the one my soul aspired to . . .' and went on to enu-
merate 'causes of failure', chief among them:

'I have lacked the gift of inspiring confidence and loyalty, two
qualities of which I myself had a great provision at the start.'[1]

We are 'at the start', when the foundations of Berenson's connoisseurship were well and truly laid. Nothing short of his own
confidence in his knowledge and his visual memory could have tided
him over this period into the writing of *The Venetian Painters of the
Renaissance* and the *Lorenzo Lotto*, and (what he does not refer to,
nor does Mary, at any point) into noting, with taste already backed
by considerable knowledge, those pictures in private collections
which would in due course pass through his hands out of European
houses across the Atlantic into American collections—provided their
owners would accept offers for them.

The operative word in the early quotation from the letter to
Mary is *enjoyment*. Clearly, for this young man, after his five years
of close and first-hand study of paintings of the Italian Renaissance,
enjoyment included the enjoyment of knowledge.

Why did his most precious and comprehensive enjoyment turn
into the despised 'technique' referred to in the second quotation?
The obvious retort is that art cannot serve God and Mammon, and
that the horror began when the connoisseurship was harnessed to
yield an income. But that would be too simple. The income was
desperately necessary for the pursuit of his activities: 'Not only did
it enable me to pay for assistance in any work, for comfort at home
and abroad, and for expensive journeys, but it gave me the means
to acquire the books and photographs that my study and research
required.'[2] All his life he was fairly delicate, quick to react unfavourably to overwork, draughts, physical hardship. Years of
standing in the ice-cold galleries of Europe (long before they were
heated as they are now) did not improve matters. Comfortable
travel has always been expensive. He never enjoyed that comfort until
he was thirty years old. Berenson offers some answers of his own to
the clouds that darkened the pristine days when his work (in his own
words) left 'the morning as fresh as after the first dawn and the
evening as cool as when the Lord walked in the garden'.[3] We shall
come to them in due course—in the first decade of the next century.

It was at the end of 1893 that Mary and Frank Costelloe obtained

[1] *S.S.P.*, pp. 61–2.   [2] *S.S.P.*, p. 41.   [3] *S.S.P.*, p. 72.

a separation, a divorce being out of the question. Mrs Whittall Smith now looked after Mary's two girls, Ray and Karen, most of the year. Mary rented part of a small villa at the foot of the hill at Fiesole, a minute's walk from the Villa Kraus where Bernard rented his rooms. In 1894 he bought his first picture for Mrs Gardner—a Botticelli narrative painting on wood—representing the story of Tarquin and Lucretia. The Catalogue of Fenway Court compiled by Philip Hendy[1] in 1931 tells one a great deal, in a quiet unobtrusive way, about all the great painters who are represented in Mrs Gardner's collection and about the ways of patron and painter in their day.

It is the Italian masterpieces which make this collection so famous. As Sir Philip Hendy puts it:

'There are less than sixty pictures definitely attributed to Italian painters but the reader . . . will see that it contains almost all the great names of Italian history . . . the majority of painters from Giotto to Guardi are represented at Fenway Court. . . . The honour of recommending to Mrs Gardner the purchase of the greater part of her collection rests with Bernhard Berenson her constant adviser. His attributions . . . have been the basis of the author's studies, and his recent opinion is quoted on all the important Italian pictures, as are those of Crowe and Cavalcaselle and of their modern editors Douglas and Borenius.'[2]

That constant advice is the main subject of the Berenson–Gardner correspondence from now onward. It is a unique correspondence, a mixture of art appreciation and salesmanship, of friendship and commerce, if such things can be. Again and again Berenson tries to lift the commerce on to a plateau of national American concern. It was after all the first great private collection to be formed in the United States. He takes 5 per cent on all the prices he charges. That first Botticelli he purchased direct from Lord Ashburnham. Almost all the others he purchases through Colnaghi's of Bond Street; but Colnaghi's records for this period have all been destroyed. It is therefore fruitless to inquire whether the prices they offered correspond to the prices which Berenson charged her. Throughout the collecting period she sent her cheques directly to his bank in London.

[1] Now Sir Philip Hendy, Director of the National Gallery.
[2] Philip Hendy, *Catalogue of the Isabella Stewart Gardner Museum*, pp. v, vi, ix. Boston, 1931.

CHAPTER VIII

Fenway Court

No one who visits Boston should fail to visit Fenway Court. My first visit happened to coincide with the entry on a warm June day in 1955 of about fifty be-hatted and be-gloved middle-aged ladies, *en masse* as it were, each paying two dollars for a conducted tour, tea and a concert. I learned that they belonged to the local St Patrick's Society. Boston today is more Catholic than Protestant, owing to the great influx of Irish and Italian settlers. I seldom visit museums in a troupe, but here, in a new land and on the threshold of a place in which I knew I was to spend many hours, I thought it would be fun to enter with the eager ladies. It was. I paid my two dollars and there we were, in an immense rectangle of a courtyard, brimful of flowers of every hue of white, or so it seemed to me. They came down in tiers to a central little court with a fine old Roman mosaic floor and a fountain. Surrounding this enormous rectangle were the walls and windows of nothing less than a four-storied warm pinkish Venetian palace, brought, we were told, stone by stone, from Venice. Of that there could be no doubt. The fourth side was locally designed.

The whole was covered with an immense glass roof, enabling the courtyard beneath to be filled with flowers all the year round.[1]

Up we all went to the first floor and gathered into an expectant circle. The young guide began, more or less as follows:

'This collection was made by Mrs Gardner. Mr Gardner had three million dollars and Mrs Gardner had two million dollars. It was grand that they started collecting when they did twenty years before Mr Mellon and the others began, because Mr Mellon had a hundred million dollars to spend, and they could never have bid

[1] See Plate No. IV. Neither on this, nor any other occasion, was I aware, in this courtyard, of any echo of Venice. The phrase 'What a whim' kept recurring to me. These Venetian façades, without water, seemed to be turned inside out to make the walls of a superlative hothouse.

against him. Mr Berenson, who still lives in Florence, helped Mrs Gardner to choose most of the pictures.'[1]

At this point I went searching on my own, immediately aware that the paintings were badly hung, very often between windows, nearly always too high. I heard the guide say:

'Mrs Gardner endowed Fenway Court and its concerts and laid down in her Will that nothing in the museum should ever be moved or altered from the way it was at the time of her death in 1923.'

More than one visitor has regretted such an unfortunate clause. Happier ways of hanging pictures and of arranging museums are devised every year both in the United States and in Europe: but none may ever be introduced at Fenway Court.

The Patricians were moving rapidly. I rejoined them in front of the amazing and immense Titian. What a bull, what a girl, what a sea and hills, what a sky, and what a dolphin! The gorgeous blues and whites and reds of *The Rape of Europa*, the immense action in the great picture, the whole of it, takes one's breath away. The visitors were impressed when the guide told them that a *Conservateur* of the Louvre-Paris-France had declared there was nothing like it over in Paris, yet they wanted to get back to the nearby little 'Giorgione' (which Sir Philip Hendy decided to be a Palma Vecchio), the singular sideways-glancing head of a very Venetian Christ, bearing a brightly grained cross.[2] A chair and a small vase of flowers is always in front of this small painting.   One of the visitors bade me sit upon the chair, 'for only then can you see that tear on our Saviour's cheek'. Of all the paintings in Fenway Court this one undoubtedly appealed most to the Roman Catholic ladies and they could hardly tear themselves away from it. It was the only one which Berenson did not choose for Mrs Gardner. She insisted upon having it. The guide said, 'the laws of the time forbade its export, so that a copy had to be made of it to hang where it came from'. I was to find that its purchase was a prolonged and dramatic affair.

Among so many sculptures, hangings, *objets d'art*, and master-

---

[1] Actually Andrew Mellon made his first 'grand tour' in Europe when he was twenty-eight in 1880, but he was not then a centimillionaire. Henry Clay Frick made his when he was thirty, in the same year.   [2] See Plate IX.

pieces, Italian, Dutch and Spanish, there was one I knew well from a catalogue at home, for it had hung for seventeen years in Oscar Hainauer's collection in Berlin,[1] whence it was purchased with the whole collection as Joseph Duveen's first venture into picture buying on the big scale, in 1907. As I was looking at this rather repellent but splendidly painted *Woman in Green and Crimson* by Piero (or Antonio?) Pollaiuolo, a Museum official suggested I hurry down or else I should miss tea.

The fifty visitors were filing in to a grand spread, showing their half tickets on the way. I searched and searched, but had lost my half. There is no teashop within a mile of Fenway Court, so that was that. I went back to the pictures and then into a dark wood-panelled hall about 100 feet long with a platform at one end where a young woman with a violin and a girl with music which she placed upon a grand piano were getting ready for the concert. There would be room, I thought, for five hundred people at least in that dim hall. We were not more than sixty.

It was an agreeable concert of violin and piano sonatas. Once again Mrs Gardner's Will and her Endowment loomed very large in the proceedings. She would have it this way, twice a week, for ever and ever. Reason murmured that this legacy was a kind of patronage for young musicians. Maybe.

I sat at the end of an empty row at the back, quite near a portrait of the Pamphili Pope Innocent X, not a prepossessing figure even in Velasquez's famous three-quarter length sitting portrait of him in the Doria Gallery in Rome. That very morning in the Boston Athenaeum, the beautiful early nineteenth-century library overlooking the slate and stone tombstones of Old Granary Churchyard, Mr Morris Carter, now retired from the Directorship of Fenway Court, had mentioned this Innocent X as 'one of B.B.'s mistakes', so I looked and looked, and decided there and then that I could see the badly drawn shoulder all right; the face was unmistakably that of the Doria Pope, even if the reds of his Cardinal's biretta and cassock were nothing like as vivid as those at the Doria Gallery in Rome. Sir Philip Hendy rejects the picture as an original Velasquez, but thinks it a copy of the Hermitage Velasquez. It is now in the National Gallery, Washington.

The concert was over. St Patrick's ladies went out to their neatly parked cars and drove away. I walked ten minutes to my roaring

[1] Oscar Hainauer was my maternal grandfather.

tram which dived into a long tunnel and brought me to Park Street underneath Boston Common where another 'Subway' took me back across the Charles River to my lodgings in Cambridge. Next day and for all the remaining days in Boston, I returned to Fenway Court to read the Berenson–Gardner correspondence from 1887 to 1922, which was kindly put at my disposal by Mr Morris Carter and by the present Director, Mr George Stout, assisted in every kind way by the Secretary, Miss Evelyn Burr.

*   *   *

The present Director of the National Gallery, when quite a young man and an Assistant Keeper at the Wallace Collection in London, had been invited by Mr Morris Carter to come over and catalogue the Isabella Gardner Collection. The work took three years. It disputed some of Berenson's attributions as they had appeared in previous catalogues, but in each case Hendy quoted (alongside other opinions) the opinion given in a kind of omnibus letter from Berenson to himself, of February 4, 1930, which brought Berenson's previous attributions up to date, as they would appear in his own Italian Renaissance *List of the Principal Artists and their Works*, to be published at the Clarendon Press in Oxford in 1932.

Unique the Gardner Collection certainly is. Each visitor will always have his favourites: each art historian his own especial pleasures in such a collection. The art historian who catalogued Fenway Court in 1930 was especially pleased with the great altarpiece signed by Giuliano da Rimini (dated 1307) 'the first document of the Riminese school', and he finds in it a hieratic mysticism which carries him back to remote times and places. To any visitor the static and wonderfully placid figures still convey, as they must have conveyed in those equally troubled times nearly seven hundred years ago, motherhood surrounded by calm if heroic saints, the whole against a plain gold background.

The other favourites of the cataloguer are the Simone Martini, the Fra Angelico, Mantegna, Pesellino and Botticelli panels, the Piero della Francesca *Hercules*, Raphael's portrait of *Inghirami* and, of course, the plum of the whole collection, Titian's huge *Rape of Europa*. And he closes the list of his favourites with the Italian Moro and the Spanish Coello portraits.

*   *   *

Mr Morris Carter, who wrote a memoir of Mrs Gardner, recalls that from 1862–76 she lived at 150 Beacon Street. Then the Gardners purchased No. 152 and joined the two houses together. In 1884 Mr John Lowell Gardner inherited a fine house and garden in Brookline called Greenhill, where the Gardners spent their summers when not travelling in Europe.

Mr Carter was very modest. 'I knew nothing about Art', he said:

'I was Mrs Gardner's librarian. My predecessor told me that she had employed a Boston architect to plan out her Venetian palace on Beacon Street, a house surrounding a garden, something of the same idea as Fenway Court. Then on Christmas Day 1898, just two weeks after Jack Gardner's death, she called the architect and announced that she had purchased the Fenway land, and all the plans had to be scrapped and new ones made from scratch. Clearly the land had been purchased in Mr Gardner's lifetime. . . . Mrs Gardner firmly believed that when a thing or an idea belonged to her, it was all right.'[1]

The latter is, of course, a characteristic of the self-made. When money is new, with no inherited obligations, the strangest results ensue. In this case, because of the fenny nature of the ground, the house had to be built, just like a Venetian one, on hundreds of stilts, and a Venetian architect was engaged to assist in the building. Mr Carter remembered the existence of a Mr Coolidge at Harvard in the 1880s who used to bring prominent undergraduates to see Mrs Gardner and to help on public days. Public days were rare and never more than two hundred and fifty visitors were allowed, nor could they stay more than three hours. The undergraduates ushered the visitors forward. No lingering or turning back was allowed.

What Mr Carter most regretted was what he called 'B.B.'s failure to acknowledge his debt to Mrs Gardner'. He said the correspondence was full of gratitude, but that in print there was never an acknowledgement. This, now that I have read all the correspondence, is perfectly true. The correspondence may roughly be divided into three parts. The first belongs to the pre-purchasing period, and the reader has already learnt from it some of the first European impressions of the young Bernard in 1887–8. There is a gap between

[1] In conversation with the author in Boston, June 1955.

1889[1] and August 1, 1894, coinciding with Berenson's first meeting and travels with Mary.

And it is with this letter of 1894 that we take up the threads of the Berenson–Gardner story again. This letter begins what may be called the second or middle period, for every letter hereafter is chiefly concerned with suggestions about pictures she should buy, about the despatch of pictures she has bought, and about pictures she has agreed to buy but too late, so that they are already sold to someone else (who is never stated).

The third period began roughly from the moment when Mrs Gardner almost ceased to purchase pictures in the first years of the new century, and Mary (now married to Berenson) joined in the correspondence (after getting to know and to like Mrs Gardner on a visit paid to Boston in 1903).

The second period, with which we are here concerned, opened with Berenson's announcement from 13 Lord North Street, London, that Lord Ashburnham has a Botticelli—'about £3,000'—and that Berenson thinks he could obtain it, adding: 'It would be a pleasure to me to be able in some sort to repay you for your kindness on an occasion when I needed help'.[2] She sent him the cheque and thereby purchased her second Italian Renaissance painting.[3] Hitherto she had collected French Impressionists in a small way (with the advice of Charles Eliot Norton and others) and had patronized a considerable number of New England painters. She formed friendships with John Singer Sargent and Whistler and bought works from them. In this memorable year of 1894, memorable for Berenson and for Mrs Gardner, Berenson asked for a photograph of the full-length portrait Sargent had painted of her after eight unsuccessful attempts in 1888, and when the photograph finally arrived he wrote: 'Many thanks for the photograph of your portrait. It is a great work of art, but could my hand follow my brain, my portarit of you would be greater.'[4]

There are several portraits of Mrs Gardner at Fenway Court. One by Whistler lacks a face altogether; one by the Swedish painter

---

[1] The last letter before the gap announces something quite new in the correspondence, that by the end of that year he hoped to be 'quite picture-wise, not unlearned in the arts, and perhaps they will enable me to turn an honest penny'. Her attention must have been held by this.

[2] See p. 152 below.

[3] The first (attributed by Sir Philip Hendy to Bono da Ferrara) is a *Madonna and Child* and is 'perhaps the picture bought by Mrs Gardner [in Venice] in 1892'. Catalogue, p. 57.   [4] See Plate V.

Anders Zorn is like a snapshot in oil and one by Sargent of Mrs
Gardner just before her death is remarkable, but may not be
reproduced.

Berenson probably met the German art critic, dealer and collector
Dr J. P. Richter at the big London sales he had attended. In 1895
Berenson persuaded Mrs Gardner to purchase from Dr Richter's
collection a *Santa Conversazione* by Bonifazio Veronese, one of those
happy Venetian family picnic pictures of enchanting mothers and
babies. His third recommendation was a great solemn Venetian
picture by Catena, *The Delivery of the Keys to St Peter*, also from
Dr Richter's collection. Both purchases were made. Now the purchases followed thick and fast.

In the same year Berenson bought a Cima da Conegliano (called a
'contemporary copy' in the catalogue) for Herbert Cook, with whom
we know he had become friends and with whom he visited many an
English collection. This *Madonna and Child* was repurchased from
Cook by Berenson two years later, in 1897, for Mrs Gardner.
Berenson then suggested a Tintoretto portrait of the 'Florentine
poet and grammarian *Varalia*'. Mrs Gardner agreed, but too late.
He returned her cheque and promised 'solemnly, to get you one in
every way surpassing the delightful one you missed'. In the same
letter he told her he was looking everywhere for 'a Filippino, and
almost every other day I have things suggested or sent to me that
are charming and nice and "somewhere about there", but never yet
has a picture by the master appeared. However, at last, *je suis sur la
piste* . . . but you could not ask for a greater rarity'. She knew
what she wanted. He knew what he wanted for her. Usually
he won.

This letter is from the Villa Kraus in Fiesole. He was getting
known now. Innumerable suggestions were made to him and
pictures brought to him, as to one who was known to have his purchasers outside Italy. Now Berenson does most of his business
through Colnaghi in London. They buy pictures at his behest; they
make payment to the vendors he buys from, and they always do the
packing. But it is he who finds the pictures. His bankers are Baring,
and his 5 per cent commissions begin to come in, from Mrs Gardner,
Herbert Cook, the Museum of Fine Art in Boston and doubtless from
other purchasers.

The year 1896 saw the purchase of three very great pictures for
Mrs. Gardner by Berenson. He gave his plan a new fine frame in a

letter to Mrs Gardner of December 18, 1895: 'If you permit me to advise you in art-matters as you have for a year past, it will not be many years before you possess a collection almost unrivalled—of masterpieces, and masterpieces only.'

For a young man just turned thirty, the plan was bold. Also it was good salesmanship. Also it must have given some sort of moral comfort. The year 1896 began with the arrival at 150 Beacon Street of a fine Rembrandt *Self-Portrait* dated 1629, the first large self-portrait and the first to bear a date. Sir Philip Hendy writes of its 'power and romance'. It came originally from the Duke of Buckingham's sale at Stowe House in 1848, and through a number of purchasers it landed up at Colnaghi's, from whom Berenson purchased it for £3,000. The second great purchase, and the one which brought all concerned the greatest fame, was the Titian *Europa* (nearly 6 feet by 7 feet). Berenson purchased the masterpiece direct from Lord Darnley at Cobham Hall for £20,000. It had been painted for Philip II of Spain 'as we know from Titian's own letter to the King, despatched to Madrid [from Venice] in April 1562', Berenson wrote to Mrs Gardner. He had found it 'in every way of the most poetical feeling and of the most gorgeous colouring'. He told her how seventy years later 'that greatest of all the world's amateurs the unfortunate Charles I of England' had it given to him when he was at Madrid negotiating for the hand of Philip IV's sister. The negotiations came to nothing and the picture remained carefully packed for many years, which 'partly accounts for its marvellous state of preservation'. In the eighteenth century it passed to the Orléans family and then to the Darnley family, where it was now available 'for the not extraordinary sum of £20,000'. The only problem was that Mrs Gardner had been contemplating the purchase of Gainsborough's famous *Blue Boy* for which Berenson said she would have to give £30,000. The Duke of Westminster, however, held on to the *Blue Boy* till later and then it passed Mrs Gardner by. As for the *Europa*, Berenson really needed a quick reply. He had offered the picture to Mrs S. D. Warren in Boston because 'I hated it going anywhere than to America', but this offended Mrs Gardner. Once before, Berenson had brought her into rivalry with someone else, and she had asked him to promise never to propose a picture to her at the same time as he was proposing it to someone else. He in turn had asked her 'to let me know directly when any of the wishes you have expressed me have been satisfied by others'.

PLATE VIII Bernard Berenson and Mary Costelloe at Fernhurst, Sussex, in 1895

PLATE IX 'The singular sideways-glancing head of a very Venetian Christ'
(By courtesy of the Director, the Isabella Stewart Gardner Collection, Fenway
Court, Boston, Mass.) (Also pp. 132–133)

The pact was a good idea, but neither could stick to it. Both Mrs Gardner and Berenson were far too mobile, too full of ideas and too richly acquainted with picture owners and dealers ever to observe such a pact. She indeed engaged in 'orgies of buying' on her biennial visits to Europe and Italy, and from time to time she would still buy through Charles Eliot Norton, or some Boston friend or some New York dealer. Moreover, he was buying not only for her.

To obtain *Europa* Berenson had to outbid Dr Wilhelm Bode who was trying to get it for the Kaiser Friedrich Museum in Berlin.[1] When the great painting arrived in Boston, Mrs Gardner invited all her friends to celebrate the occasion with music and a feast. She always gave her greatest acquisitions a royal welcome. It was, in many ways, a joy to collect for such a woman, even if what Berenson called 'the fray of bargaining' with the vendor and the purchaser was often a most exhausting business.

All Berenson's letters are written in his own hand. He had none of the modern office staff and equipment which would now be considered indispensable. His bank book was his accountancy. His letters were written with pen and ink, without copies. They, and a single entry book formed the only record. His memory for paintings which might have become available, and for news of others which were suddenly in the market, was prodigious. There is no evidence that Mary was connected with this side of his life at this time. His successes clearly released much tension in him: his handwriting in this year of 1896 loses all its quaint flourishes and becomes smooth and sloping, as it was to remain. And the tangible benefit, the financial reward, meant that at last he could afford the essential books and photographs, and equally important, the possibility of travelling in greater comfort. From now on, when in London, he stayed at Garlands Hotel (which stood most decoratively at the end of Suffolk Street until a bomb destroyed it in 1941). His personal disciplines were such that neither at this time, nor at any other, was he ever inclined to fritter away wealth. His dream was a home, a library, friends to stay and to visit, somewhere in the hills above Florence. When the news began to arrive at 'Friday's Hill' that Berenson was making an income by selling pictures, Mary's mother

[1] Bode in a conversation with Sir Philip Hendy in 1928 (Catalogue, p. 374). Dr Bode formed the Hainauer collection, and many others. He had been a practising connoisseur since the 1860s, and in 1896 was the Director of the Kaiser Friedrich Museum.

called it 'fairy money'. She would not believe that a living could be earned thus.[1]

There are many references in the letters to the labours his new work now entailed. Gainsborough's *Blue Boy* had meant 'six weeks of continuous plotting and managing'. The 'only consolation is that in our lifetimes the *Blue Boy* will not leave its present owner without its going to you if you continue to want it'. But it went, early in the following century, to the Huntingdon Collection in California.[2] Another time (June 1896): 'There's nothing so resembles picture buying as trouting, and at times it almost seems impossible to land your fish. . . .' From Ancona in October 1896, 'I collapsed with *seeing* the livelong day'. And again: 'I am doing all I can in the absurdly indirect diplomatic way one must proceed in these matters. . . . Picture owners are so absurdly capricious. . . .' And from Florence in the spring of 1897, 'Thank heaven there are other things than business. There is Homer and Flaubert and Charles Lamb and music, and this springtime when it is so lovely that you can say to the moment with a whole heart "Stay, thou art so fair".'[3]

The third great acquisition in 1896 was the purchase of a full-length portrait of Juana of Austria with her minuscule niece Margaret, daughter and granddaughter of the Emperor Charles V. Berenson at first thought it was not by Titian and later, for a time, believed that it was. In the end he attributed it to either 'Coello or Pantoja de la Cruz'. (Sir Philip Hendy gives it to Coello.)

This painting he purchased directly in Forli from its owner the Marquis Fabrizio Paolucci de' Calboli, for £15,000. The year 1896 is rich in further purchases. There is a Guardi, a Van Dyck ('his Mona Lisa' Berenson called it) from the Duke of Osuna's collection in Madrid. This *Lady with a Rose*, together with one of those splendid Velasquez portraits of *King Philip IV of Spain*, and a (Jacopo) Tintoretto *Venetian Senàtor*, were the first great portraits of the collection. The most priceless and historic ones were soon to follow: Masaccio's *Young Man in a Scarlet Turban*, painted about 1428, one of the very earliest non-religious portrait paintings of the Renais-

[1] Bertrand Russell to the author, at Richmond, 1955.

[2] Mr S. N. Behrman who had access to Duveen's correspondence through Mr Louis S. Levy, employed at one time as a lawyer by the firm, states that Mr H. E. Huntingdon paid 620,000 dollars for the *Blue Boy* in 1913, of which (he states) the owner received one-third. S. N. Behrman, *Duveen*, p. 139, Hamish Hamilton, 1952.

[3] *Verweile Doch, du bist so schön*, from Goethe's *Faust*.

sance, with a 'splendid virility' of characterization,[1] purchased by Berenson in 1898 in Florence from Constantini, the dealer. Mrs Gardner herself purchased the almost contemporary *Young Lady of Fashion*, attributed by Berenson to Domenico Veneziano, by Sir Philip Hendy to Paolo Uccello. Third among these three early Renaissance lay portraits Sir Philip Hendy places the Pollaiuolo *Woman in Green and Crimson*, which did not, of course, join the collection until after the Hainauer sale in 1907.

*　　*　　*

Berenson stepped outside his chosen Italian period (from Giotto to Titian) several times for Mrs Gardner, and with such success that it is no surprise to read in a letter of November 1896 '. . . my fame increases at such a pace *que je commence à me sentir quelqu'un*. Believe me success is sweet because I think of the pleasure it will give you, and a few—very few—other friends'. For her he purchased, as we know, the Rembrandt *Self-Portrait*, and two years later two other paintings by the same Dutch master, *A Lady and Gentleman in Black* and *Storm on the Sea of Galilee*. Rubens's great portrait of the *Earl of Arundel* joined the collection in 1898, and the following year Berenson was swiftly and successfully after the Pole-Carew Holbein twin portraits of *Sir William and Lady Butts*, which had been deposited (Sir Philip Hendy tells us) at the National Gallery in London pending a court order to break the entail upon them. As soon as the court order came in March, Colnaghi offered £17,000 for them, for Berenson had already obtained Mrs Gardner's deposit of £25,000 for them, in reply to his letter in mid-February 1899. As always in such circumstances he wrote to tell her exactly what sums he was left with after deducting his usual commission and Colnaghi's expenses; in this case he had £3,115 in hand, he said—and suggested two 'small' purchases, one of which was nothing less than a superb Simone Martini altarpiece (painted about 1340), which he bought in the very place where it had been painted, at Orvieto, for £500—an astonishing bargain even for those days.

Dürer's great portrait of '*Lazarus Ravensburger*' (painted in 1521), Manet's portrait of his mother *Madame Auguste Manet* (painted about 1863) and Degas's *Madame Gaujelin* (1867) are among the non-Italian paintings Berenson purchased for Mrs Gardner.

*　　*　　*

[1] Catalogue, *op. cit.*, p. 236.

The year 1896 is also the one in which Mrs Gardner announced her wish to possess the Giorgione *Head of Christ*[1] in the Palazzo Loschi Collection at Vicenza. Berenson wrote that the Boston Museum of Arts was also after it and had asked him whether he thought it genuine. He thought it was, but he regarded it rather as a 'sublime illustration than a work of art . . . it is not the kind of thing I think of for you'. But she insisted.

The pursuit of this painting took two years. Turbulent local politics came into play. The picture proved very troublesome to obtain, partly because Count Zileri's father had bequeathed the picture originally to the town of Vicenza, but had altered his will and left it to his own family. The authorities knew of the change in the will, but still hoped for the picture. Berenson, on this visit to the family at Vicenza, found the windows smashed. The eldest of the Zileri brothers had just been the object of an anticlerical demonstration in the town, because being Mayor that year he had decided that Vicenza's annual celebration of the town's rising against Austria in 1848 should be celebrated by a Mass and not, as previously, by political processions.

The Palazzo Loschi, where the Zileris lived and where the Giorgione picture hung, presented a sorry sight, and the family was not anxious to discuss a sale. The picture, if it were sold and exported, might rouse the crowd again. For four hours Berenson had to negotiate with the men of the Zileri family. Then there was the question of an export permit, which could be one of the greatest obstacles then, as now, in transferring pictures from one country to another. With some of these pictures, for instance the Forli Titian, a Government export permit, after payment of duty of 1 per cent, seems to have been not too difficult to obtain. But in other cases the export permit presented great difficulties, and this was one of those cases. It is the only one fully described in the Berenson–Gardner correspondence, but others are hinted at. The clandestine export of Italian works of art was going on continually, and still goes on today under more stringent circumstances, and therefore on a smaller scale.

In the twentieth century the Italian Government listed those *painters* of the Renaissance whose works could on no account be exported. But at the time we are concerned with the Pacca Law was still valid. The Pacca Law was an attempt by Cardinal Pacca (1756–1844), Secretary of State to Pius VII, to stem the departure

[1] See Plate IX.

of masterpieces from Italy, in which Napoleon I was the chief culprit, quietly looting (for the Louvre) wherever he conquered. Pacca had drawn up two lists of *collections*, the 'inalienable' and the 'free'. From the first list nothing could be moved without a permit from the Holy See (after 1870 from the Italian Government). For the second type of collection no permits were needed. A great number of pictures and frescoes fell into neither category.

At the end of 1897 the Giorgione *Head of Christ* was still in the balance. There might be a lawsuit about the second will. If the town of Vicenza went to law there might be a chance in a hundred that it could win the case. Finally it was agreed that the picture would only be sold on condition that it would be returned at the price paid, if such a lawsuit were brought and won against the second will. Moreover the Italian art expert Adolfo Venturi had decided that the picture was a copy (Berenson wrote to Mrs Gardner), so that a permit should be easy to obtain. On June 6, 1897, he wrote of the Giorgione: 'I think all the pictures I have got for you, put together, have not been such a trouble to me!'

No permit was obtained. A copy was made of the picture and hangs in Vicenza today. The Loschi Giorgione crossed the Alps 'swaddled up like a baby in a blanket', to London. The leading critics—Morelli, Cavalcaselle, Richter, Frizzoni, and Berenson himself—attribute the picture to Giorgione. Hendy gives it to Palma Vecchio, Bode and Adolfo Venturi to 'an anonymous follower of Giovanni Bellini', and Venturi's son (Lionello Venturi) reverses his father's attribution and gives it back to Giorgione. It is the kind of picture which will make art historians and connoisseurs, young and old, disputatious for generations to come. Not only the good ladies of Catholic Boston will give it a kindly and compassionate thought from time to time. It is a picture admired by a good many others.

It would not be possible to run through all the purchases which Berenson made for Mrs Gardner picture by picture between 1894 and 1914: the exquisite small Giotto, Giovanni Bellini's *Madonna and Child* (painted 1460–70), and the Moro *Mary Tudor* and so many others. For those who are interested Sir Philip Hendy's catalogue of the collection may be studied in any good art library. Berenson purchased (as far as I could ascertain) forty-six pictures for Mrs Gardner, of which sixteen came through Colnaghi in those twenty years. In the early days he devised a little telegraphic code by which she could, in one word, agree for example to purchase or not to purchase a Titian or a Van Dyck: the single word in the telegram would be either YETIT or NOTIT, YEVAN or NOVAN. He, on the other hand, would occasionally wire prices in one word such as XVM, meaning £15,000.

One striking feature of Berenson's letters is that he never repeats himself. He thereby trained Mrs. Gardner to take his letters seriously and to make up her mind. Allowing for a few disputed attributions and even mistakes, the excellence of Berenson's recommendations is widely recognized. If the purpose was to create a limited but a great collection, he and his collector achieved the purpose. By the age of thirty-two, within two years of starting to buy for her, he had already picked up more than two dozen masterpieces for her. It was a flying start. The correspondence is relieved by descriptions of nature in phrases which were to appear again and again in later letters throughout his life.

He speaks of the golden weather in which he is basking in January in Florence. He feels 'the radiance of summer in winter' as one often does in Italian winters. And that kind of winter day makes him feel, on his afternoon walks, 'an embodied joy, with more than my share of mortal happiness'. At this time (in 1896) he was beginning to meet Gabriele d'Annunzio, and wrote, 'Yes, his prose is music', but he straightway found Hawthorne's *Scarlet Letter* infinitely superior to d'Annunzio's prose. Mrs Gardner thanks him for his first book, *The Venetian Painters of the Renaissance*, but there is little indication that she wrote more than 'pleasant words', for which he is grateful. One never gets a feeling that she was interested in literature.

Mrs Gardner was anxious to hear something about his loves. 'You ask me about my heart', he writes: 'it exists, but it is not to be written about. Some day with leisure before us I shall tell you. Meanwhile a good bit of it throbs for your Museum.' From Scotland he writes that it is 'as a dream of magic . . . it is Greece—it is the Roman Campagna in the north'. Suddenly in Munich he develops a new passion for Mozart. Beethoven takes second place and his favourite Wagner drops into third. He has seen some ballets at the opera, and he tells her that the music and the ballets and 'all this is going to be treated in a book which I mean to publish on my fortieth birthday, thereafter binding myself to keep the peace': *Aesthetics and History* was certainly casting its shadow before, as all good books should, but it was not to be published until he was eighty-five.

* * *

In 1898 Berenson sent the second of his five-yearly reports to Harvard, as all the members of the 1887 Class were expected to do. The first report[1] in 1893 reads:

'I am trying to fit myself to write about Italian painting, soberly and appreciatively. I spend the winters in Florence, the springs and autumns elsewhere in Italy, the summers in Paris and London, or else in Germany.

'My permanent address is Messrs Baring Brothers & Co. London.'

The second report, dated April 22, 1897, is much longer.

'I live at Fiesole, where I spend about eight months of the year. The summer months I pass in travelling chiefly in Great Britain, France and Germany. It is my plan to revisit the principal picture galleries of Europe each, every two years.

'I have published *The Venetian Painters of the Renaissance,* now in its third edition; *The Florentine Painters of the Renaissance,* which is being honoured with a translation into German; and a monograph on the Venetian painter, *Lorenzo Lotto.* The work has been well received by the competent. I have in the press *The Central Italian Painters of the Renaissance*; and at present I am at work upon a book on the drawings of the Florentine painters—a work which will contain some 160 facsimile illustrations. Occasionally I write articles for the *Gazette des Beaux-Arts,* for the *Revue Critique* and for the *New York Nation.* I forgot to add among my publications a pamphlet on the exhibition of Venetian Old Masters, held in London in the winter '94–'95.[2]

'I remain single and live a very retired life. Writing, talking and the classics occupy my time when I am not travelling.'

No one could have guessed from the Harvard report that Berenson had already become the leading agent for the sale of Italian Renaissance pictures in Europe and that six miles away from Harvard, in Boston itself, the first pictures of his choosing were being hung by Mrs Gardner at 150 Beacon Street—three years before Fenway Court was planned.

[1] Harvard College Class Report, 1887. Secretary's Report, Nos. 3 and 4. Burlington Free Press Association, 1893 and 1898, Cambridge, Massachusetts.

[2] See pp. 147–49 below.

One of a collector's chief pleasures is to be thought of as exceptionally discriminating, perhaps because so few are. Collectors rarely mention their advisers. Many collectors seem to be engaged in something very like speculation on the Stock Exchange, or simply in capital investment.

Of both Mrs Gardner and Bernard Berenson, posterity has judged that their aim in one respect was single and devoted, and accomplished with the greatest simplicity. Boston has its own great museum; Fenway Court,[1] a stone's throw away, remains a unique legacy to the capital of Massachusetts.

This is the picture which Harold Acton paints of it, when he visited it after the First War. 'If you admire Henry James', Acton maintains,

'it will fascinate you, for it is similar to his prose. . . . Fenway Court develops like his ponderous leisurely sentences, and among the iron eagles, green velvet copes, red velvet baldaquins, carved chests and Gothic credences, one is aware that each of these objects reflects the taste of this ambitious despotic woman. But her unique collection of paintings could not have been formed without the expert advice of Bernard Berenson. . . . This must remain one of the last monuments to the era of private patronage; and while the public may prefer the change in favour of Town Councils and anonymous corporations, I doubt if artists do. That Mrs Gardner evoked the gratitude of artists seems to be proved by her correspondence with them and by Whistler's inscription in a copy of his *Baronet and Butterfly*: "To Mrs Gardner—whose appreciation of the work of art is only equalled by her understanding of the artist".'[2]

Returning on my last day in Boston for a long look at the pictures, I felt at moments the throb of all the labours and controversies, nego-

---

[1] One visitor to Fenway Court in 1930, Miss Naomi Royde-Smith, makes the point that Berenson chose Mrs Gardner's pictures before the 'incredible stereotyping of Fenway Court' into 'if-ever-a-place-was-haunted-this-one-is'. Miss Naomi Royde-Smith, like all other visitors of ordinary sensibility, had become aware of the haunting presence also. She takes a strong view of Zorn's portrait of Mrs Gardner and calls it a portrait of 'cold and concentrated greed'. For her 'there are only three pictures on earth that floor you'. Needless to say, Titian's *Rape of Europa* 'floored' her. (Roger Hinks and Naomi Royde-Smith, *Pictures and People*, Gollancz, 1930.)

[2] Harold Acton, *Memoirs of an Aesthete*, pp. 244–5, Methuen, 1948.

tiations and heartbreaks which had gone to the making of the collection. Nearly every other large private collection in the United States of America has found or is finding its way into the big public galleries. These, by the way, are not State museums, but generously supported by art-loving people. Fenway Court seems adequately endowed to continue its own existence unless some major world disaster disturbs the life of the American continent.

CHAPTER IX

Into Print

In 1894 there appeared simultaneously in New York and London *The Venetian Painters of the Renaissance.*[1] It was a slender volume, Berenson's first, a mere 138 pages with one illustration. It remains to this day a most exhilarating introduction to the Renaissance itself. In the account of Berenson's successive writings to which I now pass, it stands high in merit.

The first three tiny chapters recapture the spirit of the Renaissance in Venice, as one gifted young man seized it after five or six years of living with its masterpieces. The writing is inspired with the desire to communicate with the reader, and communication is rapidly established. It glows with the warmth of Berenson's own impressions.

Perhaps the fact that only one illustration accompanied the original edition in 1894 compelled the vivid and simple language. When photographs in abundance could be included there was hardly a sentence which did not exactly fit the illustrations. The prose unfolds from the great Venetian pageant picture to the Venetian easel picture, from the Renaissance sculptor's and the medallist's portraits to the Renaissance painter's portraits, and to the first Venetian full-face portrait in the early sixteenth century. Landscape slides into Venetian painting as smoothly as it slides into the text. And there is a fierce lash at the painful subject of the Counter-Reformation in Chapter XI, if only to bring out more clearly a certain Venetian immunity from it:

[1] Published by G. P. Putnams at the Knickerbocker Press. This essay, together with the other three short volumes, *The Florentine, The Central Italian* and *The North Italian Painters of the Renaissance* were republished with 400 illustrations in one volume by the Phaidon Press in London in 1952, at a moderate price, with the aid of the Kress Foundation.

This edition is referred to henceforward as I.P.R. By 1958 it had sold over 100,000 copies in five languages, and was about to appear in Japanese and in Russian.

'We therefore find that towards the middle of the sixteenth century, when elsewhere in Italy painting was trying to adapt itself to the hypocrisy of a Church whose chief reason for surviving as an institution was that it helped Spain to subject the world to tyranny, . . . in Venice painting kept true to the ripened and more reflective spirit which succeeded to the most glowing decade of the Renaissance.'[1]

Ruskin abounded in such 'digs'—so did most English writers on Italian art. Berenson mostly reserved them for conversation. And from the 'more reflective spirit' to the Venetian painter upon whom Berenson and Mary had been working for most of 1894—Lorenzo Lotto—was but a short step. The book on Lotto was to come out in 1895. Already in *The Venetian Painters* one miniscule chapter (XII) is devoted to Lotto, although the passage is swift, and the reader is already on the wing for an examination of Tintoretto. With the Bassani and Palma Giovane, Berenson passes to a quick glance at the later Venice of Longhi ('an all-pervading cheerfulness distinguishes Longhi's pictures from the works of Hogarth, at once so brutal and so full of presage of change'), of Canaletto, Guardi and Tiepolo. So the slim volume ended, throwing out the suggestion that the author could easily have shown how much the Flemish painters led by Rubens, and the English painters led by Reynolds, owed to the Venetians. But it would not have been to his purpose, he told the reader. These things he often spoke of in conversation.

All he wanted was 'to explain some of the attractions of the [Venetian] School, and particularly to show its close dependence upon the thought and feeling of the Renaissance'. He had found in the Venetians 'complete expression of the riper spirit of the Renaissance' and that was why they attracted him so much:

'We, too, are possessed of boundless curiosity. We, too, have an almost intoxicating sense of human capacity. We, too, believe in a great future for humanity, and nothing has yet happened to check our delight in discovery or our faith in life.'

In view of everything that has happened in the world since 1914, that ending from the pen of the young man of twenty-nine happily (and prosperously) immersed in his chosen profession, could not pass

[1] *I.P.R.*, p. 20.

without comment by the man of eighty-seven when the Phaidon Press edition came out in 1952. In a little bracket he writes 'N.B.— Written in 1894!' Otherwise the early text stands.

In *The Venetian Painters of the Renaissance,* as in *The Florentine Painters,* an equally slim volume with one modest illustration which was to appear in 1896, and in the other two far more voluminous and laboured surveys which were to appear in 1897 (*The Central Italian Painters*) and in 1907 (*The North Italian Painters*), the whole vast period is covered with discrimination. Lesser painters are left out. The reader is not confused by any desire on the part of the author to show off. It is possible today to look up almost any notable painting of the Italian Renaissance in these volumes and to have the essence of the picture brought vividly to mind in a few brief words. And people often do so.

In the *Florentine Painters* Berenson for the first time elaborates his idea of 'tactile values'. He launches the then revolutionary notion of a physical response to painting in a mere dozen paragraphs. 'I must have the illusion of varying muscular sensations inside my palm and fingers' corresponding to the various projections of the painted figure 'before I shall take it for granted as real, and let it affect me lastingly'. Sight alone could give no accurate sense of a third dimension. The painter had to provide his own third dimension and 'he can accomplish his task only as we accomplish ours, by giving tactile values to retinal impressions'.[1] The painter's first business was there-

---

[1] Bertrand Russell (in conversation with the author) maintained that Berenson's reading of the philosopher Berkeley and of his theory of vision had set him thinking along these lines, and that Russell and Berenson had argued much about it on a bicycle tour they made together in Lombardy in 1894. Of that tour Lord Russell said, 'I remember I was amazed at his reading. He it was who first put me on to Fustel de Coulanges' *La Cité Antique,* for which I have always been grateful, and he first put me on to reading Ranke. I read his *Venetian Painters* in manuscript and felt he was under a misapprehension in following Berkeley's mistaken theory of vision [that we see everything in two dimensions and ourselves supply a third]. I put B.B. on to William James's *Psychology* to dissuade him from this view, and he subsequently modified his theory and clarified it greatly.'

One must, I think, remember that Berenson had been a pupil in William James's class for three years at Harvard. His theory of tactile values was his own, and he used it continually all his life. Anyone who visited a gallery with him remembered how he might suddenly stop in front of a favourite Madonna and child saying: 'Look how that child rests on its mother's arm. One can almost feel the impress he makes. There—those are tactile values.' He would

fore 'to rouse tactile sense, so that one could have the illusion of being able to touch a figure'.

If the first impact of a great painting was to rouse the sense of touch, the lasting impact of painters who gave Berenson a 'vivid realization of the object' was an altogether enhancing stimulation of the imagination, a 'sense of greater physical capacity', of 'an ever-heightened reality' and a 'real source of aesthetic enjoyment'. He even went as far as to say:

'. . . art stimulates to an unwonted activity psychical processes which are in themselves the source of most (if not all) of our pleasures, and which here, free from disturbing physical sensations, never tend to pass over into pain. For instance: I am in the habit of realizing a given object with an intensity that we shall value as 2. If I suddenly realize this familiar object with an intensity of 4, I receive the immediate pleasure which accompanies a doubling of my mental activity. But the pleasure rarely stops here. Those who are capable of receiving direct pleasure from a work of art are generally led on to the further pleasures of self-consciousness. The fact that the physical process of recognition goes forward with the unusual intensity of 4 to 2 overwhelms them with the sense of having twice the capacity they had credited themselves with: their whole personality is enhanced. . . .'

No one has quarrelled with this. None has formulated it better.

remark them in the texture of a house, a cloud, a meadow, if they were present, and presently one would remark them too.

D. S. MacColl, in *Recollections of a Keeper*, maintained that Vernon Lee first launched the idea of physical expansion and ease in the presence of beauty. I am told that he made light of the phrase 'tactile values', and called them 'pneumatic values'. It is, of course, possible to make fun of anything. Sir Kenneth Clark takes a different view. He suggests a line of descent for these ideas from the Swiss art historian Heinrich Wölfflin, as follows: 'Wölfflin's laws that works of art develop according to their own internal laws and not against a background of political history were to a large extent borrowed from the theories of the German sculptor Adolf Hildebrand, who in turn had derived them from a philosopher named Conrad Fiedler. Indeed, I think it could be shown that Fiedler's ideas, contained in letters to Hildebrand and the painter Hans von Marees, were the real origin of that new direction in applied aesthetics which led to Mr Berenson's theory of tactile values and Roger Fry's doctrine of significant form.' (Sir Kenneth Clark, 'The Study of Art History', *Universities Quarterly*, May 1956, pp. 223–38.)

141

Nor had the great qualities of Raphael and Piero della Francesca in composing their interiors and their landscapes in depth, height and width ever been so happily described as in Berenson's paragraphs on 'space-composition'.

'Space-composition is the art which humanizes the void, making of it an enclosed Eden. . . . Painted space-composition opens out the space it frames in, puts boundaries only ideal to the roof of heaven. All that it uses, whether the forms of the natural landscape, or of grand architecture, or even of the human figure, it reduces to be its ministrants in conveying a sense of untrammelled, but not chaotic spaciousness. In such pictures how freely one breathes—as if a load had just been lifted from one's breast; how refreshed, how noble, how potent one feels; again, how soothed; and still again, how wafted forth to abodes of far away bliss!

'The feeling just described is one that, at happy moments, many of us have had in the presence of nature and it is one that we expect, but too seldom get, from landscape painting. Yet space-composition is as distinct from the art of landscape as it is from architecture. . . .'[1]

The effect of these ideas seems to have been electric. In the immediate neighbourhood of Florence the English and American colony, which was large in those days, talked of nothing else but the *Trecento* and the *Quattrocento* in a way which had not happened since Walter Pater's *Renaissance* came out in 1873. Somehow the phrase 'tactile values' caught on and spread far and wide, and is often used today. The two little books set the whole art world talking. There was something in them 'in reaction against all Berenson's nine-teenth-century predecessors, alike in his philosophy of art and in his aphoristic style, a contrast to the purple splendours and irrelevancies of Ruskin and the dreary long-drawn dullness of Cavalcaselle'.[2]

Ponderous writers on art were really shaken up, at least for a time. Berenson's theory of space composition and of tactile values opened up a whole new school of appreciation. One American writer says that Gertrude Stein (a neighbour in Florence) 'thought that everyone was doing their best to look like some person out of a bygone day— and she fled', but he hastens to add that Gertrude Stein, after all, believed (like Emerson) 'that nothing is anything more than it is to

[1] *I.P.R.*, pp. 120–1.
[2] Van Wyck Brooks, *The Confident Years*, p. 460.

PLATE X The green garden at 'I Tatti', looking towards
San Martino a Mensola and Galluzzo

Right: 'I Tatti', Mary Berenson's room and balcony overlooking the Arno valley. (Photo, Guglielmo Alberti)

PLATE XI The Ilex wood and balustrade stairs leading to the green garden at 'I Tatti'. (Photo by Guglielmo Alberti)

Pomegranate and lemons in the upper garden at 'I Tatti'

oneself'[1] which is, after all, a very dreary doctrine, 'oneself' being often limited, sick or cross.[2]

Nowhere outside these two books has Berenson himself stated so clearly the kind of thing that might happen to anyone who went into the National Gallery in a receptive mood. He himself had undoubtedly enjoyed his first revelation when he first looked at Giotto. With Byzantine ikons, or even with Cimabue, he had had to work at deciphering the representations. 'With what sense of relief, of rapidly rising vitality, we turn to the Giotto!'

Giotto he found 'on a high plane of reality', and he asks himself how Giotto had managed to be first among the Italian Renaissance painters to get there.

'Now what is behind this power of raising us to a higher plane of reality but a genius for grasping and communicating real significance? What is it to render the tactile values of an object but to communicate its material significance?'[3]

Before Giotto there had been 'generations of mere manufacturers of symbols, illustrations and allegories'. If a painter now appeared who could give material significance to what he painted, it must mean that he had 'a profound sense of the significant'.

For Berenson, familiar from childhood with the Old Testament and from manhood with the New, the first experience of the Cappella degli Scrovegni in Padua where the best of Giotto is to be seen in one place, and the upper church of St Francis at Assisi, where his other great fresco series adorns both sides of the long nave, the meaning and purpose of the painting could not baffle, as it frequently baffles those young tourists from northern Europe who are no longer brought up on the Bible or those from the East whose mythology is Marxian, Islamic or Confucian.

It is probably unwise to attempt any sightseeing in Italy without reading at least the New Testament. Berenson takes it for granted that you have, and that you are no great stranger to the chief myths and legends of Greek and Roman antiquity. But then every Victorian

---

[1] Van Wyck Brooks, *The Confident Years*, p. 448.

[2] Among many memories of Gertrude Stein in later years in the Berenson household there was one which persistently recurred: that she would borrow books from the library and fail to return them, and that when they were finally recaptured they were not in a very good condition.　　　[3] *I.P.R.*, p. 45.

tourist in Italy knew his Bible and those without Greek and Latin had read Mrs Jameson's *Sacred and Legendary Art*—a book which admirably illumines the classical and the mediaeval inheritances in Renaissance painting. Since Mrs Jameson's day this subject—called by the German writer Panofsky iconology—has rallied a host of learned researchers to its ranks. To make a science of the subject may be part of our twentieth-century mania for method. Mrs Jameson certainly had a fine way of marrying all her research to her appreciation.

To the end of his time Berenson would acknowledge how much he owed to Mrs Jameson's books (she wrote another volume on *Legends of the Monastic Orders*). He liked her inquiries into all the various symbols, attendant animals and objects, which belong to the paintings and sculptures of saints, early Bishops and Martyrs, and which had become unintelligible since the Reformation to most English-speaking students of Italian art. In her day those students knew and recognized all the Greek classical figures, the gods and heroes, who appear in later Renaissance art, because most of them had had a classical education. But of mediaeval Christian symbolism they knew little. For them taste had replaced knowledge. Berenson liked her descriptions of pictures, her lists of patron saints of cities and her analysis of the meaning of colour and her chapter on Angels— probably the best in the two volumes. After reading it one has a new eye for cherubs and angels wherever they occur:

'. . . angels . . . as intermediaries between heaven and earth—are introduced into all works of Art which have a sacred purpose or character, and must be considered not merely as decorative accessories, but as a kind of presence, as attendant witnesses; and like a chorus in the Greek tragedies, looking on where they are not actors.'[1]

To Mrs Jameson even the wildest mediaeval legends of the saints probably rested on some basis of local tradition, and were, in any case, an intense expression of 'those crushed and outraged sympathies which cried aloud for rest and refuge and solace and could nowhere find them'.[2] She spent six years collecting the scriptural and legendary attributes of a vast number of saints, giving two or

[1] Mrs Jameson, *Sacred and Legendary Art*, two volumes, p. 61 (Vol. I), Longmans, Green, 1879.   [2] *Ibid.*, p. 2.

three versions of their history if these could help in understanding
the representations of them in mosaic, in paint and in marble.

She had very naturally been interested in the Byzantine inter-
pretations of the chief figures in the Christian story. Another contemporary writer, who was among the first to rescue Byzantine art
from the opprobrium into which it had fallen, was an American,
W. J. Stillman, who for many years was *The Times* correspondent in
Rome. In his spare time, which must have been considerable, he was
a passionate amateur of Italian Renaissance painting. He wrote: 'As
decorative art nothing that we know surpasses certain Byzantine
work from the fifth to the eleventh centuries' after he had studied
the monks' illuminations in the Laurentiana Library in Florence.[1]
Students were beginning to become interested. At Oxford, William
Richmond at this time gave the 'Stack Foundation' lectures which
first drew attention (before any frescoes or mosaics of the period
had been found) to the treasure house that Constantinople must
have been before the sack of the city in the Venetian (Fourth)
Crusade in 1204. Here, in pre-1204 Constantinople, Berenson
believed, probably were the artists who then became refugees all
over Italy and brought with them the skill of the silversmith and
the painter—in a word the earliest visual inspiration of the
Renaissance.

Berenson was to write down these beliefs a little later, in his book
on Sassetta, published in 1909.

*   *   *

Only the briefest attempt is made here to link Berenson's writing
with the prevalent books and articles of the period. Mary has
described the main sources—the handbooks—with which they
travelled. Writers on the period today must still use those reference
books, for the study of painting is a relatively new subject, and the
nineteenth century in Europe, and especially in England, Germany
and Italy, produced the keenest scholars and researchers in the
subject. In the enormous output all over the world of illustrated
'art books' after the Second World War, a volume which adds to
their research is rare. Even Roger Fry, who launched the Post-
Impressionists in the Anglo-Saxon world with such enthusiasm in
1910, was at this time unable to cope with all he saw in Italy.

[1] W. J. Stillman and Timothy Cole, *Old Italian Masters*, p. 4, The Century
Company, New York, 1892.

Eventually he produced a little monograph on Bellini which altered no one's taste, and a more important essay on Giotto.[1]

However solipsistic Berenson's theories may seem to some art scholars, his 'looking' was continuously fresh, his reading was wide and he was never averse from changing a number of his own attributions to much debated pictures. He took as long as twenty and thirty years to decide some attributions. This can be seen in the various modifications he made to the lists attached to his books and then reissued in the 1932 Lists. Many of his inspirations came to him with the speed of lightning. Many of course he absorbed from his predecessors and contemporaries, with that nod of recognition which is a delight in any branch of knowledge.

The tradition in which Berenson writes is John Ruskin's. Ruskin's conversion to the 'joyousness' of the Italian Renaissance was to Walter Pater and to Berenson like dew in the gardens they tended. Berenson found much of Ruskin, especially his later writing, was governed by religious dogmatisms, which turned easily into propaganda for and against an artist's conception of a religious theme. Ruskin's biographers in this century have given a score of medical reasons why he began to fantasticate, and having (in our twentieth-century clinical way) dissected him, they forgot to appreciate his greatness. Like Ruskin, Berenson found that the great schools of Italian painting after the death of Titian were ruled by 'the masters of exaggeration', so that religious pictures began to be affected and farcical or just mannered, and secular painting suffered accordingly. Contemporary art historians would look first to the condition of society in which such painting occurred. Berenson shared with Ruskin the view that a civilization survives by its deeds, its words and its art, 'but of the three, the only quite trustworthy one is the last'.[2] Ruskin was immensely distressed by the ignorance of this fact in expanding industrial societies, and fought with his pen and his voice to get the fact recognized. Berenson was not a fighter on social problems, least of all a reformer. One shudders to imagine what a lone voice his would have been had he attempted to carry such a

---

[1] Virginia Woolf in her biography of Roger Fry says that on his third trip to Italy he was still being overcome by the sight of so many masterpieces and wrote home: 'Italy makes one lose one's nerve—a malarious infection of humility creeps over one's soul' (p. 103). The first shadow of his wife's insanity was, at the time, cast on this journey. Roger Fry was a year younger than Berenson. See footnote, p. 186.   [2] John Ruskin, *St Mark's Rest*, Preface.

banner in his adopted America; even more isolated than Ruskin's was in industrial, jerry-building England. These were (and are) outrageous times for lovers of beauty. In Berenson's *Painters of the Renaissance* there shines a very fresh and infectious love of beauty. This was the revolution: for the first time the viewer became quite as important as the work of art. Here was a writer who spoke directly to the man or woman in front of a work of art, and gave that person new confidence. Few art critics realized what had happened. The art merchants were quick—as always—to sense a new voice and a new language.

Among the many reviews of the *Florentine Painters*, friendly and hostile, there was one in *The Studio* of August 15, 1896, signed 'Mary Logan', which expressed 'surprise' at the 'thoroughly original treatment of the most essential problems of representative art'. She, who had accompanied him on innumerable visits to galleries and collections since 1891, pretends she has just come upon the book. She enthusiastically confirms the 'life-enhancing' experience of great art. The review, despite her frivol of 'surprise', certainly reveals what had been going on in those long hours of joint looking.

*   *   *

In 1895 they both went to an 'Exhibition of Venetian Art' in London, composed largely of loan paintings from private collections. It was being held in what was then called The New Gallery. The catalogue stated 'The Committee cannot be responsible for the attributions', a statement which, after one visit, spurred Berenson to entirely re-write the catalogue. Mr (later Sir) Herbert Cook had the new catalogue 'printed in haste, at his expense', and in Mary's words this is what happened:

'Without a word of explanation or apology, he [Berenson] named all the pictures according to his views, and this aroused a great scandal and excited much hostility. We drew up the catalogue together in a curious kind of innocence, not thinking about the effect it would produce, and not realizing how fiercely the owners of the pictures held to the big names that had traditionally been attached to their works of art. It did have, however, the effect which I at that time judged important for the future, of making his name known to all collectors of Italian pictures; but the result was not really planned for him or by me, although it gave us the undeserved and unsavoury

147

reputation of schemers and hunters of publicity—a reputation further enhanced by my writing an article on the 'New Connoisseurship' for the *Fortnightly Review*. I wrote it because I was so keen on the subject, . . . I admit that it certainly looked like a planned campaign!'[1]

Of the thirty-three 'Titians' Berenson would attribute only one to the Venetian master, and that one Mr Ludwig Mond's *Madonna*. Twelve of the 'Titians' had 'no connection' in Berenson's view, five were copies and the rest were by other painters. The official catalogue had gaily listed eighteen Giorgiones. Berenson would have none at all. He only ventured an opinion on seven: a Catena, a Buonconsiglio, a doubtful Schiavoni and so on. The exhibitors included Lord Cowper, Lord Brownlow, Louisa Lady Ashburton, Lord Battersea, Lord Powerscourt, Sir William Farrer, the Duke of Westminster and a host of others. They must have been horrified by the new catalogue. In it Lord Malmesbury's Moroni was not a Moroni, nor was Lord Battersea's. Lord Pembroke's *Judith* was ruled out as a Mantegna, because its 'gaudy pink and yellow were un-familiar'. However, Berenson hesitates about this picture in 1901 and finds it 'more puzzling than ever'. Out of ten pictures attributed in the official catalogue to Cima da Conegliano, Berenson would only recognize three. His notes were fierce. There was, for instance, a portrait of a lady professor of Bologna by Giorgione. He noted that she was neither a lady, nor a professor, nor of Bologna, and least of all by Giorgione.[2] Seven Montagnas were listed of which he would allow only four. Of the four Carpaccios he would allow none.

One can guess, if only from the Giorgiones, of which there are not eighteen in England, that the organizers simply used the owners' attributions, many of which were traditional ones, handed down from generation to generation. Berenson later revised some of the attribu-tions he had made in his rapidly printed catalogue. All the attribu-tions (if the paintings were masterpieces) had to be revised and brought up to date for his great 1932 *Lists*. Moreover, many had changed hands by then and had sometimes passed through more than one auction room or dealer.[3]

It now became apparent that to keep track of the masterpieces it

[1] U.L.   [2] Now in the Ashmolean Museum, Oxford.
[3] The art scholars have doubtless kept pace with these pictures: the mere amateur can hardly hope to pursue them to their present position, geographic or hierarchical.

would be necessary to collect catalogues of all the great sales in London, Paris and New York, and to collect information about as many private sales and movements of pictures as possible. Little wonder that the magical universe in which Berenson acknowledges that he had lived up to that moment began to cloud over with an immense vista of tasks to be performed:

'Until thirty or so I was young enough to live in a magical universe, a universe full of glamour through which I saw what was for the time being conventionally regarded as the actual world, as if through a prism. And till then almost everything that meant anything was IT. Then something happened. I was pushed out of Eden and found myself in a realm where men and women did not live for IT but were invariably doing something for the sake of something else. True the most fortunate did it with gusto, with the satisfaction of healthy functioning. They were, however, so preoccupied with the next that they found no time to feel how much they were enjoying the passing moment.'[1]

Berenson was thirty in 1895. The 'they' might well refer to himself, after the bombshell of his dramatic attributions at the Exhibition of Venetian Art, that year in London. At just about the same time he was entering the buyers' world. Henceforward there would be two worlds, the magical one of the passing moment, and the unmagical one of all those who had pictures to sell, or had to be wheedled into selling them, and those others who had to be likewise wheedled to buy.

That autumn the *Lorenzo Lotto, An Essay in Constructive Art Criticism*, his second book, appeared (again with G. P. Putnams in New York and London). With this book Mary helped him a great deal. It was a long work, and a good deal of it had to be revised for the grand edition which appeared no less than sixty-one years later, in 1956, when he was ninety-one, with four hundred illustrations instead of thirty.[2] Very few authors are able to revise their books sixty-one years after publication.[3]

[1] *S.S.P.*, p. 121.
[2] Bernard Berenson, *Lorenzo Lotto*, pp. 486, The Phaidon Press, London, 1956.
[3] The revisions were chiefly the work of a young Florentine art scholar, Signorina Luisa Vertova, who worked with Berenson from 1945–55, and then married the editor of the *Burlington Magazine*, Mr Benedict Nicolson.

The main revision was the detachment of Lotto from the close association with Vivarini which Berenson had insisted upon in the 1894 and in the 1901 edition, and the whole arrangement became much smoother than in the earlier edition. The important—the very remarkable—final essay entitled 'Resulting Impression' remains unaltered. In it Berenson enters into the artistic personality and genius of this painter, whom he calls the first psychological portrait painter of the Renaissance. There are some magnificent passages, which undoubtedly established Lotto in a way that no other writer on art had established him before among the great Venetians. In Lotto's lifetime the Venetian world was moving towards conformity. Lotto was 'evangelical at heart in a country upon which a rigid and soulless Catholicism was daily strengthening its hold'.[1]

Berenson found Lotto not only a great and humane portrait painter but a psychological master of religious paintings also. Here is a typical passage:

'The Madonnas of Botticelli, if we may trust Mr Pater, are so wholly out of sympathy with the Christ-child they bear in their arms that they feel Him like an "intolerable honour" thrust upon them. The exact contrary is the truth about Lotto's Madonnas. They seem to realize to the full what new life the Child brings, and they do not humbly treasure the secret in their hearts, but long rather to enlighten the world, and to fill it, in like measure with themselves, with the new hope and the new joy.'

Berenson found it likely that Lorenzo Lotto was in some contact with the Venetian Reformers who were so much hoping (at the height of the Counter-Reformation) to achieve some reconciliation with Protestantism. In the little mountain village of Cingoli, in the Marches, he found an altarpiece, a large Madonna and fifteen small pictures above and around her, in which

'. . . Lotto treats each one of these episodes [from the lives of Christ and the Virgin] with a depth of conviction, with a sublimity of conception, with an earnestness of piety, with an eloquence of appeal, which have a kindling power such as the early Protestant preachers are reported to have had over those who heard them. We have here

[1] *Lorenzo Lotto*, p. 278, George Bell, 1905. In the Phaidon edition fifty-one years later, 'Catholicism' is changed to 'Vaticanism'.

150

the expression of a noble and inspired soul endeavouring to reconcile itself with eternity by the only means within its reach, the symbols and allegories of Christianity. The gulf between the human and the divine has never been indicated with more spiritual suggestiveness than in the last scene, the *Coronation of the Virgin*. Lotto here attains a sublimity which can be compared with Milton's.'

Most people who enjoy this picture remember the wonderful wicker tubful of rose petals in the foreground, from which three enchanting small angels are scattering the flowers, and they hardly glance as far as the little medallion in the extreme right-hand top corner which so won Berenson's devotion. Now that single large reproductions of these medallions are given in the 1956 edition their piety and earnestness are apparent.

*   *   *

The writing of these books was accomplished mainly in the Villa Kraus. But Fiesole now had a new brass band and Berenson gives the band as his reason for moving away. In the Christmas week of 1897 he moved to San Domenico di Fiesole. His income from picture sales enabled him to rent a little house at 5 via Camerata. His first thought, however, was for his parents. He swiftly made it possible for them to move away from Minot Street and its shunting trains to a pleasant house at Roxbury outside Boston. He described his own new dwelling at San Domenico to Mrs Gardner with all the pride of a very young householder. It had two floors. He was living on the second and had turned the lower floor into a hall with a guest chamber. He says he chose 'pistachio green' for the walls of the hall, which was bare except for a big desk. Upstairs the passages were 'monastically whitewashed'. There was a library room with white bookcases and, at last, the longed-for cases made of walnut to house his ever-growing collection of photographs of paintings. Then there was the green room for his treasures. It contained a mirrored Venetian desk and some fine Venetian hangings and a 'gorgeous cope' which Mrs Gardner had bought for him a few months before in Venice. In that memorable spring visit of 1897 she had, as often, rented the Palazzo Barbaro from the Ralph Curtis's, a Boston family who owned it and spent many months of the year in it. The fifty-seven-year-old collector had invited the thirty-two year old Berenson to stay there for a fortnight. He told her, in Venice, all about Mary. Mrs Gardner seems there and then to have confirmed what was already a friendship and already a proven respect for his competence and his unerring taste. She must have been convinced then, if ever, that he was buying well for her, and not overcharging her.

The winning of her confidence seems to have been sealed anew in that fortnight in Venice in 1897. Writing about it to her twenty-six years later, from Palazzo Barbaro this time as the guest of Mr and Mrs Cole-Porter (on July 29, 1923, a few months before Mrs Gardner's death) he says:

'It was enchanting arriving in this milky opalescent soap-bubbly world early, early, being met by an Arab I knew on the Nile and the gondoliers of Casa Curtis. And I shall never get over that fortnight in 1897—how you made me feel as if you had nothing in the world to think of except my happiness. Yes, it was wonderful, and if I ever sigh for anything in the past it is for those days.'

She had long ago ceased buying pictures when he wrote this letter.

In his treasure room at San Domenico there was a fireplace with a sofa in front of it, and in the corners 'some resplendent chairs, covered with mossy green'.[1] The floor was covered with an Aubusson carpet 'so that on the whole the effect is gorgeous'. To complete the green room he hoped to hang 'two or three pictures on a gold ground'. There was another room on the second floor—his bedroom —and he wondered whether, at the sight of it Mrs Gardner would not, like his other friends 'burst into fits of laughter'. They had said such a room was 'not made for a bearded monster but for a delicate creature'. The walls were white. The floor was covered with Japanese matting. The bed was a low and narrow divan 'but with a *baldacchino* which with the bed cover is of pale blue green silk— Louis XVI—with a design *painted* on it'. He tells her there is 'a charming mirror' and 'a nice canapé white and gold covered with a pretty silk'. An old marble topped table on carved white and gold legs and an Intarsia bureau completed the room. It was a place 'after my own heart', and he adds: 'Dear Friend, I never never forget how much of this I owe to you.'

Mary was still at Fiesole, and now living in the Villa Kraus. In

[1] See Plate VII.

1898 he describes to Mrs Gardner how 'we are cooped up in our several houses because of the rain'. Mary Costelloe had her brother Logan staying with her; Robert Trevelyan was staying at Poggio Gherardo with Mrs Janet Ross and her niece, Lina Duff Gordon (who later married a painter, Aubrey Waterfield). Herbert Horne was staying with Berenson and the young people were all to go off on a bicycle tour to Volterra and San Gemignano. Berenson had bought a bicycle the previous year.

The expedition begins a half-century's friendship with Robert Trevelyan and with the lady who later became Mrs Waterfield. Of her he writes:

'Miss Duff Gordon is a charming graceful creature, a descendant of Scotch lairds and of many generations of women renowned in letters. Trevelyan is a delightful creature, aristocratic and unworldly, wholly devoted to poetry.'

These were happy days. Berenson describes how they are all reading 'The Bible, the poets, Greek, Latin and English, aloud, and listening to Robert, who was writing verses of his own'. On Shrove Tuesday evening they meet a crowd of boys and girls coming down from Fiesole in the twilight, singing, and swinging torches of grass. The troupe is like a Bacchanalia, 'so pagan, so antique, so uncontaminated with Christianity . . . almost I felt that the lights held over the cornfields were meant to help Ceres in Lethe search for Proserpine'. Robert Trevelyan must have been translating his Lucretius, for Berenson finds 'a certain pathos' in seeing Lucretius 'speaking with such glow of what are now the commonplaces of science primers'. The expedition to Volterra is a great success, 'we form a merry party, talk much of poetry and enjoy ourselves'. There are distant views 'of the Appennines glistening with snow and amethystine with shadow'. He was never so happy as with such a crowd of English contemporaries. And such expeditions were never quite divorced from work. In San Gemignano Mary and Berenson separated from the party to spend hours in the Cathedral looking for and identifying frescoes by Pier Francesco Fiorentino. Then they go off into the neighbouring villages with the rest of the party to enjoy and identify or just to identify more paintings and to spend the evenings 'by the fire in the improvised sitting-rooms of primitive inns', with 'roaring talks about poetry'.

Mrs Gardner was laid up with a broken leg in Boston, and, as always when Berenson's friends were laid low by illness or accident, he took especial pains to cheer her up by letter. This seems to have been a universal experience of those who were his lifelong friends. As soon as Mrs Gardner was better he would begin writing 'business' letters again, but not before.

*   *   *

Back in Florence he now spent days, months, years, in the print rooms of the Uffizi Gallery. The time had come for a thorough study of the drawings of the Florentine masters. In a letter to Mrs Gardner about the great book he was planning he sees the work with extraordinary clarity. The only flaw is the date by which he hoped to finish it. The *Drawings*

'. . . has to be a work *de grand luxe* with some sixty facsimile reproductions and a hundred more modest illustrations all chosen by me, with a text giving an appreciation of the quality of each master's genius as a draughtsman. I am bound to have this ready by Christmas '97 . . . then my head is swimming with ideas on the what and wherefore of art, which I am dying to write down in full. In my *Florentine Painters* I have attempted to write down the few most essential ideas, but in a form too curt to be obviously intelligible.'

He was now planning his tasks for years ahead, and he makes no mention of the continual flow of essays rather than articles (twelve between 1890 and 1900). Some of these articles were reviews of art books, but most of them were original studies of individual painters and sometimes of individual pictures.

Today hardly an exhibition of paintings takes place which has not some of an artist's drawings in it, except for those not infrequent exhibitions devoted to modern painters who do not know how to draw or whose drawings would best be forgotten. Before Berenson's book appeared, exhibitions rarely showed a painter's drawings. Berenson's *Drawings of the Florentine Painters* is to be found in every great museum of the world today. Many of the greatest, including the Louvre, have not yet been able to go through the vast treasures of the drawings of the Italian masters which they possess. 'Hardly a week goes by without our consulting Berenson's *Drawings of the Florentine Painters*', said the head of the Print Room in the Louvre, fifty-two years after the first edition appeared.[1] But outside the museums the two volumes remain almost unknown.[2]

The book goes into much detail about every painter of importance among the Florentines of the Renaissance, and enables new connoisseurs to set about identifying more and more unfathered drawings in the known collections, or as they may turn up in odd places.

By far the most exciting pages in the first great folio volume were naturally devoted to the most exciting draftsman of the Renaissance. One might guess that this would be Leonardo da Vinci, whose 'continuous studies from life gave him such an intimate acquaintance with the workings of bone and muscle', but it was not. This 'horsey man' ('there is a sheet at Windsor with heads of horses . . . with a look bordering on the maniac'), this 'master of draperies and of brilliant heads', never really won Berenson's devotion either in line or in colour. Berenson does not really like what he calls the parallelism drawn so often by Leonardo between the nature of animals or plants and human conduct. In this he finds Leonardo mediaeval, symbolical and allegorical. As for Leonardo's excursions into military and aerial machinery, which so enthralls the practical Englishman, it is not mentioned.

Michelangelo is the man. 'Michelangelo's chief, nay only, interest was the nude and nothing but the nude.' Berenson even forgives Michelangelo his tumble of horses out of the sky, and thinks it may have arisen out of envy, because people in Florence were saying 'leave horses to Leonardo'. Berenson claims that hardly a day has gone by in years without his looking at some sketch or other by Michelangelo. Thirteen pages of the *Drawings* are devoted not so much to Michelangelo's drawings for the famous tomb of Julius II,[3] as to refuting two alleged drawings for the tomb, and another four alleged Michelangelo drawings (in Vienna and in the Louvre) for

[1] Madame Saupique, Head of the Drawings Department in the Louvre, to the author in February 1955 in Paris.

[2] In September 1954 the Italian Radio printed a selection of the drawings of the Florentine Painters with extracts from Berenson's text, in a limited and beautiful edition as a New Year gift to its senior staff members. In this edition fifty-three drawings are reproduced in the most careful facsimile we are ever likely to see, finer than those in the first and second editions in 1902 and 1938. In a brief introduction to this R.A.I. edition, Berenson hoped that the effect of these drawings would be to 'keep out the invasion of so-called *primitivism* and worse still *infantilism* . . . the two most dangerous enemies art ever had since man has been man' (p. 121).   [3] Intended for St Peter's, Rome.

the tomb of the Medici,[1] because they had 'obstinately stood in the way between ourselves and any understanding of the tomb of Julius'. Berenson draws a gloriously vigorous picture of Michelangelo's untidy genius, his hasty drawings, his listlessness, his snatches from Petrarch scribbled between drawings, his own verses, and his relations with his employer, Pope Julius II, a major version, one feels, of Berenson's relations with his patron in Boston. Berenson really got to grips with Michelangelo's drawings.

This labour enabled him to wade through all the Sebastiano del Piombo drawings at the British Museum which were then passing as Michelangelos. It enabled him to discover how Michelangelo was copied, imitated and forged 'by a host of Bolognese and other mannerists' and to be grateful to one Austrian professor, Franz Wickhoff, for sorting out almost all of the imitators—except Sebastiano del Piombo. That Venetian's horses 'betray the child of the lagoons'. Berenson was not the first to note that Venetians could not possibly know anything about horses and therefore used the four bronze ones of St Mark's when they needed a horse in their pictures. One could always recognize a Venetian painter's horse, and often a Florentine's horse, once the magnificent bronze steed had been placed in the Piazza della Signoria—a horse which many used as a model.

Just then the British Museum had acquired a drawing of the famous *Pietà* in Viterbo as a Michelangelo. Berenson attributes it where it belongs, to Sebastiano del Piombo. (It belongs to a very famous painting, little appreciated or known then except by Berenson.) So he proceeds with a score of other alleged Michelangelo drawings, at Windsor, at Chatsworth, at Christ Church, Oxford, in the British Museum and in Venice, not to mention the 'Augean Stable', as he called it, of alleged and authentic Michelangelo drawings in the Uffizi.

Berenson's preferences continually associate the reader in decisions about beauty and non-beauty, achievement and failure. He himself cares passionately. For instance, a note of the most awful regret creeps into the text when Berenson considers Sebastiano del Piombo's 'claw-like hands, tapering legs and excrescent ankles'. The imitator of Michelangelo is uncovered. Imitators, he finds, always copy just the exaggerations of their masters and thereby create their own mannerisms. Other imitators are identified by Berenson and named.

[1] At San Lorenzo in Florence.

Everyone knew that Leonardo was left handed. Berenson discovered that Michelangelo also used his left hand, but only 'if it could help out the right'. Berenson foresaw that the mannerists—Baccio Bandinelli, 'the father of so many art lies', the 'forger Passerotti'; 'a worse and even cleverer mannerist, Luca Cambiaso'; and the 'scissor and paste artist Bacchiacca'—might all come into fashion again quite soon (which, in fact, is happening in the 1950s, partly because the dealers have run out of masterpieces and they would like the smaller fry to be written up). But Berenson remained adamant. 'While I try to do justice to a mannerist of no matter what clime or date, I can never consider him an artist.' He expected any great artist to possess a vigorous visual memory. If an artist wanted to delineate movement he would have to rely on his imagination and his memory of it since one could never draw as fast as a movement. To copy or repeat someone else's visual memory and imagination of movement—that led to mannerism. No one had ever written so lucidly about this as Berenson did here, nor has anyone done so since he wrote it.

Berenson's stigma on the mannerists, whom he associated with the decline in nearly all painting after the death of Titian, angered many art historians, and all the dealers. He appreciates painters like Andrea del Sarto, Pontormo and Bronzino, and then pinpoints details of drawing in which he discovers 'a loss of artistic, no less than of moral concentration', or 'an effect of hit or miss, of seeking for winsomeness' or the pursuit of sheer novelty, for its own sake (another mannerism, and perhaps the most common of all).[1]

The *Drawings* introduce a moral criterion into aesthetic theory. A certain kind of line shows 'moral concentration'; artistic concentration is identified with 'seriousness of purpose'. On such grounds Berenson places 'Pontormo, despite his mannerism, alongside the great men'. On such grounds Berenson quarrelled very politely with the famous Swiss art scholar Professor Wölfflin:

'Your genuine Cinquecentist was not satisfied with the largest figures a composition could bear. He wanted them just large enough to seem out of proportion to the space at command, and so packed

[1] Perhaps the easiest literary analogy for an English reader would be the 'mannerist' word-coining imitation of that poet's poet, Gerard Manley Hopkins. Dylan Thomas and many others were guilty of this from time to time, and the habit never improved their poetry.

as to produce an impression of breathlessness. This fact was first systematically observed and stated by Professor Wölfflin in his *Klassische Kunst*. I congratulate him on the discovery, and I understand how the constantly increasing attention to the figure inevitably led to it *but I do not share his aesthetic approval of it.*'[1]

The italics are mine. Neither wild horses nor gold would drag aesthetic approval out of Berenson if he did not feel it. There is morality in this also. When he did feel it, as for example in a fresco by Pontormo in the nearby Poggio a Cajano, on a neighbouring Florentine hill, his language almost dances. That fresco he describes as

'. . . a midsummer afternoon's frolic of folk half rustic, half gentle and altogether Arcadian, enjoying under the suffused light of the shimmering sky the breeze that tempers the heat. Take it for what it is and everything pleases. Why should not the children be sporting on the parapet? Why should not the grown-ups loll in the sunshine? Why should they not lie about as suits refined picnickers?'

He preferred the painting to the grander scheme of the Uffizi sketch for the painting,

'The colouring too takes my fancy. I love its freshness and newness. It has tones and harmonies of a gaiety and an audacity which wellnigh make it seem a creation of today rather than of four centuries ago—and I pity the man who has not felt the delight of encountering, when he least expects it, a touch of ourselves in the midst of ancient things.'

[1] Wölfflin was venerated by generations of German art students at Munich University where he taught them to see and to enjoy Greek and Italian art. His *Klassische Kunst* is a remarkable book, not unlike Berenson's work. Wölfflin's tastes and preferences are all passionately held. It is not easy to share them all.

One of his pupils (the German Cultural Attaché at the German Embassy in London in 1957, Dr Eugen Guerster) remembered in after years a lecture which Wölfflin ended with: 'You can take the parts of a Renaissance façade apart bit by bit, but if you try to pull a Baroque façade apart, the blood flows', and the students left the class wildly enthusiastic for almost any Baroque façade. 'He justified Baroque art at a time when it had not a single other supporter, and *Klassische Kunst* was written, he tells us, to correct the exaggerated admiration of *quattrocento* art.' (Sir Kenneth Clark, 'The Study of Art History', *op. cit.*, p. 234.)

Sometimes his aesthetic appreciation takes the form of repulsion. Of an Antonio Pollajuolo drawing in the British Museum, of a handcuffed prisoner being brought before a judge, he writes: 'As an illustration his drawing repels and and yet fascinates, like those bas-reliefs expressive of high scorn and hissing cruelty where-with Ercole Roberti was wont to adorn the thrones of his Madonnas.'

Berenson's prose can sway the novice into believing he has looked as Berenson has looked. In the *Drawings* Berenson devotes para-graphs to this likelihood and suggests that such a reader 'will divest himself of the stranger's vision with the same enthusiasm wherewith he took it up, and with equal ardour he will put on a new pair of spectacles'. Berenson thinks of everything, even of shaking up his readers when they are about to absorb his text lock, stock and barrel. But who except the constant traveller can verify all these matters? The layman isn't really meant to read the *Drawings*, but if he does he becomes aware of the astonishing genius and power and variety of these Florentine drawings. They dwarf almost any drawing executed in one's own lifetime in the twentieth century, including Picasso's classical heads. The very power of re-creating movement in line seems to be disappearing in our day.

Michelangelo remains the central figure of the *Drawings*, 'not only for the quality of his draftsmanship but for the splendour of his ideas'. The rehabilitation of Pontormo as a great artist was never challenged after the *Drawings* appeared. Cellini and Rosso introduced the Michelangelo tradition into France, but of Rosso, Berenson complains that he could be fantastic and monstrous with his palsied thumbs 'in a way that anticipates the worst northern engravers of two or three generations later'. With the formlessness of Rosso, 'form in line has almost disappeared'. Henceforward 'over desert and marsh and stagnant pool we can dimly descry the banners of another school—the school which strives for form not in line, but in light and shade and colour'. For Berenson such a technique cheats. It is a trick. The Caravaggists loom on the horizon like a dark cloud. So ends the first volume of *Drawings of the Florentine Painters*. There follows in the second volume a *Catalogue raisonné* invaluable to the Print Rooms of museums, in which the majority of known drawings of all the Florentine artists were attributed and listed—a total of 2,801—a fairly large number to have survived nearly five hundred years. These vast labours only have two pages of additions and corrections.[1] More and more drawings began to be studied and collected after this book appeared. New drawings came to light. Revision inevitably went on in the course of the years and could be incorporated in the second edition published by the Chicago University Press in 1938.[2] In 1957 Berenson was engaged on a third edition of this monumental work.[3] Nowhere else can one penetrate the methods used by Berenson and appreciate his integrity in matters of art, except in his three *Essays in Method* written a score of years later. By then a didactic note had crept in. In the *Drawings* he is an explorer.

*   *   *

These labours compelled a holiday. To Mrs Gardner he wrote that not one in a hundred of the drawings ascribed to Michelangelo had proved to be by him. The work on the *Drawings* in the ice-cold Uffizi had really told on Berenson's bodily health and, it seems, on his spiritual health also. In a curious way, in the years to come he regretted what he called 'competing with the learned',[4] which of course he identifies with the writing of the *Drawings*. He knows he was the first in that field, but he thinks

'it is a pity that I spent so many years on a task which others might have done as well once the path was laid out. . . . This book, in two folios too heavy to lift, has never been seriously reviewed either in the first edition or in the second, but with the public it established my reputation as an authority.'

Berenson recalls that on his next visit to London after the book's publication one connoisseur told him 'with choking voice that in

[1] *Drawings of the Florentine Painters*, classified, criticized and studied as documents in the History and Appreciation of Tuscan Art, with a Copious Catalogue Raisonné, John Murray, London. Volume I had 330 pages (the text) and 72 illustrations; Volume II (the Catalogue) had 200 pages and 106 illustrations. Both volumes were *in folio* and cost £25 in 1903.

[2] The second edition was *in quarto* and in three volumes, Volume I (text), pp. 367, Volume II (Catalogue), pp. 388, and Volume III contained 1,009 illustrations and no text. These, published by Chicago U.P. in 1938, bore the plain title *Drawings of the Florentine Painters*.

[3] So keen did the interest in drawings become that more than one Museum Director in the U.S.A. (where all Museums have to find their own funds) collected any minor drawings on his European travels for sale to museum visitors at home, towards the upkeep of the museum.   [4] *S.S.P.*, p. 35.

PLATE XII The main library at 'I Tatti'

Above right: The entrance to the library at 'I Tatti' (architect, Cecil Pinsent) from the main corridor of the house. Statue of Buddha in alcove. (Photo lent by Signor Guglielmo Alberti)

Right: Bernard Berenson at the foot of the green garden at 'I Tatti' in 1938

PLATE XIII Portrait of Bernard Berenson painted by William Rothenstein in 1907 ('I Tatti' Collection)

Bond Street my word was law, and that it stood in the way of his career'. The man had apparently turned 'not into an adversary but an out and out enemy'.[1] He adds that he too might have hankered after authority at that moment had he not already possessed it. So it seems to him, looking back at the age of eighty, when he had held authority in these matters for nearly five decades.

The study of the Florentine Renaissance drawings during those last four years of the nineteenth century gave Berenson the grammar of that great period of painting. Now he could not only more easily classify other drawings of the period from non-Florentine schools, but he could work with new confidence in those schools of paintings which the great Florentines influenced—and since their drawings passed from hand to hand in the sixteenth and seventeenth centuries all over Italy, he was continually rediscovering their importance.

Familiarity with these drawings inevitably revealed a real and sometimes a deliberate flouting of draftsmanship among many of the fashionable contemporary twentieth-century artists. This offended Berenson. No truce was ever reached, even if there was a brief and early appreciation of Matisse, and an essay on Picasso after the Second World War.

[1] *S.S.P.*, p. 36.

CHAPTER X

A Home in Italy

I N 1899 Mary's husband Frank Costelloe fell ill and died. The
following year Berenson wrote to Mrs Gardner:

'I am going to get married, and as you may imagine from what
I told you three years ago, to no other than Mary Costelloe. Her
husband died last autumn, most unexpectedly, and when the decent
year is over we shall marry. For ten years Mrs Costelloe and I have
been constantly together, sharing every thought and almost every
feeling. Marriage can bring our minds and our ways of feeling no
nearer than they already are. I am ridiculously bashful about communicating it to anyone. . . . I do not know why I am so. Perhaps it is
that I had made up my mind to a continued bachelor existence. . . .
She understands me and my needs and my interest as no other
person, and I am sure she will try to make me happy—I am too
shy to say more.'[1]

He told only his mother and Isabella Gardner. Henceforward
Mary wrote fairly regularly to his mother. He himself wrote to
Mrs Gardner on the first day of the year, until her death, and five or
six times a year in between New Year days. Then there were the
'salesmanship' letters to her in which he was a Duveen *avant la lettre*.
These grew fewer, and finally ceased in about 1905, except for one
or two offers by Berenson for 'first refusal', once he had become
associated with Joseph Duveen in 1907.

The death of Frank Costelloe and the marriage a year later seemed
'a stroke of great good luck', to Bertrand Russell, looking back, on
what he seemed almost to envy, Berenson's half-century of marriage
to the same wife.[2]

Before the wedding Berenson decided to take a summer holiday
of a few months in the kind of bracing fashionable resort—the only

---

[1] See Plate VIII.
[2] Lord Russell in conversation with the author, Richmond, 1954.

one he ever liked—where he could be sure of good conversation, good food and exhilarating mountains and skies. The place was St Moritz. It was frequented every August in those days by the Duchesse de Rohan, Lady de Grey, the Cuban-born Countess Serristori (a lifelong friend from Florence) and two other devoted friends from Nervi near Genoa, the Gropallo sisters, and a host of other lively people. Women, 'especially certain society women are more receptive, more appreciative and consequently more stimulating',[1] than colleagues, he wrote, 'who seldom draw each other out'. Berenson held that before monastic society had left its dour impress upon the universities of the world in what he called 'the hard competition in a verbal prize fight'; the ancient Greek philosophers (as well as many other men of science and men of letters since the monastic period) had also chiefly frequented 'the adolescent-minded and seldom the over-mature'.[2] It is all a rather grand way of saying that Berenson's greatest gifts were in large part intuitive, whether about pictures, people, or situations. Women liked his intuitions, and he appreciated theirs. Argument was a great effort for him. Sometimes he had to engage in it in print; in conversation he avoided it like poison. So, of course, did 'society women'; they were brought up not to argue, but to enjoy. They were restful, agreeable and always well turned out. 'I Tatti' was seldom without such a visitor in the years to come, whether from America or from Europe, or from nearby Florence, although the Florentine ladies who called at 'I Tatti' were relatively few and nearly all engaged in some intellectual pursuits alongside the keeping of great houses and estates. None, I think, kept anything remotely like the open house that 'I Tatti' was soon to become. It is four centuries since Italians have 'entertained' in the English or French sense.

From St Moritz Berenson wrote to Mrs Gardner that he was glad by his marriage 'to step out of the equivocal position I (and far worse a person I loved) had been in for years'. To complete their happiness Mary and B.B. had found 'a house at Settignano, very snug and warm and at the very entrance to the most beautiful strip of rock and forest country that we have near Florence'. He said they hoped in time to make a real home of it, and that one could hardly imagine what a paradise the environs of Florence were.

For the present they could only rent 'I Tatti'. Its name was curious. One explanation which Berenson used to give was that it

[1] *S.S.P.*, p. 17.   [2] *Idem*.

lay on the land of a family called Alessandri. The diminutive of Alessandro in Italian is Tatto—pluralized into Tatti. Maybe. Tatto also means tact: needless to say, the name gave rise to joking about tactile values. The house itself was plain, square, roomy, just like a score of prosperous Tuscan farmhouses built on three floors. It stood on a knoll immediately above the small fifteenth-century church of San Martino and its manse. The usual cypress avenue led uphill to its side entrance. Behind it and on either side were gentle rounded hills. Vines grew on the slopes below the house, and olive trees dotted the vineyards. Among one of the earliest visitors in the spring of 1903 was the English painter and illustrator Charles Ricketts. He noted in his diary:

'his villa faces an ideal landscape where all the delicate trees and growths are like filigree. The air lets one see too much detail . . . we basked in the garden which is more pleasant than beautiful, whilst the lizards crept about. After tea Berenson showed us his house which is spacious, cool, pleasant in wall colour, white grey, grey-green, decorated with old furniture, some of which is exquisite. . . .'[1]

Gardens take long years to mature. This one, so memorable by the mid-twentieth century that visitors came from far to see it and friends returned often to enjoy it, had not even been planned when Charles Ricketts visited in 1903. 'I Tatti' was still a plain roomy farmhouse, with no great library, courtyards and wings built round them. It only possessed an incomparable view across the valley to soft hills studded with villas and farmsteads like itself.

*　　　*　　　*

Mary Costelloe and Bernard Berenson were married by the Mayor of Florence on December 18, 1900, at the Palazzo Vecchio. Two days after the civil ceremony they were married five miles outside the city in the little chapel adjoining 'I Tatti' on the Settignano hillside. It was a brief Roman Catholic ceremony, 'over in about five minutes', Berenson wrote to Mrs Gardner, 'although we did have two priests to officiate, both of us, you see, being nominal Catholics'. Berenson came from Poggio Gherardo, the adjoining estate which belonged to Mrs Janet Ross. Just before the wedding he sent Mrs Gardner some wild tulip bulbs from there. Mary came from the Villa Kraus.

[1] *Self Portrait from the Journals of Charles Ricketts*, edited by Cecil Lewis, Peter Davies, 1939. See Plate XIV.

A Home in Italy

The wedding breakfast at 'I Tatti' was followed by music from a string orchestra—the first of many Saturday concerts.

In her Unfinished Life of Berenson, Mary wrote that once the house had been rented neither of them ever envisaged living anywhere else. If fortune were kind they would one day purchase it, and then it would be home.

' "Home", what is it? (Berenson asked himself years later). Is it the place where one is born, where one's forbears were born and died, where one spent one's earliest years? Few in America, even if native, can claim such a privilege; still less those who were brought there with other memories already filling their heads.'[1]

Americans faced with this problem have invented the word 'home town'. In Europe the concept of home usually means nationality. At 'I Tatti' newcomers were often puzzled not by the fact that Berenson's nationality was American, but by his intensely developed home-feeling for Boston. It grew with the years. Distance lent enchantments which neither Nashua nor Minot Street ever could have possessed. But Harvard and its life he followed closely. In time its professors and its students came to call. They recounted its alterations, the gossip of the place, the topographical changes in Boston, the social changes in the city. The same thing happened with Philadelphia, with New York, with Paris, London, Berlin and Madrid. Berenson had a thirst for the gossip of the city, its latest craze, its newest books, the adventures of its political or royal or aristocratic or merchant figures, and the very latest scandals if they were big enough. Life, warm and actual, famed or ill-famed, was grist to his mill.

His memory was excellent. He could add to his stock of knowledge by asking the right questions of a new caller. People were astonished at his familiarity with the places they came from. His very profession kept him informed, for he was never long without visits from the museum directors and keepers who came from the four corners of the earth. And they often, indeed usually, live interesting public lives and must attend public functions where they meet public men and men of science and letters. Many of them, especially in the United States, also led private social lives, and invited the great and the learned to their houses. This kind of exchange of news was

S.S.P., p. 129.

165

carried on at 'I Tatti' in four and sometimes five languages. No wonder the place became a beehive of current opinion and information exchanged in gay and witty conversation at meals, or on walks in the hills beyond Vincigliata. The pace of the household was swift, but only at these times. The main part of the day was spent working, each in his own room or in the library, once the first wing of it had been built. Without that discipline the enjoyments would have been thin. Indeed the amount of reading in that library was considerable. With the years, visitors came to appreciate the enormous historical and literary knowledge inside Berenson's mind. It was very difficult to catch him out. People tried, but when they looked the matter up, he was usually found to be right or as nearly right as mattered.

Such a man leading such a life was bound to take a wide and frontierless view of humanity. 'The individual I meet in England, France, Germany or Italy is, in all but language and what language carries with it, pretty much the same human being. . . . National differences are in fact so superficial that on acquaintance they disappear.'[1]

One day early in the century, during one of his rare visits to Boston, Berenson was asked, at a dinner party there, to describe what Italians looked like.

'I glanced around at these Boston worthies, all of uncontaminated Anglo-Saxon blood, and said: "Gentlemen, everyone of you could pass for an Italian, and as far as appearances go there is not one of you who could not be a Milanese, a Piedmontese, a Venetian, a Florentine, or member of a distinguished family from Rome, Naples or Palermo."

'The truth is that it is only the less evolved man or woman who has stamped indelibly on his mask the map of his country. The stage Englishmen and Frenchmen are caricatures.'[2]

*   *   *

For centuries English-speaking people had visited and settled in Italy. At times the visits were essential: young men had gone to learn astronomy and mathematics from Galileo. Long before that the most advanced banking systems could be observed only in Genoa and Florence. Where else could one study diplomacy so well as in the Vatican? And where archaeology, and architecture, decoration

[1] *S.S.P.*, p. 60.   [2] *S.S.P.*, p. 61.

166

and silk manufacture so well as in Pompeii, in Rome, on the Brenta
or up in Como?

By the nineteenth century the big English colonies in and around
Florence were mainly composed of writers and artists in search of
cheap living, the sun, wine and the delights of a beautiful city within
walking distance. But the Brownings, Landor, the Trollopes, Isa
Blagden at Bellosguardo and the Levers had very few Italian friends.
Elizabeth Browning was passionately concerned with the cause of a
United Italy. It was even rumoured that the news of the death of
Cavour precipitated her own death. And Browning caught something
authentically Italian in many of his poems. But the voluminous novels
and notes of the others never conjure up more than an Italian coach-
man and servant to fill in the background. They neither spoke
Italian nor knew Italians. Bulwer Lytton and George Eliot never
conceived a contemporary Italian plot at all. The Italy of their day
might as well not have existed except as a setting in which to search
for the background of *Romola* and *The Last Days of Pompeii*, or the
Rienzi story. They loved Italy, not Italians. Marion Crawford was
an exception, and there must have been others who left little record.
The art historians in general had many Italian acquaintances and
some friends, Layard and Morelli, Crowe and Cavalcaselle, for
example.

In the twentieth century the English colony in Florence was no
longer composed of writers, sculptors and painters. It had become
social. In the giant upheavals of our century ex-royalty very naturally
found that a villa near Florence would make a happy asylum.
Royalty attracts royalty, and royal visitors came, Edward VII and
others. For many a year Mr and Mrs George Keppel were the
'undisputed King and Queen of what was left of the English colony;
their Ombrellino villa up at Bellosguardo was if not a Palace at least
a Residency. Alike socially and politically they remained *au-dessus de
la mêlée*, a timely reminder to the present generation of what a
genuine governing class is like, taking themselves for granted, as
others without question took them for granted both as regards
personal distinction and mode of life. They were neither more
intelligent nor more moral than their neighbours: they were just of
a different caste. It would never even have occurred to them to
doubt the superiority of England, at any rate their England, in
everything that mattered. All the most important people of every
nationality living in or visiting Florence came to their house . . . so

far as their mantle has descended on any one person, it has descended on the American, Bernard Berenson, as different from them in origin, in intellectual and personal attributes as could well be imagined. Even at that time he exercised a social hegemony similar to theirs, a hegemony which after their disappearance became equally incontestable.'[1]

Mr Francis Toye, who wrote this, was head of the British Institute in Florence after the Second World War. He found it an unforgettable experience to hear Berenson talk: 'He never seemed to transfer all that wit and vitality into his writings.'

The 'undisputed kingship' which Mr Toye makes Berenson inherit was laughingly referred to by the owner of 'I Tatti' as an 'institootion'. 'I have become an institootion—one of the sights—which the traveller to Florence has to see.' By the end of the Second World War, he really had.

*   *   *

In those early days at 'I Tatti' Mary immediately arranged the household in such a way that friends could be entertained to any meal. She loved company. She had always had troops of friends round her, so had her mother. In the sunny, easy climate of Italy, with never a shortage of domestic help, abundance of fresh fruit, vegetables, fowl and wine, the effort required to entertain is almost non-existent. One might overdo it. One might spend too much money—but given a liking for guests at luncheon, tea and dinner, here was the perfect setting for conviviality, for the summer evening meal out of doors with long hours of mild air and talk, good talk, witty talk, news from afar and plenty of gossip. In winter there was the big sitting-room with a blazing wood fire, very English, just like Fernhurst. Upstairs some of the bedrooms had chintz for wallpaper and chintz on the chairs. Mary wanted a clock on the house, but not yet. None of the big changes could come till 1907.

Why, one might ask, if conditions were so ideal, did not more English people settle in Italy? In this century none except Eugenie Strong down in Rome settled quite like this. Up in Rapallo Max and Florence Beerbohm bought a villa overlooking the bay in 1910 and lived in the greatest retirement, with occasional visits to London. They certainly had no Italian friends except for one Rapallo family.

[1] Francis Toye, *Truly Thankful*, pp. 22–3, Arthur Barker, London, 1957.

Passing friends were English. Sir Max Beerbohm and Bernard Berenson met but once, early in the century, and it was not a success. It could not be. Had not Max complained that 'Pater treated English as a dead language, laying out "every sentence as in a shroud—hanging, like a widower, long over its marmorial beauty or ever he could lay it at length in his book, its sepulchre"'?[1] They never had more than three close friends in common, and they met curiously enough at the bedside of one of them, in a London nursing home.[2] Berenson's impression of Max remained vivid but very wide of the mark. He mistook Max's way of talking for a kind of cockney. He disliked his cane and his straw boater *in* the room', and there was an end to it. He could not read him. None of that chiselled prose really rang a bell for him; none of that penetrating subdued humour made him laugh. Sybil Colefax, in whose room they had met, was probably the most indefatigable bringer together of the famous and the aspiring. She never attempted to bring them together. This meeting had been mere coincidence. A half-century later a young admirer of both had planned a meeting in Rapallo itself, but by then Sir Max was already too ill, so that it never took place.

By far the most constant and intimate English visitor to 'I Tatti' in these early years of the century was a neighbour—none other than Vernon Lee, ten years older than the Berensons and living in nearby Villa Palmerino, with her devoted friend and companion, Kit Anstruther Thompson. Even if the whole of Europe had been Vernon Lee's nursery, she graduated towards England with an exile's love. 'She should have lived in Olympian circles, discoursing. She would have made a perfect Sybil', wrote her friend and executor, Irene Cooper-Willis.[3] All are agreed that Vernon Lee had a rich gift of conversation. Miss Cooper-Willis, who often stayed with her until her death, recalls her as

'a brilliant talker and peculiarly witty. But her mind was too immediately fertile, and her practical experience too narrow, for her theories to be always sound. . . . She was a magnificent improviser, an impressionist who straight away spun her impressions into elaborate theories and then embroidered them. When she talked

---

[1] J. G. Riewald, *Sir Max Beerbohm*, p. 175, Marinus Nijhoff, The Hague, 1953.   [2] Bernard Berenson to the author.
[3] *Vernon Lee's Letters*, privately printed, reproduced by permission of Miss Cooper-Willis.

she needed an exceptional amount of elbow room and unlimited attention from her listener—approach to argument with her could only have been secured by the introduction of traffic signals, and these she might have ignored—but as a talker she was always interesting and often arresting. Her unique personality, those intensely inquisitive (though not penetrating) eyes, almond shaped and set slightly aslant in the small but long Hapsburg type of face, her slow, foreign articulation of the syllables of words and the peculiar range of her voice, compelled attention.'

That is the picture drawn by her friend and executor, Miss Irene Cooper-Willis, in the preface to Vernon Lee's privately printed letters.

The vagaries of human beings, and especially their matrimonial adventures, did not interest Vernon Lee. Her sensibilities were directed to landscape and 'the spirit of places'. She would therefore have gradually come to feel (as a regular visitor) somewhat at sea in the knowledgeable talk about 'people' at 'I Tatti'. But to walk with her in the Florentine hillside seems to have been a sheer delight. Miss Cooper-Willis says that she had 'a Chinese eye and a Chinese power of drawing sustenance from what is beautiful', and that there was not 'an atom of sham or affectation in her tastes'. If there was affectation and mannerism in aesthetic talk in London, there was none in these hillside gatherings round Florence. The beauty was too real and close and accessible. There was plenty of sparring and some rivalry of course.

Vernon Lee's friend, Kit Anstruther Thompson, often sat at the feet of Berenson, drinking in his new theories of tactile values in paintings and drawings of the Italian Renaissance. This talk she carried back to the Villa Palmerino. The story goes that the two once rushed down to one of the Florentine Galleries to pose in front of a Renaissance picture in the same attitudes as the figures in the picture, hoping in this way to achieve a new interpretation of 'tactile values'.[1]

Vernon Lee incorporated all this into an article in the *Fortnightly Review* which reached the new tenant at 'I Tatti' and greatly annoyed him. The article cribbed many of his phrases in the conversation with Miss Thompson, and the next time she walked over, he said to her,

---

[1] Miss Cooper-Willis in conversation with the author, June 1954, in London, and all that follows about Vernon Lee.

'I always knew you were an angel, but I did not know you were a recording angel'. The poor girl was so upset that she went back to England. Thus ended a joint household arrangement with Vernon Lee which had lasted for nine years. 'Vernon Lee was lonely after Kit Anstruther Thompson went back to England, and "I Tatti" was for years closed to her. She missed all the interesting people one met there.'

About 1907, after three years of this sad cold war, 'Mary Berenson managed to smoothe things out a bit'. Vernon Lee would then come over with friends to whom she wanted to show the treasures of the Berensons' house and garden. She would stay to lunch and 'B.B. and Vernon Lee would have one or two scraps at lunch, but little conversation. The old talk never took place again'.

Professional quarrels of this kind are terribly frequent in the literary and art world because both those worlds depend enormously upon the sensibilities of the citizens who inhabit them. One of the deadly sins is of course plagiarism. Plagiarism seems to be the chief cause of jealousy and strife, but only when the stolen idea is not acknowledged to its proper author. Is it modesty or rather a lack of it which so tempts the plagiarist? Vernon Lee stands out with her fair share of wilfulness in another portrait drawn of her by Percy Lubbock in his *Portrait of Edith Wharton*:

'Vernon Lee, tall and angular and vestal in her stiff collar and her drab coat, fixed in rumination . . . she pondered, she reconnoitred as she talked. She wound her way through suggestion, sensation, speculation—she threaded a labyrinth . . . and then again she slashed right and left . . . she thumped out with a judgement, a maxim, a paradox on a croak or chuckle of her crusted laughter. It all took time, but it was worth while to wait for her. While she talked on, with her pungent and guttural deliberation, a scene unrolled, brilliantly peopled and displayed—a drama was evolved. . . . Most surprising, most interesting, most exasperating of women, in her power and her humour, her tenacity and her perversity . . . what a figure!'[1]

[1] Percy Lubbock, *Portrait of Edith Wharton*, p. 113, Jonathan Cape, 1947. Mr Lubbock settled in Lerici, near La Spezia, early in the century. He married Lady Sybil Scott who was the daughter of the Earl of Desart. She had been *en première noces*, the wife of an American, Mr Cutting, and then the wife of Geoffrey Scott, Berenson's private secretary for twelve years. Her daughter by Mr Cutting subsequently became the Marchesa Iris Origo.

171

That was a portrait of Vernon Lee after the reconciliation with 'I Tatti'. She became an ardent pacifist during the First World War and supported the movement in speeches, in writing and with money, and was in favour in 1918 of a mild peace treaty with Germany. Bernard Shaw, himself a pacifist, reviewed her book on the subject, *Satan, the Master*, in *The Nation*, and thought she had 'the whole European situation in the hollow of her hand . . . knows history philosophically . . . is a political psychologist'.[1] Vernon Lee died in Florence just before the outbreak of the Italo-Abyssinian war. Her works became source books for young travel writers on Italy, and remain so. She wished that no life of her should be written before 1980, and all her papers have now gone to an American university.

Another and most welcome caller in those earliest years of the century was Carlo Placci. Berenson has left a most vivid portrait of him:

'When I first knew him he was like most advanced young Italians in the early 1890s, like most young writers of those hopeful days, a declared atheist, a positivist, a fervent socialist, and all else that then was up to date.'[2]

Before the turn of the century Carlo Placci returned with fervour to the Church and became 'as vehemently as aggressively reactionary as he had been "leftish" only a few weeks before'. Berenson thinks that when he lent William James's *The Will to Believe* to Placci it gave him 'the pragmatical justification for choosing the principles which his whim of the moment and his tropism led him to prefer'.

Anyone who remembers Carlo Placci today remembers him as a kind of Italian Oscar Wilde in conversation. He was always well dressed, well informed, witty, good company, 'with an irresistible impulse to show off, a pillar of a man with a vast chest, dark eyed with massive hair and a protruding lower lip'. He was an early devotee of the motor car, and often took the Berensons with him. The likeness with Oscar ends with the conversation. Berenson's sharp portrait of him after thirty years' friendship and much travel together, reveals him as a man of immense acquaintance. He introduced Berenson to all his friends, 'I might almost say [he] forced

[1] *Vernon Lee's Letters*, ed. cit., Preface
[2] *Rumour and Reflection*, pp. 23–40.

172

me upon them, including the most exalted', and Berenson found that, 'like most Latins, Placci made a clear division between his private and his public self . . . what an Italian thinks remains his own treasure hidden away in a safe, to the unlocking of which he alone guards the elaborate secret'.

Others gathered round the Berenson table at 'I Tatti' in those first years of the century. There was Gaetano Salvemini, fresh from remote Molfetta in Apulia and at that time 'an unkempt lad, with his huge square head, broad shoulders and provincial accent' who was destined to become one of the fighting historians of Italy ever in battle with the Papacy and later with Fascism. He was to become a lifelong friend. Writers and artists then on the threshold of their careers like Papini, Soffici, Prezzolini 'and other equally rubber-neck exploiters of the moment', would be caught by Placci 'on their first flight' and brought to 'I Tatti' 'for us to sample'. A regular visitor and neighbour at the Capponcina villa was Gabriele d'Annunzio, 'such delicious company when you had him to yourself, talking always impersonally of literature, of poetry, of books, with the keenest zest for words, rare and sonorous words which he would caress as a jeweller caresses precious stones'. Berenson already noticed how d'Annunzio became a different person when he was not alone with him. If a woman was present d'Annunzio lost interest in everything except in the impression he was making. Many a time Berenson noticed some of the most charming and intelligent women, quite unaware of the change in d'Annunzio, gradually becoming 'subdued, enticed, bewitched and confessing that they could not resist him'. As for Placci he drew Berenson out, 'anxious to let no word pass unappreciated . . . in a way that would elicit one's best'. But he was quarrelsome and usually disappeared to Paris and London and Rome for their Seasons before one could wholly tire of him or wholly quarrel with him. In the end he became obsessed by the number of people he knew, and could talk of nothing else, and it palled, as such things do.

Frau Cosima Wagner was brought by Placci up to 'I Tatti'. To Mrs Gardner, Berenson writes that she bewitched him.

He took the great musician's widow as he took many of his notable visitors as 'a great aesthetic impression . . . such a person I look on as a great work of art. I think no more of the effect I may be making on her, than the effect I may be making on a picture'. That was of course not the impression which all the women visitors to

'I Tatti' left upon their host. With some he inevitably became deeply entangled, as did Mary with some of the remarkable men who called at the villa or stayed there. In a curious way, with all their dislike of Bloomsbury and its ways—the guests sitting on the floor, the earnest discussions about ultimate matters, the break-up of a good few of that circle's marriages—the Berenson marriage seems to have had some typically pre-Bloomsbury characteristics. It was entered into on that familiar but precarious principle that each would be free to go his own course, if such a situation should arise. For a good many years, from time to time, each did, and the excitements and dramas of these occasions very nearly wrecked the long voyage. The very size of the house and income probably kept disaster at arm's length. One knows who the loves were, but these are tales of long ago and no good purpose would be served by recounting them. Neither Bernard nor Mary ever lost the capacity for falling in love; it endured into ripe age. Each adventure had its own glow, and frequently its own tears. The setting in that Tuscan hillside was incomparable, and when all is said, it is likely that far more people became slightly or seriously enamoured of their handsome and fascinating host or hostess, than the other way round.

Without Mary's gift for arranging parties and the wonderfully impromptu expeditions to see the sun rise, or to see it set, or to call in at some distant church or village, there would not have been those innumerable occasions for Berenson's gift of conversation—unequalled among all those excellent talkers on the hillsides round Florence—to flower.

Mr Percy Lubbock says that Italians seem to be eternally puzzling as to what the English-speaking dwellers in Italy *do*. Do they go berserk? Are they all spiritualists like Mrs Browning or merely engaged in the pursuits of Bacchus and Cupid? Many of them of course were, but Berenson had a quite puritan horror, Jewish and Bostonian, of such excesses. It prevented him, for instance, from enjoying anyone like Norman Douglas who lived in Florence for years before settling in Capri. He would keep open house but within a composed and strict timetable. In the course of the years the routine was established with the strictness of a small court. Visitors staying in the house (and each had his own sitting-room) were left quite alone to read or write until eleven o'clock. Then the morning walk or drive lasted till noon. From noon till one o'clock Berenson dealt with his vast correspondence. With some friends he had, at periods

almost a daily correspondence, and over the years a weekly one.[1]
Some of these correspondences were routine and almost trite, others
vigorous and lively.

At lunch the language of the day might be any one of four:
English, French, German or Italian. People who only spoke one
language were considered a little trying. The week's invitations had
to be reshuffled on their account in order to achieve some linguistic
harmony at meals. If that was not possible then the unilingual
guest would very likely be farmed out to some neighbour. After
coffee at two-thirty everyone retired to where they had come from
or to a siesta in the house. Nor were the staying guests expected to
be available again until four o'clock. The afternoon walk or drive up
into the hills above Vincigliata, or down along the Arno valley lasted
till five-thirty—tea time. More guests would drop in to tea, often
Italians. From six-thirty till nine silence again descended upon the
house, and on summer nights dinner was spread at a long table
under the cypresses, where an electric light hung from the trees.
At eleven o'clock punctually Berenson always went to bed, for he
was up working very early in the morning, usually at six-thirty.

Mary's grandchildren claim that the routine gradually became
'fossilised' and rigid, but that the outline was always the same—only
the drives used to be forty kilometres instead of five or six. Everyone
who visited 'I Tatti' before the first war, when Mary was at her
liveliest and her best (before her serious illnesses), remembered her
as a woman of wonderful invention and spirit. She was always full of
notions—once she thought how delightful walks might be, if everyone could have two small hydrogen balloons fixed to each shoulder,
just big enough to lift one off the ground so that one could skim
effortlessly down the road, across the fields, touching down every
now and then. She would write to a firm or two to find out whether
they could make the balloons, and be fearfully disappointed when
they replied that they could not. She was, after all, only anticipating
the tiny single-seater helicopters which American parachutists used
in the 1950s, or the inflated single-wing airplane invented in

[1] Nearly all the letters of any consequence which arrived at 'I Tatti' were kept
so that an enormous archive of letters accumulated with the years, and in
course of time it is to be hoped that some of them will be published: there were
long correspondences in the early days with Henry Adams and William
James, but not with Henry James and not with Proust, contrary to the commonly held belief. There was nothing Jamesian or Proustian in Berenson's
direct approach to people.

England a few years later. She was game for almost any experiment, and lived completely in the present. Berenson, looking back, was never quite sure about it all. He found in her 'no feeling for the "numinous", no awe before the universe, no ever-present sense of the precariousness of human life. . . .'[1]

* * *

In the first half of the twentieth century it is almost as impossible to think of Florence without Bernard Berenson as it is to think of Rome without Eugénie Strong, Assistant Director and Librarian of the British School in Rome from 1909 to 1925, author of *Roman Sculpture, The Apotheosis of the Imperial Figure and its Influence on Design*, and of many contributions to the *Cambridge Ancient History*, and resident in Rome till her death in 1944.

Of course they knew each other since the 'eighties in London, but they were 'enemy-friends', or sometimes just inimical. Very few young people moved from the glowing orbit of the one into the glowing orbit of the other; not only twelve centuries divided their chosen fields of work, but the very order of priority in the words 'Greece and Rome'. In time, the priority was obvious: in spiritual values Rome and 'Romanità' came first for Mrs Strong. When I knew her best in the late 'twenties, she was a wonderfully vigorous and handsome woman with a profile so like that of an imperial Roman senator that one could find her three or four times on the crowded bas-relief of the *Ara Pacis*. Unlike Berenson she was a most magnetic lecturer.

From the first she had been preoccupied with the religious aspect, the thirst for divinity in Mithraic, Etruscan and ancient Roman art: no sculptured portrait of an Emperor, no stele, no new archaeological find but received that historical and religious attention from her which made her Roman lectures most memorable experiences. Generations of students, friends, passing visitors, enjoyed these lectures at the British School, and later at the Convent at 10 via Boncompagni. She was a great teacher and a fierce controversialist.

For her, Roman art held its ground on its own merits. In her notes for an autobiography, which she never completed, she recalled, 'Rome and her Empire . . . seemed then to archaeologists a mere cloud or shadow overhanging the clear world of Greek art',[2] in her

[1] *R. and R.*, p. 15.

[2] *Mrs. Arthur Strong*, a memoir by Gladys Scott Thomson, p. 34, Cohen and West, 1949.

PLATE XIV 'I Tatti' in 1906 as it was before the garden was planted and the clock tower built. (From a contemporary photograph lent by Miss Mariano)

Right: Bernard Berenson with his step grandchildren, Barbara Strachey (now Mrs Halpern) and Ursula Strachey (now Mrs Wentzel) at 'I Tatti' in 1919. (Lent from 'I Tatti' collection)

PLATE XV Mr Harry Truman and Bernard Berenson at 'I Tatti', 1955

Bernard Berenson with H.M. The King of Sweden, a frequent guest at 'I Tatti'. (Snapshot, by permission of H.M. the King)

Below: Count Umberto Morra di Lavriano, Miss Mariano and Bernard Berenson on the Sechietta above Vallombrosa, 1947. (Snapshot)

student days in Munich where the classical world, as in England, was dominated by the passion for Greek art. Her early childhood in Spain, her convent days in France, her Classical Tripos at Girton and her first visit to Rome in 1892 had already drawn her historically and religiously to Rome. Her mother was French, and she was born and brought up a Roman Catholic. She and Vernon Lee and Berenson had met in London and in Rome in the 'nineties. Significantly Vernon Lee recorded how Eugénie Sellars used the methods of Morelli in an attempt to establish the authorship of Roman and Greek sculpture in the British Museum. Then came a long period in England after Eugénie married Mr Arthur Strong in 1897. He became Librarian of Chatsworth, and concurrently of the House of Lords and (for the Duke of Portland) of Welbeck. She passed her time at the great houses studying and working and translating F. Wickhoff's *Roman Art*.

'. . . this translation, with her comments, marks the turn of thought at which she had arrived . . . to see the art of the Roman Empire not as an appendix to the art of Classical and Hellenistic Greece—but as a subject compelling attention on its own merits and for its own sake'.[1]

Berenson had little use for Wickhoff. 'Why are the Wickhoffs so eager to persuade us that the sculptors and painters of late antiquity did what they did with full intellectual awareness of what they were doing? . . . I cannot say that it makes any difference to what we are to think of their art today. If awkward and infantile, it is only more deplorable if it was carefully thought out.'[2]

At Chatsworth Arthur Strong discovered many treasures, and the eighth Duke of Devonshire encouraged him to add to the library. In its shelves he even discovered an additional chapter to *Vanity Fair*. He restored the Hardwicke Hunting Tapestries and discovered a neglected bronze head which proved to be a fine Greek antique (in the British Museum since 1957). He would invite famous scholars and archaeologists like Senator Lanciani from Rome and professors from Berlin and Vienna and the young Berenson to contribute their knowledge for the building up of the history of the collection both

---

[1] *Mrs. Arthur Strong, ed. cit.* p. 54.
[2] Bernard Berenson, *The Arch of Constantine*, p. 22.

at Welbeck and at Chatsworth. In the notes Mrs Strong left she says that her husband played with the dream of a revivified aristocracy.

'He hoped against hope that the rising generation of young lords would shake off insularity, would be educated, enlightened, enterprising and worthy of their inheritance as the privileged class, exempt from sordid care in order to pursue worthwhile ends, that in particular of serving in England so as to exalt her to her—in his eyes—rightful place as queen among nations.'[1]

The language is not Kiplingesque but positively Ciceronic. Mrs Strong is writing after her husband's death in Rome. She says he was a passionate dreamer but also a man with an acute insight into reality, and that the clash between his two visions sometimes turned to sharp satire. He died of pernicious anaemia in 1903. For five years she stayed on at Chatsworth, pursuing her own researches and often guiding distinguished visitors round the treasures in days long before the great country houses were nationalized.

After the publication of her *Roman Sculpture* she was appointed Assistant Director at the British School in Rome, then in the Palazzo Odescalchi, and later transferred to the British Pavilion in Valle Giulia which Sir Edwin Lutyens had designed for the Great Exhibition held in Rome in 1911.

There she certainly shook off any remaining insularity, and entered, heart and soul, into the inheritance of Rome, historical, archaeological, pagan and Christian—and in the end political. I found her passion for Mussolini tedious but unimportant. So much else about her was of far greater importance. This was simply the tail end of a very long love affair with Rome. She did not really live in the present: certainly not politically. It was typical of her that the first copy of *The Waste Land* to reach Italy was to be found on her sitting-room table. She knew what was being written in literary London. The signed photograph of the Italian Dictator on her mantelpiece could be treated as that of a Maecenas obsessed with digging up anything Roman in Rome, regardless of what had to be destroyed in the process. She followed these digs with boundless enthusiasm and study, delighted that Mussolini had found the money to finance them.

She entertained in the grand manner. She had a way of introducing

[1] *The Arch of Constantine*, p. 57.

the young with just enough flattery about their aspirations to loosen their tongues. She was good to the young. The old at her famous Saturday afternoons were very distinguished. Often one of the more learned Cardinals came to tea. He was met with the proper ceremony, the lighted candles, the kissing of his ring, and was then enthroned in a large armchair in a corner of the room, where Catholic visitors would gather, and one or two heretics like the writer might be introduced. She was quite bilingual in English and French. Italian and German she spoke fast and fluently with an English accent.

In the end her devotion to what must be called *Romanità* blinded her vision. Mary Berenson recorded that Mrs Strong said to her in 1940: 'Don't you agree with me that this war has been sent as a punishment on England's desertion of the Catholic Church?' In her final isolation and remoteness it was an old anti-Fascist friend, a social reformer and archaeologist, Umberto Zanotti Bianco, who often visited her in the Hotel Regina, where the Fascist Government arranged for her free accommodation. No funds could now reach her from abroad. She was eighty in 1940, and she continued to work upon what she hoped but failed to finish, a history of the Vatican palaces. She died a week or two before British and American troops entered Rome in 1944, unreconciled to the outcome of the war.

To gain something of a feeling for ancient Roman art from Mrs Strong, for its architecture and its portraiture and for the mystic rites of the pre-Christian age; to visit with her the Mithraic temples beneath San Clemente and at Porta Maggiore and to study the portraits of the Augustan Age was the happy experience of many winter visitors to Rome. To enjoy an equally vivid and inspiring introduction to the painting of the Italian Renaissance at the hands of Bernard Berenson in Florence was the privilege, of course, of a much smaller circle, because Berenson never lectured, never led small groups of keen amateurs. But wherever he was, in Florence or travelling round Italy, friends and acquaintances would often enjoy in a memorable way a visit with him to a gallery. No two finer teachers could one desire, and both are still there, in every good lending library, to read and enjoy.

Mrs Strong, Berenson, Vernon Lee—what a trio. They belonged to the real amateurs or lovers of Italy, each in their own way more anxious to communicate that love than to excel or shine above all the other stars in their respective firmaments. The traveller who

179

came under the influence of Mrs Strong or of Berenson must be considered fortunate.

Inevitably there was conflict between the two. Could it have been the young Bernard in the 'nineties who inspired the young Eugénie Sellars to try to apply the 'Morellian method' of identification to Greek and Roman statues in the British Museum? In those days Berenson maintained she was fond of him. Yet her increasing glorification of Roman art would not, clearly, have satisfied Pater's disciple, for whom the art of Europe has its fountain-head in Greece, sparkling afresh for each visitor civilized enough to enjoy it. For him Greek art, the temple, the statue, the poem and the prose possessed human, and therefore divine proportion. Rome had to acknowledge its debt to Greece—or pay the price of decline.

But there was too an incompatibility of temperament. The scholar, especially the English-trained classical scholar, male or female, always found some difficult fences in Berenson's fields. Language was the first and often the insurmountable one. English words used by Berenson in a way and in a context in which no one at Oxford or Cambridge used them—that would make the precise scholar impatient.

It is curious that in the four years I lived in Rome and often saw Mrs Strong, between 1927–31, I never heard Berenson's name mentioned in her house. In the nine post-war years when I again lived in Rome and often visited 'I Tatti', there were a good many references to the late Mrs Strong as of another 'orb'. Students and scholars who had moved in her orbit would, Berenson said, be certain to dislike and distrust himself. Perhaps this happened: I only knew one possible example of it, and in that case, I think, the distrust would have smouldered, even if Mrs Strong had never existed.

However that may be, there were some very radical differences between the two households. Mrs Strong was never well off. She received a pension for her long service at the British School and the emoluments of a Fellow of Girton. It was a miracle that she could entertain (very frugally) on the scale that she did. Berenson was, by comparison and in reality wealthy.[1] But his personal way of life was

---

[1] 'I think it is always worth remembering that he did not want to be rich in order to be rich—that it was a means to a definite end. He wanted the financial resources above all to create his library. I am sure it has always meant more to him than anything else. So many of his colleagues have never been able to forgive him for being rich: they think it immoral that he should have

quite as severe, as simple, as studious as Mrs Strong's. She had a small library at home, but she used public libraries. He could build his own, although some say he could have used the excellent library of the German Institute in Florence. In a passionate sort of way, and in the historical sense of the words (and only for those who know Rome really well), Mrs Strong 'went native', which is quite different from taking Italian citizenship. It has happened before, but it is unusual among scholars, although not so unusual among great travellers like Lady Mary Wortley Montagu, or like Freya Stark when among the Arabs. Women are in any case so naturally receptive that even great women scholars probably have to guard against too close an identification with the subjects they pursue.

Berenson never 'went native', if only for the reason that his early training and his Jewish ancestry endowed him with a general, indeed a universal sidelight, on every subject which engaged his attention. But both he and Mrs Strong were probably the most eminent and fruitful 'Anglo-Italian' settlers the peninsula has ever had, and in their respective ways, among the richest contributors to the understanding of Italian art in the English language. Berenson at 'I Tatti' left a splendid library for students of the humanities. Its 40,000 volumes covered art history, the literature of Western and of much of Eastern Europe, the history political, religious and economic of the nations of the world; philosophy, poetry, biography, memoirs abound in it. It is rich in encyclopaedias and reference books in a dozen languages.[1] In the end, after many enlargements, it occupied two halls and ten rooms.

had any instinct for making money, but they seem to forget that he wouldn't have made it at all if he had not *in the first place* combined an extraordinary flair, eye and memory for pictures with an instinctive feeling for quality.' William Mostyn Owen in a letter to the author, February 1955. (Mr Mostyn Owen was Berenson's assistant from 1953 onwards.)

[1] See Plate XII

CHAPTER XI

The Reverse of the Medal

THE word 'connoisseur' still seems to have a slightly sinister connotation in English. Moreover, hundreds would never attempt to spell it for fear of disaster, and thousands would hesitate about its pronunciation. It is beginning to return to the language in its pristine association with wine and food.

In the United States, at least among the very young, it can raise a sort of comic incredulity on the lines of 'Gee, what a profession! Didn't those painters ever *sign* their pictures?' This remark was made to me in mid-Atlantic by a young American student of the name of Berenson in July 1955. I thought he might be a relation, but he was not, though he had heard of his namesake and wanted to know some of the reasons for his fame.

At 'I Tatti' itself, the activity of ascribing a painting to its most likely author came to be called 'conòshing'. On some evenings, when a new batch of photographs had to be examined, and if the friends present were equipped for the game, a few rounds of 'conòshing' might be played. Berenson himself would encourage the hesitant with, 'In the beginning was the guess, you know'. It was just a game. Long hours of work, often months and even years as we know, went to the making of Berenson's attributions.

Whatever stigma still attaches to the word connoisseur certainly comes down from the eighties of the last century. A kind of cold war had grown up between the German art historians and the connoisseurs. Art connoisseurs—the people who claimed to know who had painted a picture or carved or modelled a masterpiece—said that many art historians hardly knew or had ever handled what they were writing about. The art historians considered the connoisseurs as drudges who picked up the raw materials (upon which the art historians then worked) in the auction rooms and among the dealers of the world. It is true that Wilhelm Bode, the German connoisseur who eventually became Director of the Kaiser Friedrich Museum in

Berlin, merged the two activities. His introduction to his collectors' catalogues are of little interest.

It took a man like Giovanni Morelli, quite unhampered by any feelings of social inferiority, equally at home in the museum or the auction room, pursuing his identifications, his purchases and occasionally his sales for the enjoyment of the thing, and then writing it all down for the aid of future students—it took such a man to define a connoisseur in the field of art as the equivalent of a botanist or a geologist in the natural world, able to distinguish between good and bad specimens, able to classify correctly and thereby to appreciate the more. There is a pretty vehement discussion between the imaginary Lermolieff (Morelli) and an Italian on this very subject:[1]

'As the botanist lives among his fresh and dried plants . . . so the art-connoisseur ought to live among his photographs and, if his finances permit, among his pictures and statues. . . . Yet, for all this, he must never neglect the study of nature. To understand a work of art thoroughly . . . he must learn to look at all around him with an artist's eye.'

By the age of thirty-one Berenson had reached this point. He was just married; he had published his study of Lotto and the three slim volumes on the *Painters of the Renaissance* which were going into second and third editions; he had finished the long weary labours in the Uffizi print rooms which had enormously increased his knowledge and given him the assurance he needed. He and Mary had the very kind of house which they most wanted, in a setting of great natural beauty. Books, photographs and works of art were being gathered in. As though to crown and confirm his abilities as a connoisseur he could look back on the purchase of no less than thirty-five masterpieces of the first rank for Mrs Gardner's collection, including a work or works by Masaccio, Giotto, Botticelli, Raphael, Titian, Correggio, Rembrandt and Holbein. But in print he never did so.

In the very first years of the new century Mrs Gardner was still buying on a considerable scale. There was an *Annunciation* (by Antoniazzo Romano) which had hung for years upon an outer wall of the little chapel-cell of St Francis, the Porziuncola (preserved inside the huge church of S Maria degli Angeli) at the foot of the hillside of Assisi. People remembered seeing it there (Mrs Water-

[1] Morelli, *Italian Painters, ed. cit.*, pp. 11–16.

field was one of those who first noticed that it had gone) and then it was purchased 'by a syndicate in London which included Colnaghi and Berenson'.[1] In those days the bold could buy even off the walls of the churches. In this painting 'the scene is not dramatically laid, but the knowledge and enjoyment of all Italy have gone into its compilation . . . the garden gateway gives upon a view which is the very essence of Italian landscape', wrote Philip Hendy in his Catalogue.[2] Mrs Gardner bought it for £6,000. In the following year she spent another £33,000 through Berenson on a wonderful *Madonna and Child with St John* by Botticini, *A Lady with a Nosegay* by Bacchiacca, *The Child Jesus disputing in the Temple* by Bordone, *Queen Mary of England* by Moro, a splendid Dürer portrait of *Lazarus Ravensburger*, a Pinturricchio *Madonna and Child* and some Carpaccio drawings.

But Berenson knew that these purchases represented her last great 'fling'. Her husband, John Lovell Gardner, had died in 1898. About five years later she began to get anxious lest she were spending too lavishly, and then she ceased to buy altogether for a number of years. It became obvious that Berenson's main income would soon have to come from other sources. He had been buying occasionally for the Metropolitan Museum in New York, for Mr and Mrs Warren, for Pierpont Morgan and for Henry Clay Frick, yet never on the scale of his purchases for Fenway Court. If life in the new home at Settignano was to proceed upon its course he would have to find another patron, or else draw in his horns, cut down on book collecting, on travel and on entertaining.

Added to the anxiety about a regular income was a fairly constant undercurrent of worry beneath all this buying activity. The art market must be among the most unpleasant of all commercial worlds in some respects.

We know about the problem of getting the works of art across the frontier and how they were replaced by copies. In 1899 one of the great prizes obtained by Berenson for Mrs Gardner was the Chigi Botticelli, the *Madonna of the Eucharist*. As in the case of the Zileri Giorgione, the picture was replaced by a copy. This time the Italian Government acted. Prince Chigi was known to be hard up. He had sold his Rome palace in the Piazza Colonna to the Italian Government (it is now the Italian Foreign Office). The Prince was

[1] *Catalogue of Isabella Stewart Gardner Museum, ed. cit.,* p. 18.
[2] *Ibid.,* p. 16.

indicted for selling his Botticelli and had to stand trial in Perugia early in the century. Berenson induced Mrs Gardner to let Colnaghi exhibit her Chigi Botticelli 'as no one knows where it is and the picture has excited the whole world and the Press of every great town'. Prince Chigi was fined a nominal 2,000 lire. Berenson next writes to Mrs Gardner that the copy also had appeared in London and had been sold by a famous dealer for £10,000. He punctuates the news with three exclamation marks.

Things could go wrong long before a purchase had reached or crossed the frontier. The pursuit of a picture could be strenuous or even fruitless. There were setbacks and they are often referred to in the letters to Mrs Gardner. Sometimes a setback 'is responsible for the great part of the miserable health I have been in this summer' (1902). He speaks of 'the fray of bargaining'. And sometimes he hands over all his correspondence, even his book reviews and his proof reading, to Mary.

The dealers themselves presented him with problems. There were no tricks they would not practice. Mary tells of one of their most ancient practices, that of hanging a forgery in a fine dim setting, surrounded by damask or velvet in the palace of an ancient impoverished family who would stoop to lending their palace temporarily to impress the transatlantic traveller in search of bargains. Tuscany was full of dealers and of frame makers. Among the latter the most highly skilled was a man called Joni, a craftsman, who lived in Siena and could reproduce an early Renaissance frame with wonderful skill. Joni could not resist the temptation of reproducing a great deal more than frames. He wrote his memoirs in later years.[1]

Joni tells a story worthy of Benvenuto Cellini, with all the fighting details of a poverty-ridden life. He was born in 1868 as the illegitimate son of an Italian soldier who committed suicide. He was apprenticed to an old restorer in Tuscany and learned how to gild. His teacher made him copy and restore little tabernacles which were then sold at a fine profit. A one-eyed antiquarian used to come to his teacher's shop and order wooden shields with plaster reliefs which sold 'just like antiques'. Joni goes into all the details of how to make a really good patina so that the illusion was perfect. He

---

[1] Icilio Frederico Joni, *Le Memorie di un Pittore di Quadri Antichi, con alcune descrizioni sulla pittura a tempera e sul modo di fare invecchiare i dipinti e le dorature*. Published by the Società Editrice Toscana, Sancasciano, Val di Pesa, Florence. (No date, but probably in the mid 1920s.)

describes how he soon made panels without even looking at the originals and how all this went into the shops at Nice to be sold there. He learnt to make worm holes in his fake coffers, using knitting needles of various sizes. Then he began to make Renaissance book bindings and panels with little Madonnas on a gold ground, and he tells how he himself was one of the people who took American buyers to see fakes in dilapidated working-class houses. A poor family would get 100 lire for lending a dirty wall, just as a palace owner would get a percentage on a sale for lending his wall complete with velvet hangings.

Joni's book is a jumble of unco-ordinated stories and hearsay—gossip of the workshop. Berenson certainly ordered frames from Joni. Joni was the best imitator of Renaissance frames alive in Italy at the time. He tells how one day 'a gentleman with a reddish beard and a fairly large wife' called upon him and ordered a fifteenth-century frame for 1,000 lire (about £40 in those days). 'The gentleman then lived in a little villa and the lady in another next door.' Thereafter the gentleman is called 'Somberen' and is described by our modern Cellini as 'a very good writer, but as an artist he does not even know how to sharpen a pencil—but he is very clever and will certainly make a fortune'. Joni complains that 'Somberen' paid him well at first and then less well. And then suddenly (on page 183) he writes (using the full name), 'Berenson visited me and admiring my new creations said, "Mind, you do not obviously imitate any master—by careful comparison your work will always be recognized with ease".'

This frank statement is followed by an account of a visit from 'Mrs Somberen with a U.S. Museum Director', urging him to purchase one of Joni's fakes 'just to show how far imitation can go'.

The Siena craftsman was making enough money between 1900 and 1920, on the rising tide of the world-wide rush into antiques as a form of real estate, to travel twice to London and once to Paris. At home he kept a tavern. Also he was a regular gymnast. He says that people who walked into his place in Siena did not at once know whether it was a gymnasium or a studio. About 1910 he worked for a middleman called Torrini,[1] and on page 210 he writes, 'Somberen told me he had sold almost all that Torrini had sent him

[1] Roger Fry, touring Tuscany with his patron and Pierpont Morgan, meets a similar middleman in Perugia called Torelli in 1907. (Virginia Woolf, *Roger Fry*, p. 141.)

of my work, and gained on it at Christie's sales in London'. He also claims he was working through 'Papini' (no Christian name is given) for Lord Westbury, for Lady Wantage and for Queen Margherita of Italy, and that he was trying 'to collect gifted unemployed Siena artists to give life to my little industry'. He tells how he gilded canvases and crumpled them up to get the desired craquelure. Then he would glue the canvas to an old panel and give it an antique varnish and add a bit of 'fly dirt' with a sharpened stick 'dipped in appropriate colouring and the result was identical with the real thing'. Not, of course, under modern scientific methods of investigation, probably not even under a strong magnifying glass.

Joni announces proudly in 1914 that he spent 10,500 lire on a Bianchi motor car and drove it himself, and one of his first calls with samples of his latest wares was on the 'Somberens'. He describes how Mr Somberen would not receive him and Mrs Somberen came to the door with a message from her husband to say 'your production is much improved'. The allusions which follow are too obscure to trace: he answers:

'Say to your husband that there will be much to laugh at over this. It cannot end here. I am told that a fine comedy was written in England to guy a famous German critic who had attributed a wax bust to Leonardo: one could write a funnier one here describing how Signor Somberen bought modern pictures made to look like old masters by Joni, and when Joni brought him old masters he wouldn't buy them, because he thought they were moderns!'

Joni seems to have been storming on the threshold of 'I Tatti'. He states that for a moment Mrs Somberen lost her composure and then 'laughed and laughed, and the servants laughed too'. He left disgusted: 'Think of it. These people come to Italy to enrich themselves, and instead of being grateful to us, they treat us as though we were a herd of tramps asking for their charity.' He says he drove away shouting imprecations at the Villa.

After other storms against 'Somberen' came a violent one against 'Berenson':

'Many say that our art is much enhanced through his work, but one might ask . . . would not the masterpieces of Botticelli, Bellini, Michelangelo, etc., have remained what they are without this gentleman's illustrations, and before him were there not Milanesi, Crowe, Cavalcaselle, Murray, Langton Douglas and so many others too numerous to recall? Did the great Masters have to await recognition as men of genius through the approval of this foreigner? . . . even admitting that we have gained glamour through his criticism, it would have come sooner or later, for have not the new generations provided an abundance of young scholars whose education is as good as that of any foreigner?'

Joni was clearly very jealous. He sold his wares as successfully as other great fakers, Van Meegeren the clever faker of Vermeer and de Hooch, and Dossena the successful faker of classical Greek and Renaissance sculpture, in our century. These last were the subject of court cases, but Joni was not. The Fascist régime took him up and gave him quite a position as Director of the Siena Academy of Fine Arts, with the special task of training young men to repair the frames of the Sienese primitives. His pupils were taught to remove posthumous silver crowns from gold background panels, as well as 'false pearls and silver hearts' which had been added to Madonnas in the seventeenth and eighteenth centuries. Joni was grateful to the Blackshirts for thus elevating him, for deep down he resented the attention paid in Italy to foreign students of the Italian arts and crafts.

'. . . even Fascism which has done so much to elevate our national dignity has not made us aware of our true value. Faced with a foreigner we always feel the need of making compliments. . . . I remember one day seeing Someberen standing in the doorstep of [the café] Donney, pontificating, and round him in a semicircle as though afraid to come too near, stood all the Directors of the Florence Galleries. Then I saw how we ourselves keep feeding the foreigners' unbounded pride. . . .'

The little craftsman with the great skill of restoration certainly fanned his resentment and became, in his curious way, the prototype of many people in the art world who envied, questioned or doubted Berenson's work. Joni shoots a final arrow at Someberen, with whom he says he visited the Uffizi one day in order to discuss whether some panels were painted in oils or in tempera: 'In the course of our discussions I discovered that he knew nothing', and Joni adds 'modern art critics should study painting'. Joni's last fling at Berenson proves that he had entirely misunderstood the nature of Berenson's approach to art. Berenson's reply to all who reproached him for not being a student of powders, glazes and varnishes, was not published till 1948 under the title of *Aesthetics and History*.

'The theory and history of art as I have tried to pursue them are concerned with the work of art as it affects the spectator, the listener, the enjoyer, and not its maker, unless he too becomes an enjoyer . . . it has been my life's work to "live" the work of art, to turn it over and over on my mental palate, to brood, to dream over it; and then in the hope of getting to understand it better I have written about it. As consumer of the art product I have the right to do all that. As I am neither figure artist, nor architect, nor musician, I have no certain right to speak of the producer. . . . I for my part have never thought of writing on art except as an experience, personal, individual, but not private, not capricious, not self-assertive.'[1]

There are reputed to be several 'Jonis' in the cellars of the National Gallery in Washington, and one in the basement of the National Gallery in London, and certainly one which belonged to a member of the household at 'I Tatti'. Joni was a dealer as well as a faker, and claims that he used the services of the late Mr Mason Perkins, the American collector and writer on Sienese primitives, when making his purchases.

Joni provided only one of the innumerable pitfalls into which the purchaser of pictures in Italy might fall. A greater restorer than Joni was Cavenaghi in Milan, who came to be used much more frequently by Berenson for the cleaning and restoration of the masterpieces he bought for Mrs Gardner and others. The famous Chigi Botticelli was cleaned and restored by Cavenaghi. One of the problems of transporting five- and six-hundred-year-old paintings to the United States, as Berenson wrote to Mrs Gardner, was that the different climate of North America might severely harm them, and they would then need further restoration. No one had yet invented air conditioning. When Mrs Gardner, eight years after forming the Italian part of her collection, began to get anxious about the state of the pictures, Berenson suggested that Cavenaghi should go to Paris and clean and varnish any future purchases, and perhaps

[1] *A. and H.*, pp. 16, 17.

189

even be persuaded to cross the ocean. The paintings survived and Cavenaghi did not go to Boston.

The art world was (and still is) divided about Cavenaghi's restorations. Berenson thought very highly of him. To Mrs Gardner he wrote, 'Cavenaghi has Röntgen rays so to speak in his eyes . . . he examines paintings eighth of an inch by eighth of an inch, and then operates on them with the same loving tenderness and sovereign skill that a great surgeon uses operating on a vital organ'. Berenson often went to Cavenaghi's studio in Milan where 'hundreds if not thousands'[1] of Quattrocento paintings were restored. Once Berenson gave him what he deemed a Bellini for cleaning. Cavenaghi kept it as was his wont for years, and then appeared with it, untouched, saying that it was a forgery:

'Very well, then, if it is a forgery let us see how it was done'. He set to work and got off the stupendous carriage varnish that in England used to be applied to every Italian Quattrocento panel, and there came out an almost intact old picture, every touch betraying the delicate brush of Giovanni Bellini.[2]

On the whole Berenson thought that the restorer, dwelling so much on how these early panels had been painted, was probably less fitted to recognize the artistic personality of an old master than the man 'who has learned to identify himself with most of the creative ways of the same master'.[3]

The faking of old and of modern pictures had always been an industry in Italy. It spread to other countries and is now become a vast enterprise with ramifications in almost every restoration studio in Paris, London and the cities of Italy. In the last decade the most notable forgeries were several scores of allegedly twelfth-century figures painted by a restorer in the Marienkirche in Lübeck. The German Government attended the reopening of the great Hanseatic church after it had been repaired from war bombing in 1948. Books and theses were written about the 'newly discovered' frescoes until the forger Malskat, in his cups, revealed how he himself had painted the whole frieze. The frescoes were finally washed off and the painter sentenced to imprisonment. In the case of Lübeck the existing twelfth-century frescoes are so gawky and coarse in outline that almost anyone could have imitated them. In Italy great skill was used

[1] *A. and H.*, p. 197.   [2] *A. and H.*, p. 198.   [3] *A. and H.*, p. 198.

and seemed always to be available, as though it had been passed on, straight down from the old masters.

Berenson wrote little about forgeries and fakings. The peril of being taken in must have been constant, and some errors must have occurred, one imagines. Nevertheless nearly all his attributions were accepted in his lifetime, and this acceptance continually increased and enhanced his reputation. The prices of Italian Renaissance works were soaring. Berenson wrote to Mrs Gardner, just after her last orgy of buying,

'With all the experience I have had in buying, and the control I could easily have of the market, advising about pictures is the path marked out for me. But you have now nearly had your fill. . . . I feel I could sell ten times as much as I do, if only I had a larger circle.'

He said he would rely on her to widen his circle. 'We want Americans to have as many good pictures as possible. You have had the cream. Other collectors will only enhance the superiority of yours.'

By now Mary was fully acquainted with her husband's purchases. In one of her earliest letters to Mrs Gardner (November 10, 1902) she writes gratefully,

'It is not only that when he was young and unknown you confided to him many honourable responsibilities—it is the way you did it— as different from most people who have sought advice, as a Queen from a petty Merchant. He loves the splendid way in which you have carried out your ideas and is proud that you associated him with them.'

That was the form in which Mary must have been initiated into the friendship, now nearly two decades old, of Mrs Gardner and Berenson, with its culmination in the vast purchases of the previous eight years, upon whose proceeds by way of price and commission the Berensons had not only been able to set up house in Italy, but Berenson himself had been launched upon the first stage of a long career of expertise.

The only printed reference to Mrs Gardner in Berenson's works, however, still carries the marks of some unaccountable resentment. He calls her 'Boston's pre-cinema star':

'While Jack [Gardner] was alive, *he* did all the paying not only abroad but at home. Isabella spent only on clothes, pearls, diamonds and, later, on almost as expensive Old Masters. When her husband died and the bills of the baker and butcher and electrician were brought to her, she got into a panic from which she never quite recovered. She who in Europe had travelled like royalty with compartments reserved for her in railways and luxurious suites in hotels, now went second class, and, frequenting the same hotels as before, would take the cheapest rooms and order the least expensive dishes. Remaining wealthy, but having had no training in the workaday use of money, she lived like a Latin *rentière* in constant fear of losing it. She all but ceased acquiring works of art on the ground that she was poor, and this at a time when those nearest to her used to beg me to induce her to buy, assuring me that she could amply afford it.'[1]

Berenson's observations may well be accurate. The elderly often develop deep anxieties lest they should fail to support themselves through to journey's end, or fail to implement their legacies by spending too much in their lifetime. Nevertheless Mrs Gardner did spend over £30,000 *after* her husband's death on purchasing old masters through Berenson. Also there was a cessation of certain incomes from Mr Gardner's paid posts when he died, and there was her determination to endow Fenway Court for all time—an ambition which she amply achieved.

The only tangible evidence of alarm in the Berenson–Gardner correspondence at Fenway Court is a hastily pencilled note on the back of an envelope dated April 13, 1921, with a postmark 'Hyères' written probably at Edith Wharton's home there.

'Dear B.B., There's a hold-up about everything. Swift has decided that I have no money for anything. I am schooling myself to have no wants. Love to both from your Isabella.'

It was not sent to Florence, or it would not be at Fenway Court. The correspondence the other way from Boston to 'I Tatti' does not seem to have been preserved. By 1921 the pageant of friends staying and visiting at 'I Tatti' is the main subject of Berenson's and Mary's letters to Fenway Court. Among a host of visitors Lytton Strachey

[1] *R. and R.*, pp. 26, 27.

192

stays for three weeks, Lowes Dickinson stays for a month, the Walter Lippmanns begin to pay their annual visits, the Duke of Alba picnics with the 'Tatti' household on the slopes of the Villa Medici gardens, and George Santayana comes over to supper. There is much to write about apart from pictures.

* * *

The dichotomy in Berenson's life—the total separation between purchaser and salesman on the one hand and the appreciator of all the arts and crafts of man on the other, was bound to have its painful side. The correspondence with Mrs Gardner tries to bridge the two Berensons who, in life, were kept in two separate compartments. The anxieties and intrigues of picture buying and selling were kept as far from the social occasions as any business talk is usually (though not always) kept from grouse shooting occasions on August moors in Scotland. But that dichotomy is accepted. This one caused Berenson pain, that it should have to exist at all. It contributes to the otherwise unaccountable sense of failure which runs like a black thread right through the tapestry of the human document, *Sketch for a Self-Portrait*, written in Berenson's silver old age. At first he attributed his exit from a happy world to the moment when he entered the ranks of the expert, which he (and the art world) associated with the Florentine *Drawings*. But by then he had already crossed the Rubicon of combining the appreciation of art with art-dealing. By then there had already been two kinds of writing, the one for the love of it, the other for salesmanship. This situation gives Berenson trouble in the *Sketch*. He keeps coming back to it. At one moment of intense self-examination he no longer names connoisseurship and the acquisition of authority *per se* as the cause for the exile from paradise.

'My only excuse is, if the comparison is not blasphemous, that like Saint Paul with his tent making and Spinoza with his glass polishing, I too needed a means of livelihood. . . . Mine took up what creative talent there was in me, with the result that this trade made my reputation and the rest of me scarcely counted. The spiritual loss was great and in consequence I have never regarded myself as other than a failure. This sense of failure, a guilty sense, makes me squirm when I hear myself spoken of as a "successful man" and as having made "a success of my life".'[1]

[1] *S.S.P.*, pp. 41, 42.

The comparison is not blasphemous but inadequate. Both Berenson's examples were men who lived in humble circumstances in order to devote themselves to their chosen or destined missions, with just enough activity of a skilled kind to keep them out of want in an emergency. Of Spinoza it was said that he could have made a substantial living, so good a glass grinder was he, but his philosophic thought took up a great deal of his time. To draw a full comparison, would it not be necessary to imagine that neither had engaged in tent making or in glass grinding, but that each had fortuitously discovered some technical and lucrative activity belonging to what they felt to be their main mission in life, and had decided to practise that activity during at least half their working day? It did not happen, and they would not have been St Paul and Spinoza if it had.

Clearly the sense of initiation, of dedication and of a mission had carried Berenson very far—so far that he had not once but often enjoyed an almost mystical act of identification with something like perfection in a work of art, in nature, in certain human beings, when the occasion presented itself. Upon such occasions he could speak briefly in an inspired and an inspiring way, so that people often thought of him as of one of the minor prophets of the Old Testament. This inspiration, and the knowledge upon which it grew, included some facts of great concern to the market-value of pictures. I suppose it became humiliating, once he had crossed the rubicon in 1896, to find that so many hours of his day and so much of his 'creative talent' had to be devoted to these humble facts, that they had to be spun out into persuasive prose and used to convince a buyer that this or that picture was the proper one to purchase, with immediate and very considerable rewards to Berenson himself.

Many art dealers, professors of art and art critics have entered the market all over the world, without turning a hair. Could not Berenson have done likewise? He could not. He belonged to no confraternity of business people, national or local. He had a keen and sharp sense of monetary value, and liked other people to have it also. But he clung to his vision of a civilized society on however small a scale at 'I Tatti', and he knew it could not be preserved without relegating the business of expertise to a closed and a secret portion of his life.[1] The rigours of this dichotomy were considerable.

[1] For those young people in our greatly slackened society who might still ask 'But why?' it is necessary to put the matter more simply. Conversations about deals are, and will always be, exercises in complaint, in cunning, in

Infringement by others—for instance if a man arrived with a picture thinking to get an expertise there and then—relegated those others to a lifelong limbo. He would never speak to such a man again. Museum directors were not so treated. They could bring photographs and examine them with him. After all they were puzzled colleagues, concerned for the reputation and improvement of their museums. Very late in life, when Berenson heard a rumour that one of his younger pupils had begun buying and selling pictures, he was horrified, and the horror was genuine. He feared for the young man lest the dealing should kill his leisure and his relationships with people. For it nearly always does.

A hundred phrases were conjured up to defend civilized life at 'I Tatti'. One was '*Unsereiner*'—best translated by 'the likes of us'; another was IT, and IT-ness; another (from Rossetti's sonnet sequence) *The House of Life*.[1] Under these terms the paradise on the hillside at Settignano was defined. With the years the terms began to signify. They were no longer mere phrases. But long before this happened some new way of earning had to be found, if the house was ever to be purchased and the library built.

intrigue and in financial compromise. As such they are incompatible with the pursuit of truth, the exercise of wit and the exchange of news which form the essence of good conversation.

[1] These phrases appear constantly in *S.S.P.*, *R. and R.* and *A. and H.*

CHAPTER XII

The Rewards and the Taint of Connoisseurship

> The work of art serves not only as a joy for all
> time, seeing that it offers permanent possibili-
> ties of life-enhancement, but from the moment
> of its completion, for generations to come, it
> serves as a model, after which the society in whose
> midst it has appeared tends through its most
> sensitive members to shape itself.
>
> BERENSON: *Aesthetics and History*

AMERICAN travellers to Italy were now beginning to carry
with them the three slim volumes of *The Venetian Painters*,
The Florentine Painters and *The Central Italian Painters*
alongside their Murrays, Baedekers and *Guides Bleus*. The best
articles which Berenson had been writing in the *Gazette des Beaux-
Arts*, in the (American) *Nation*, the *Connoisseur* and the *Burlington
Magazine* (refounded in 1903) were to be reproduced in his three
series of *The Study and Criticism of Italian Art*. In the first series
there were six essays on Vasari; on Dante's visual images; on
Venetian painting; on Correggio; on Giorgione's lost originals and
on that temporary composite figure he called 'Amico di Sandro', a
supposed friend of Botticelli, to whom, for lack of an existing author,
he attributed fourteen paintings and one drawing, hitherto variously
attributed to other Botticellian painters. Amico di Sandro was later
dropped and 'his' pictures reattributed where they belonged, or left
with the question mark which Berenson was never afraid of using.

There are all sorts of asides in these essays, and invitations to
scholars and dilettanti to embark on tasks for which Berenson had no
time or qualifications. He wanted someone to make a systematic
study of Dante's visual images. He noted that immediately after
Beatrice's death, the first thing Dante did was to sit down and draw
an angel. 'Dante could not have invented this angel. It would be

like an angel of Dante's favourite painter, Giotto. . . . Dante's visual images of the Virtues, of the heavenly hosts, of Christ and the Virgin, of St Francis, could not have been very different from Giotto's'. Berenson, who did read Dante, found that Giotto, Duccio, Simone Martini and Lorenzetti helped him to form a clearer conception of Dante's images. Botticelli's famous illustrations to Dante he dismisses as 'lineal rhapsodies'. If Dante's imagery is difficult, 'The attitude of the Renaissance to classical antiquity in Dante's time was still subjective—Michelangelo's is already quite like our own.'

The essay on Vasari warns the student to take account of Vasari's 'excursions on loop lines to kick an enemy or puff a friend'. Berenson finds that 'Vasari is not so penetrating as Mr Pater, not so fantastical and poetical as Mr Ruskin, but he is broader than either, and in closer sympathy with actual humanity'. There is an aside in the essay on Vasari which is fundamental to Berenson's whole outlook. It refers to people who 'do not take the trouble to look at the works of art they might have seen by sticking their heads out of the window', the dawns, the sunsets, the stars, the full moons, which are free to all. He insisted that all the learning in the world was useless without artistic imagination, which began on one's doorstep or one's windowsill and could not be confined to the study or the studio. This angered many art critics. But they were disarmed (almost to a man) when they visited him and went for a walk with him. 'The gift he had for making one look at skies, trees, hills and pictures with new eyes. How he communicated colour and atmosphere!'[1]

It would not be possible to run through the score of essays in the three series. The student of art history will find and read them in any case. The essay on *Rudiments of Connoisseurship* in the second series remains (with Morelli's work) fundamental to the training of the connoisseur. It is richer than Morelli. It outlines the morphological method and then discourses on the place of the nude in painting between 1400 and 1600, the use of drapery, the importance of hands, the curiously wooden quadrupeds of Paolo Uccello, Car-

---

[1] Nesta de Robeck, to the author in 1954. She was a lifelong friend of the Berensons. At first she lived in Arcetri near Florence with her parents and then settled in Assisi, whence she accompanied pilgrimages of invalids to Lourdes every year. There was no kind of distress which she did not assist to the best of her ability.

paccio's 'strange hybrid horses', Leonardo's tumbling horses. 'Animals were rarely petted in the Renaissance', therefore they are not observed with affection. Berenson confesses he had some difficulty in memorizing colour. He thought that the student who trained his colour memory might make a highly profitable use of it.

But in the end there remains the question of quality, and we are back where we started from, or almost. For quality does not fall into the category of demonstrable things. In the essay in this series on the *Sposalizio* at Caen in Normandy, Berenson is faced with just this problem. People said of course that this was another Raphael, just like the *Sposalizio* by Raphael in the Sistine Chapel in the Vatican. Of the latter Berenson writes that the breadth in the middle distances, pure and cool, filled with a soft and fresh air, gave him a sense of the utmost well-being. He found repose in the delicate horizon. And he found the colonnades of the temple in the background uplifting and soothing. After careful study of Raphael's drawing in the Uffizi, and after observation of the Caen picture, he finds that the latter is a copy by Lo Spagna. Crowe and Cavalcaselle had attributed it to Perugino.[1]

In 1903, largely through Roger Fry's efforts, the bankrupt *Burlington Magazine* was re-started, and the first of a lifelong series of contributions to it came from Berenson. In this and the next two numbers he wrote three essays on a painter of the Legend of Saint Francis of Assisi, Stefano di Giovanni Sassetta. The articles were appropriate, for there was to be an Exhibition of Sienese Art at the Burlington Fine Arts Club in 1904. Various writers were preparing the public with articles on the Sienese primitives.

Berenson had grown familiar with them on his many visits to Monte Oliveto near Siena. Since J. J. Jarves had written about Sassetta in the middle of the previous century there had been little interest. Cavalcaselle had complained that Sassetta was a painter of 'ugly types' of people. Sassetta had fallen 'into the limbo of the footnote', as Berenson put it.

So little interest was there in the early gold background pictures at the beginning of the century that few people visited the magnificent Jarves Collection which had been hanging in Yale since 1871.

---

[1] The French keep up their old attributions for this and many other Italian Renaissance works in their provincial galleries, but they are always slow to catch up in these matters.

A friend informs me that according to Professors Popham and Pouncey (1958) the picture should be attributed to Perugino.

The Rewards and the Taint of Connoisseurship

Can mysticism be conveyed in the visual arts? Berenson asks, and finds that Sassetta comes nearer than any other European artist to 'that rare and most unattainable of emancipations, the emancipation from oneself'. He enjoys the painter's cool detachment. He also thinks that a great legend like the Franciscan one of the young gallant of Assisi who took poverty for his bride and became a wandering friar living entirely upon the kindness he preached and received, was more likely to find its first expression in literature, and in St Francis's case 'in prose of angelic candour and in poetry celebrating man's recovered intimacy with nature and its Creator'. After the poems of St Francis, the painters take up the theme. At the hands of Giotto (1266–1336) in the upper church of St Francis at Assisi, and in the Sassetta (1392–1451) panels in the National Gallery in London, in Siena, and elsewhere the legend finds adequate expression. Berenson thought he discerned Far Eastern influences in Sassetta's painting: the flat colours, the plain contours, the spacing, the avoidance of chiaroscuro. No Western art came closer to Buddhist religious art for him than the Sienese fourteenth- and fifteenth-century schools. To crown his affection for this painter Berenson lived for the better part of fifty years with an immense St Francis altarpiece painted by Sassetta and hung in the sitting-room at 'I Tatti'.[1]

The three essays in the *Burlington Magazine* were republished and enlarged and appeared in book form in 1909. Others have since written on Sassetta without Berenson's affection for this painter's candid way of painting the legend of poverty as a quality of saintliness. Berenson's *Sassetta* has been out of print since 1909, except in France—a great loss. It is a book of deep poetic appreciation.

This experience of Sassetta and his contemporaries gave Siena a special place in Berenson's affection. No other city has indeed produced so many saints. Elsewhere Italy remained 'pagan and classical even in Christianity. . . . They never knew what it was to have the feeling of mystery which haunts the north, that sense of being in the presence of unknowable and unimaginable though almost tangible powers', he wrote in the essay on *Renaissance Churches*. 'Lacking this

---

[1] It was a part of the high altar of St Francis at Borgo S. Sepolcro (the contract for it was dated September 5, 1437). It stood there for 308 years, and was then dismantled in 1752. Early in the century Mary came upon it quite by chance in the shop of the dealer Bardini in Florence and bought it for a song.

feeling, their art lacks it. Their literature has no touch of weirdness; their painting, if it has magic at all, has only the sun-flooded magic of a midsummer day. Their architecture has nothing inspiring about it.' Nevertheless, Renaissance churches gave Berenson 'an effect of space and harmony produced by the simplest means'.

*　　*　　*

The way one looks at things 'is largely determined by the works of art with which one is acquainted', Berenson wrote in one of those essays. Living in daily sight of Renaissance art himself, he often saw men and women as Botticellis, Carpaccios, Turas, or as though they had walked out of a Florentine, a Venetian or a Ferrara fresco into his drawing-room. Or they might recall some esoteric head among his Persian and Indian bronzes.

Recalling an evening long before the 1914 war, when friends were gathered for dinner at 'I Tatti', Nesta de Robeck said:

'how handsome all those young people were, B.B., Mary, Lady Sybil Cutting, Geoffrey Scott, Cecil Pinsent—all the beauty and wit seemed to be gathered together. I felt quite a misfit. . . .'

'And you looked it!' was her host's jovial comment, forty-five years later, in the garden of 'I Tatti'.

Mary on her travels in England had met two young men whom she invited to 'I Tatti'. Geoffrey Scott and Cecil Pinsent had been at Oxford together. One wanted to be an architect and the other (who had studied architecture) wanted to be a landscape gardener. Geoffrey Scott[1] had lately won the Newdigate and the English Essay prize at Oxford. When the painter William Rothenstein was invited to Florence to paint Berenson's portrait in the autumn of 1907,[2] Geoffrey Scott took him visiting round the churches and galleries of Florence. Rothenstein wrote, in his memoirs:

'Dark eyed and pale, he looked strikingly like a Botticelli portrait; indeed, he was more Italian than English in appearance. Scott had come to stay at "I Tatti" for a week; but after several months

---

[1] He was a cousin of C. P. Scott, editor of the *Manchester Guardian* from 1872 to 1929.　　　　[2] See Plate XIII.

he was still there, and no wonder; he was the most inspiring and entertaining of guests . . . a wonderful talker, his talk at the Berensons' was something to be remembered. Berenson, too, with his astonishing intellect, delighted in the play of ideas; he could illuminate regions, however remote, not of art only, but also of literature, philosophy, politics, history, ethics and psychology. And sometimes we gossiped: for there were armed camps and fierce rivalries in Florence then, as in past times; but the fighting was far less bloody, concerned as it was with attributions rather than with Ducal thrones. Berenson, Horne, Loeser, Vernon Lee, Maud Crutwell, all had their mercenaries—and their artilleries.'[1]

Geoffrey Scott stayed on for twelve years at 'I Tatti' as Berenson's private secretary, and then married Lady Sybil Cutting. Mary put him on a pedestal from which he never descended to give her encouragement. He wrote two memorable books, *The Architecture of Humanism* and *The Portrait of Zélide*. In the first he acknowledges his debt to Berenson. It had been the intention of the two friends, Scott and Pinsent, to set up in Florence as architects and landscape gardeners.

Cecil Pinsent, the gentlest of men, with a powerful imagination about plants, trees, views and flowers, performed the miracle of laying out the garden at 'I Tatti' in such a way that after fifty years of steady growth, the sight of its evergreen spaces in the heart of the 'Tatti' landscape was as varied and as satisfying as a Bach fugue. I have walked round that garden with him several times. I never asked the acreage: perhaps no more than fifty acres. Within it he and Berenson imagined that a man might take a fairly long and varied walk passing from one landscape and mood to another, not with violent change but imperceptibly. The walker might have to take some zigzag route (fifty acres is no great area for a half-hour walk), but there would be a choice of routes, again imperceptibly suggested—few paths, no fences. At first, when the trees were young and small, Berenson believed the miracle would never happen. As they grew mightily there was fear that the garden would get out of hand. But it never did. Four gardeners tended it. Through the years Pinsent came to see it grow and to legislate about the trimming of the great yew hedges and the ilex trees, and to establish the

---

[1] William Rothenstein, *Men and Memories*, 1900–1922, p. 122, Faber and Faber.

placing of those statues and grey stone benches in the dark shady places where one might sit and read.

To visualize this garden one must imagine it falling away at the sides and in front of 'I Tatti', downhill on every side. The green garden, evergreen with box and yew, ran down straight from the centre of the house by a path through the orangery where lemons and oranges were sheltered from the frost in winter. The path then became a double stone staircase surrounding a pool and rapidly descended in a flight of broad pebbled stairs to two simple long stone pools far away at the bottom. On either side of this descent there were terraces upon which box bushes formed patterns and the whole wide descending green pattern was enclosed by what became a gigantic yew hedge in flat broad tiers, on either side, like some giant's stepping-stones into the valley. Papyrus and lotus grew in the pools and grey benches and statues, at some distance from them, formed another frame beneath the yew hedge to these airy spaces.

Besides this green garden there were two long avenues of trees and three 'other gardens', all very good to walk in. One of the avenues was the main approach on foot to the house, with cypresses thirty feet high, the other a gentler affair of ilex trees descending to another round pool, surmounted and enclosed by trellis crowned with a trellis cupola open to the sky. An evergreen jasmin grew on this trellis. The reflection in the water, as you looked over the stone ledge of the pool, made you think of Mantegna's ceiling in the wedding chamber in the Palazzo Ducale in Mantua.

The other three landscapes were a kitchen garden dotted with fruit trees whence the southern views to the hillside of Corbignano and distant Vallombrosa were constantly delighting the eye. There was a meadow too—as English a meadow in springtime as one might ever hope to see south of the Alps. In spring its grass slopes were dotted with anemones and daffodils, and fritillary. From it, in summer, came the smell of new cut hay. And there was a wood of young ilexes growing in rugs of moss, with a grotto with more water and a statue. Looking back from that grotto and upward, one saw 'I Tatti' high in the distance, too far to read the time on the clock which Mary had built into a stone cornice over the centre of the façade, but not too far to hear its slow clear chimes at the hour and the half-hour. The whole garden was a bird sanctuary on a hillside hardly ever free of local bird trappers and shooting butts.[1]

[1] See Plates X, XI, XII, XX.

The Rewards and the Taint of Connoisseurship

The sound of running water in this garden came from a stream, a tributary of the so-called torrent, the Mensola, whose waters formed a boundary to the property. Beyond the Mensola the land rose again in olive-clad hills belonging to the neighbouring castle of Poggio Gherardo (Mrs Janet Ross, and later inherited by her niece Mrs Aubrey Waterfield), and the villa of the last descendant of Comnenius, Emperor of Constantinople, which was later grimly enlarged and became a Jesuit seminary. In time even Poggio Gherardo was sold and broken up into a housing estate, so that 'I Tatti' remained the only sizeable estate on that hillside. It had farms and fields beyond the garden whence came the wine which was drunk at meals and some of the flour used for making bread. As on all Tuscan farms, the tenure was share cropping (*mezzadria*). Once Berenson became the owner he had to supply the seed and the cattle and tools. The produce and the young cattle were shared in a proportion fixed by the government of the day.

Geoffrey Scott and Cecil Pinsent and Berenson planned the enlargement of the house in 1907. It took three years to complete. Cecil Pinsent further enlarged the house and garages on two later occasions.

'My house, I trust, does express my needs, my tastes, and aspirations. It is a library with living-rooms attached. These are both spacious and comfortable yet with a touch of the old Italian severity that might depress the happy victims of our "interior decorators". . . . The pieces of furniture are of a size suitable to that purpose, and so is the rest, the hangings, the paintings, the few art objects. . . . When the house was at long last furnished and the works of art in their place. . . . It took the scattering of most private collections all over Europe to make me realize that mine was one of the best remaining.'[1]

That collection of over two hundred Italian Renaissance paintings and a host of Oriental works of art did, in truth, never have the appearance of a gallery. It was scattered in the bedrooms, in the corridors, in the sitting-rooms, never crowded, at eye level, easy to enjoy.

Berenson came to love the house he had rebuilt and furnished: 'Although I had so gifted an architect as Cecil Pinsent, who often

[1] *S.S.P.*, pp. 132–3.

understood my wants better than I did, it half killed me to get it into shape . . . now after many years I love it as much as one can love any object or complex of objects not human.'[1]

Cecil Pinsent worked in many Anglo-Tuscan houses and laid out some beautiful gardens. The library he built and twice enlarged at 'I Tatti' had eventually to house some 40,000 volumes on two floors, and thousands of photographs of paintings, with desks in the centre and in the alcoves for students and readers. What students and what readers? In Berenson's lifetime himself, Mary, his assistants and his guests—rarely an outside student. Yet, very early, he must have had a vision of students at those desks. I remember being astonished one day in Massachusetts in June 1954, when visiting the three Curtis sisters on the north shore, to hear from one of them that she remembered, when visiting the Berensons in Florence in 1909, already then hearing from Berenson the outline of a plan to bequeath 'I Tatti' to Harvard. The Curtis sisters were all over eighty in 1954. One of them had been the famous golf champion and donor of the Curtis Cup. Another had founded an agricultural college in the Gobi desert. The one who recalled her memories of 'I Tatti' was still a student of Italian art and a most knowledgeable one.

*   *   *

The buying of 'I Tatti', the building on to it, the planting of the great garden and the making of the collection—all these delights began in 1907, the year in which Berenson entered the service of Joseph Duveen.

Berenson's last three big offers to Mrs Gardner met with no success. The first was no less than the offer to get her Titian's *Sacred and Profane Love.* It is still in the Borghese Gallery in Rome, for the Italian Government, hearing that the impoverished Borghese family were negotiating (with the Colnaghi–Berenson syndicate) about it, offered to purchase the whole Borghese Gardens and the villa with its contents in 1902. The Borgheses then sold it.

The second offer was an El Greco for 40,000 dollars, but when Mrs Gardner's wire did arrive it came too late and another purchaser had bought it. The third was Lord Lansdowne's *Mill* by Rembrandt, which Berenson offered to get for her for £40,000. But she said she could not afford it.

The years from 1903 to 1906 were so encumbered with the

[1] *S.S.P.*, p. 133.

worries of picture buying and selling that even Mary began to be distressed. 'I feel the only way to really live is to be free from possessions', reads like a *cri de cœur* in one of her letters to Mrs Gardner. The Berensons paid their first joint visit to the United States in 1903, but Mary's account of it reveals more worry connected with sales and with attributions. From Bryn Mawr (where Mary lectured) she wrote to Mrs Gardner:

'Poor B.B. gets so upset, he feels like quitting art altogether and settling in some wild Western place, where the connoisseurs cease from travelling and the critics are at rest.'

They travelled as always in Italy, every spring and autumn. In 1905 Berenson spent the spring in Duino Castle, five miles from Trieste, where Princess Marie of Thurn and Taxis held her small court, with the poet Rainer Maria Rilke often a guest. From there he explored Aquileia and Grado. Then in 1907 he was in London, looking at pictures, attending auctions. There is some discrepancy about the date.

Mr. S. N. Behrman, in his effervescent, brilliant portrait of Duveen, written as a series of articles for the *New Yorker* and published in book form in 1952, puts the date of meeting in 1906, in Duveen's shop in London, where the Hainauer Collection had just arrived. But the Hainauer Collection (according to Sir Philip Hendy in the Gardner Catalogue) was sold in 1907. The meeting may have taken place in 1906 and the Hainauer Collection may not have been in the shop, or else the meeting took place in 1907. In any case, it resulted in an association which was to last thirty years, until 1936. According to Mrs Dorothy Burns's (Lord Duveen's daughter) account,[1] Berenson received a salary of £20,000 a year and a commission of 10 per cent on the price of every picture sold, to which he had given an authentication.

During those thirty years Duveen built up a monopoly in Italian Renaissance pictures by a process which has been fully described in Mr Behrman's book, so that there is no need to go over the ground again here. In the chapter on Berenson there are inaccuracies; for instance, that Berenson's ancestors were rabbis, that Marcel Proust's reflections on art were gained on walks with Berenson, that Duveen acquired Berenson's eye or that Berenson's eyes were blue.

[1] In conversation with the author in London, 1955.

In Duveen, Berenson undoubtedly found a new patron at the very moment when he most needed one. The new Duveen patronage was not only financially welcome; it transferred the whole of the tedious and nerve-racking business of persuading people to sell and other people to buy, lock, stock and barrel, into the hands of Duveen Brothers. So the days ended in which those hundreds of letters written in Berenson's own hand about the buying and selling of pictures had often been a nightmare. Henceforward the process was quite different and much simpler. Berenson would still learn of pictures for sale and visit them. Then he would write his first letter acquainting the Duveen Brothers with the discovery, and ask for a cable about whether the picture should be reserved. The second letter might answer certain queries from the London or New York end. (By 1915 these queries were often concerned with whether the subject of a picture was 'too painful' for Duveen's pleasure-peace-and-plenty-loving clients.) The third letter would be an official authentication, without which the American purchasers had been schooled by Duveen to refuse to buy. Three such documents about a Piero della Francesca *Crucifixion* are preserved at Fenway Court, because Berenson wished Mrs Gardner to have first refusal of this picture. She was exempted from the Duveen–Berenson arrangements owing to Berenson's long association with her. If she wished for a picture she would get it at a lower price than that paid by Duveen's 'squillionaires', as Berenson called the big collectors. (She did not take this one and it went to the Rockefeller Collection.) Compared with his writing and his conversation, a Berenson authentication is dull stuff, but since so many hundreds were written, it may be of interest to reproduce this typical one:

                          ' "I Tatti", Settignano. November 18, 1915.
'Dear Messrs Duveen,
      'The "Crucifixion" that you ask about is an autograph painting by Piero della Francesca. Although of small size it is large in scale and produces nearly the same impression as his famous frescoes at Arezzo. What differences there are, are rather in favour of your painting.
      'Besides the qualities of grandeur, aloofness and impersonality, besides the qualities of drawing and modelling which we find in all his authentic works, your "Crucifixion" shows qualities of colour and handling that are a revelation. I should be at a loss to point to

any other Italian work that was of a colour at once so powerful and yet neither warm nor cold, but fused in a manner soft and harmonious. We are reminded of Giorgione, and, indeed nothing could be more Giorgionesque in colour than, for instance, the soldiers throwing dice for the raiment of Our Lord.

'Other paintings of Piero must have had such strong, beautiful coloring, but elsewhere it has faded, leaving paler and feebler tints behind.

'The handling of your little picture reminds me of Cézanne. It has become a commonplace to assert that this greatest of modern French masters had a sense of form and a feeling for atmosphere and placing singularly like Piero's. It was left to your "Crucifixion" to reveal how curiously like these two great artists are in handling as well.

'I trust you will let me know the ultimate destination of this most precious painting.

'Truly yours,
'Bernard Berenson.'

In the course of the next thirty years hundreds of these Berenson certificates would accompany Duveen's Italian pictures when he showed them to the great collectors in the United States. About the collector, Berenson has nothing kind to say:

'Such a one loves to compete, to get the better of the seller, to gloat over the object as a scalp or trophy, and finally either to enshrine it in his halo of self-satisfaction or to sell it at a high profit in money or pride.'[1]

Mr Behrman has this to say:

'. . . after having spent a lifetime making money, Duveen's protégés were rich enough to go anywhere and do anything but didn't know where to go or what to do or even how to do nothing gracefully. . . . There were no noble titles to be earned—or bought—and lived up to, as there were in Europe, and if they ever made an attempt to do nothing gracefully, they were hampered by the Puritanic and democratic tradition that held such a life sinful.'[2]

[1] *S.S.P.*, p. 132.   [2] S. N. Behrman, *Duveen*, p. 63, Hamish Hamilton.

One may speculate or even know what these great collectors wanted, but the only one who really succeeded in achieving what he wanted—and he disclaimed being a collector—was Berenson himself. So the collectors sometimes came over to see what he had done. One of them, Mr Paul Getty, whose company Berenson appreciated, said afterwards:

' "I Tatti" and Bernard Berenson are an event and a privilege I shall always remember. I have never been more impressed in my life.'[1]

After a few years of picture hunting even that exhausting activity could be abandoned. The pictures for Berenson's expertise began to arrive in consignments from Duveen Brothers. Those who knew 'I Tatti' before the 1914 war remembered sometimes seeing the long corridor between the main and the garden entrance stacked with paintings and panels, queueing up as it were for examination. These were now the chores of his profession. No longer could he look at the paintings of his choice, which remained all his life the paintings of the early Renaissance, before the human figure became contorted and began to fill canvases and walls in vast and ever-increasing medleys. Now for years he had to look at all that was sent, all that Duveen's scouts had picked up—anything painted or alleged to have been painted between Giotto and Tiepolo. In time, as photography became more and more expert, there was no need even to send the original painting. Photographs of details and photographs from every angle served equally well, strange as this must seem to the layman. Berenson was the first connoisseur to use the photograph daily in his work. He was also the first to advise the photographing of details.

The first and immediate result of the association with Duveen was 'one whopping piece of news' to Mrs Gardner. 'We are buying our house', he wrote to her; 'our landlord has lost his all at Monte Carlo so we are getting the place at a very reasonable price.' Luck at this moment was definitely on his side. But he did not mention in the letter how he had come to be able at last to purchase 'I Tatti'.

*   *   *

Writing of the period, Harold Acton, a lifelong friend and neighbour, recalls the descent of art historians of every nation upon the city

[1] Ethel Le Vane and J. Paul Getty, *Collector's Choice*, p. 225, W. H. Allen.

of Florence, pursuing their investigations, splitting hairs over the most obscure Tuscan masters, while others, like Roger Fry, entered wholeheartedly into the business of restoring Renaissance panels. The visitors and the 'locals' were almost all hoping to find an American patron. Roger Fry found his in Pierpont Morgan.

Harold Acton's father was engaged in the purchase and sale of Italian pictures and *objets d'art*. So was Mason Perkins. Adolfo Venturi, the famous Italian art historian, charged handsomely for his opinion on a picture. Like lawyers charging for advice, the art experts also had their fee, and still have. There are probably more dishonest art experts than lawyers. A favourite habit was (and still is) to organize a large exhibition of some classic painter or period with a fine catalogue written by an art expert, only to include in it some worthless pictures which might sell to an unsuspecting purchaser, because they had hung in good company. In these matters Berenson was a ruthless 'de-bunker'. Dealers and purchasers knew it and were afraid of him. His attributions were sought after. One has heard fearful tales of attempts to wrench attributions from him, even of thefts of photographs from 'I Tatti', on the back of which he had written tentative appraisals in his own feathery handwriting. Some of these were found on sale in New York soon after the Second World War, and had been lifted bodily from the photo library at 'I Tatti'. The culprit was known, but no action was taken.

*   *   *

Relatively to the millions of dollars which changed hands in the Duveen organization, Berenson's retainer was not excessive. The rub is in the 10 per cent. A lesser man than Berenson might have been tempted into giving a noble attribution which would bring in the 10 per cent, when no such attribution or a lesser one would be a dead loss. Few of us are equipped to assess the integrity of the connoisseur. The views of those who are so equipped are therefore important.

'People were prepared to say anything about Berenson, especially those who had never had occasion to meet him. They would say that the whole Harvard Bequest was blood money—reparation for years of mis-attributions. Nothing could be farther from the truth. The instruments of Berenson's trade were his own; he had created them. They were his child, to bequeath to something for which he had a tender feeling—his university.'

That was the view of an Englishman, Mr W. G. Constable, a descendant of the painter, for twenty years Curator of Paintings in the Boston Museum of Fine Arts, and the author of many works on painting.

Another important opinion comes from the late Mason Perkins. He had first met Berenson in 1898. He was himself a collector, a writer, and in a small and constant way, a dealer. He was a man with a finely chiselled face, a small and beautifully-shaped head, like that of a miniature Roman senator. His wife had discovered a Perugino fresco, reputed to be his last, in a stable that was once a chapel, on Lake Trasimene. First they lived in Florence, then in Assisi. In 1902 Mason Perkins wrote a serious small book about Giotto (for George Bell). He left his collection to the town of Assisi, which made him an honorary citizen. He was never rich, and he might well have been envious. Berenson always called on him when passing through Assisi. He said:

'Of course the long association with Duveen was bound to give Berenson a taint. All such associations in the dealing world do—but I don't believe Berenson was capable of giving an attribution of which he was not convinced. He made mistakes—we all do—but they were never and could never have been deliberate.'[1]

*   *   *

This chapter closes on a note of regret. It will be recalled that Berenson himself said that the first thirty-six years of his life were by far the most important. He was thirty-six in 1901. We are already years beyond the 'important' period and, for the second time, engaged on refuting tangible as well as shadowy allegations against his probity. Probably he foresaw that any account of his career would have to meet these obstacles and take them in its stride. What he may not have appreciated was that almost all his problems arise in one form or another, sooner or later, and in every country, for those who embark upon the career of art historian, art critic or museum official. A Duveen will not again appear to tempt them, but many

[1] To the author in Assisi in 1954.

other lucrative propositions which are just as compromising assail those who enter the art world as a career.

No one was more aware of what Mason Perkins called 'the taint' than Berenson himself. It is now generally accepted that his break with Duveen in 1936 was desired by Berenson rather than based on their sudden clash of opinion about Lord Allendale's *Nativity*, which Duveen was trying to sell that year to Andrew Mellon as a Giorgione, while Berenson held it to be an early Titian. It hangs in the National Gallery in Washington today as a Giorgione and is so recognized in Berenson's comprehensive *Lists of Venetian Renaissance Paintings*, published by the Phaidon Press in 1957, with the additional rider that it was 'probably finished by Titian'.

The clash was abrupt. Berenson would not authenticate the picture as a Giorgione at the time and Mellon would not buy it, for the very peculiar reason that he had 'enough' Titians. Mellon's taste, like that of so many collectors, was inclined to be statistical.

However, after the break Berenson did not cease authenticating pictures. Not only had the work become less alien, but by then he had an additional objective for earning and saving: the endowment of 'I Tatti'. He worked for various private collectors, but mainly for Georges Wildenstein in Paris and for Count Contini Bonacossi in Florence, both of whom had many clients in the United States.[1]

His authentications must stand beside his published work. Without his books they would not have the value which is likely to be attached to them for many generations to come.

[1] See p. 248 below.

CHAPTER XIII

The First War, the Middle Ages and La Belle Ferronnière

Nous sommes si malheureux, que nous ne pouvons
prendre plaisir à une chose qu'à condition de nous
fâcher si elle réussit mal: ce que mille choses
peuvent faire et font à toute heure.

PASCAL

EUROPE's great conflicts in the twentieth century have not inter-
fered with the buying and selling of works of art. Rather the
contrary. So great were the economic upheavals consequent
upon the years of fighting, the re-drawing of frontiers, the fall of
monarchies and the rise of republics, that many of those with great
possessions were forced to sell them, while many of those who
profited by the wars, or who speculated successfully in gold, in
diamonds and then in oil, were always looking for 'something safe'
into which to put their constantly accumulating wealth. Some
National Galleries, like the Hermitage in Leningrad, sold numbers
of their masterpieces. (There were over a score of Rembrandts in
the Hermitage. Mr Mellon bought seven between the wars. The
Rijks Museum also purchased one.) Also, of course, the new collectors wanted wealth with honour—the posthumous honour for
which men long, which might come when their priceless investments
would be bequeathed to the great galleries of Washington, New
York, Boston, Philadelphia or their nearest city, providing always
that the investment would not have to be realized in cash, which
rarely happened. The buying and selling of masterpieces therefore
went on steadily during and between the wars of 1914–18 and
1939–45.

In the spring of the fateful year of 1914 there appeared a notable
appreciation of Berenson's work by a well-known young Italian
writer, Emilio Cecchi, in a daily paper called the *Tribuna*.[1]

[1] April 28, 1914.

PLATE XVI   The painting of Bernard Berenson by Derek Hill
(1953) in possession of the author

Below: Berenson on the terrace of
the Villino, Winter 1955.
(Photo by Derek Hill)

Above: Bernard Berenson receiving the
honorary degree of Florence University
in 1956, at 'I Tatti', listening to the
Public Orator

PLATE XVII Count Vittorio Cini, Bernard Berenson and Miss Mariano at an exhibition in Venice, 1955

The Italian painter Renato Guttuso with Bernard Berenson at Vallombrosa

Cecchi was to become Berenson's first translator into Italian, but not until the remarkably late date of 1936. Only then did the *Italian Painters of the Renaissance* appear with Hoepli in Milan. Before that year Italians could not read Berenson in their own language. Another translator, the then young Roberto Longhi, delayed for years in doing the work.[1] From time to time would-be translators turned up at 'I Tatti' with translated chapters from one or other of the four volumes, but in vain. A contract had been drawn up. By Italian law no one else could translate the work until a fixed number of years had passed. This caused a very long coolness between Professor Longhi and Berenson, and healed only when the Italian art historian came up with the dignitaries of Florence University to confer an honorary doctorate on Berenson in 1955. Thereafter Longhi and Berenson found much to compare and discuss and the Professor frequently came to visit.

Meanwhile Emilio Cecchi, coming freshly upon the four little volumes in English in 1914, expresses great astonishment that Berenson's works had hardly ever been mentioned in Italy, while his name perpetually recurred in any catalogue of Renaissance art.

'His book on the Venetians would bring honour to anyone . . . what new experiences! He is like a dawn breeze across a landscape illuminating the horizon of European painting. Tiepolo explains Goya. The Bassani foreshadow the lazy animal heaviness of Velasquez, and the strawberry reds, sharp greens and silver whites of Veronese filter through and pullulate in Manet, Renoir, Cézanne.'[2]

Cecchi enjoys Berenson's 'tactile values'—'the sense of touch assisted by muscular sensations, helping us to feel depth'. He enjoys Berenson's analysis of 'the masters of the decorative line, and of spatial composition'. He likes the way 'the drawing-room sensual softness of de' Predis, Boltraffio and other followers of Leonardo is exposed'. No one in Italy was looking at 'pretty Pintoricchio' any more. Cecchi likes the way Berenson discovers in him 'one who can in his distances, bring a breeze of spring air'. Cecchi finds Berenson has a wide historical sense: it is he who has begun to marry Giotto and Cézanne, Pollajuolo and Degas, as well as Pater and Morelli.

[1] Signor Cecchi suggested that the real cause of delay was Professor Longhi's inadequate knowledge of English, later remedied, but too late to be of use as a translator.　　　　　　　　　[2] Compare *A. and H.*, p. 60.

'Certainly no art critic in Italy, and I do not know who outside, can provide such a vigilant and concentrated arrangement, such independence and such mental vigour as Berenson, all well hidden under a virile scepticism—like steel in velvet—providing us with the vivifying impulse of an ethical as well as an intellectual example.'

Most of all Cecchi appreciates, and in this he joins very many appreciative readers of Berenson's works, 'the hundred and one suggestions raised by his ideas about naturalism (Uccello), about the impersonal in art (Piero della Francesca) or arcadism and the ancient world in art (Mantegna) or the graceful in art (the Milanese)'. Cecchi finds that others need an essay to say what Berenson says in a line. Berenson's work is 'a catechism of those who live in a world of sentiment and of photographic painting', and it demands translation into Italian.

*   *   *

The 1914 war came so explosively into the kind of world of art appreciation and discovery we have been concerned with and caught it so utterly unawares that its inhabitants were suddenly stunned. Berenson coined a word for the war. He called it 'a manquake'. He, as we know, had for his own purposes and curiosity, and partly because Duveen's clients were interested, been delving into what might be the Oriental fountains of some streams of Renaissance art. This he was to pursue now, for a number of years, even though, as he writes to Mrs Gardner, 'we are being hurled back to the dimmest depth of the dark ages'. Mary had been caught, a few days before the lapse of the ultimatum on August 4, 1914, in Metz. Berenson was on a summer visit to England. She hurried to England and wrote to Mrs Gardner on August 11th from Arundel in Sussex to say that she found some comfort in 'little Barbary, my grandchild, who knows nothing of war, and her laughter and her pretty ways drive it out of our heads sometimes'.[1] For the first two months of the war the Berensons stayed with Mary's daughter (Mrs Oliver Strachey, Barbara's mother) near Arundel, uncertain what to do. Mary wrote to Mrs Gardner:

'All we speak of is the war, the horror of this sudden plunge into savagery, the pity of killing our friends the Germans and the incredible dislocation of all the habits and plans and pursuits in the countries engaged.'

[1] See Plate XIV.

Mary wrote that Bernard might go back to the United States for the winter, whereas she had had all the social life she could digest for five or six years, in the previous winter's visit, and she would not go with him. Probably they would end by 'creeping back to Florence', for there was no place like home. The war (she thought) had cut into their finances and they were doing without a secretary.

'A war throws one back upon real things, real values, and I can conceive of reorganizing our lives in a better way and on a simpler footing. Bernard maybe then would begin to write again. You cannot serve both God and Mammon.'

Mary was troubled but clearly unaware of the source which supplied the income of her great household in Italy, with its ten servants, four gardeners, chauffeur, secretaries and *fattore*. The income continued, of course.

Her other daughter, Karin, was to marry the son of Leslie Stephen and Virginia Woolf's brother, Adrian Stephen, on October 21, 1914. Karin had won a fellowship to Newnham in the spring of 1914, and both were to live in Cambridge, where Adrian was doing hospital work. Mary writes proudly to Mrs Gardner of her two daughters' marriages, 'to men whose families appear, along with the Darwins in Galton's *Hereditary Genius* as examples of talent belonging to several generations and spread into all the branches, so I am counting on one or two clever grandchildren'.[1]

Mary's children and grandchildren bound her in a maternal way to England. The Berensons were Americans, and America was not to enter the war till 1917. Mary was still thinking of her German friends in 1914. Among Americans Mrs Gardner was to remain fairly pro-German, 'not with her whole soul on the right side', as Berenson put it in a letter to her. But as he always avoided a clash of political opinion with friends, he would not argue with her. Mary reported that the fall of Antwerp and the Zeppelin raid on London in 1914 had made everyone anxious 'except for the fighters—*they* enjoyed it and are full of courage and clash and excitement'. Mr Robert Benson was thinking of sending his collection to safety in the

---

[1] One of her grandsons, Christopher Strachey, was to become, with his assistants, the constructor of a remarkable calculating machine, which he christened 'Pegasus'.

United States but Mary thought that the English fleet, the aeroplanes and the army made panic unnecessary.

Berenson suddenly felt 'unattached . . . and at bottom quite indifferent. The world consists of one's personal friends, one's thoughts and one's dreams and one can manage to live anywhere with these three'. The mood persists when they both go to Paris in November 1914 to stay with Edith Wharton. Neither yet feels involved; their letters from Paris are purely aesthetic. Paris is beautiful in the sparkling winter, the streets empty, the smart shops closed, no theatres, few restaurants, 'one's French friends so grave, so earnest, so calm'. The Oriental dealer, Vignier, with whom Berenson is in constant contact, has plenty of bargains, and Berenson sends Mrs Gardner photographs of Chinese figures for her to choose from.

The mood changes as soon as Berenson gets home to 'I Tatti'. In Italy he always feels very American; elsewhere he feels wellnigh stateless. Now, in January 1915, with d'Annunzio (and the young Mussolini) passionately clamouring for Italian intervention, and numbers of Italians 'anxious to join the crusade against the accursed', Berenson writes to Boston that there 'will be all the more reason for staying here, and trying to help with all our substance'. He is being drawn in by the heat of the battle. He also tells her that if only he were starting out again in life 'I would devote myself to China as I have to Italy'. In Boston Mrs Gardner was celebrating the arrival of her new Chinese and Persian treasures by a Chinese party in which she appeared in her 'Tao dress'.

In 1916 the Berensons are again in Paris. He attends for the first time a Harvard dinner, at the Ritz. He is caught up in the frenzy of war, and can only write about the 'Boches' and hope that something will 'induce the Spaniard to see that Germany is hell'. In the midst of the terrible casualties Duveen was angling for the biggest fish he had yet sighted in Italian Renaissance painting, the Duke of Northumberland's Bellini—the Bacchanal painted for Alfonso d'Este in 1514 and known as *The Feast of the Gods*. Berenson would have liked Mrs Gardner to buy it for half a million dollars. He gives her a vivid and exciting account of its incomparable beauty. He had never met anything 'so inexhaustible' and then 'such a picture seems to say: sell all that thou hast and follow me'. God and Mammon were certainly becoming confused.

This is the only time in the correspondence that the word

'peddling' is used. 'Please don't think I am bluffing or peddling.' It is like a far echo from Minot Street.

He had long ago settled his parents in the countryside near Boston, and had indeed brought them over to Europe for a visit.[1] He had built a house in Cambridge (Massachusetts) for his eldest sister Rachel and her husband, Professor Ralph Barton Perry. All his life he gave his other sisters (Senda and Elizabeth) allowances.

'An influential friend', hearing that Berenson was eager to do his bit in the war, recommended him to the head of a department of the American Red Cross at the Hotel Crillon. He describes how he waited a whole hour in the great man's ante-chamber, hearing the murmur of talk and merry laughter, after which 'one of the prettiest and most frivolous of American Parisians' came out, and Berenson was ushered in, but was too furious at having been kept waiting for so long and for such a reason.

'The interview was frosty. When I told my friend of this result of his effort to put me in touch with the high placed, he laughed and assured me that waiting around was the lot of the subordinate in all business, whether public or private. How glad I was that I had passed already the greater part of life having so little to do with either!'[2]

There follows, in Berenson's *Sketch for a Self-Portrait,* a disquisition upon the ideal relationship of individuals in a civilized society.

'I dream of a society composed of individuals, each realizing himself entirely and the by-products of these realizations combining to make a civilization and a culture. There would be no prestige connected with one occupation rather than another. There would be no rewards. There would be thus no ambition to attain power and

[1] Bertrand Russell remembered meeting Mr and Mrs Albert Berenson in the last decade of the old century. 'I think I am one of the few people alive who met B.B.'s father and mother, only it is so long ago that I cannot remember where, but I rather think it was in France. It was at tea and they were both (to me) really simple peasant people, dressed in black, small, and very, very proud of their son. I liked them, I hardly felt they were American, nor indeed did I ever feel that B.B. was. He was soft spoken, and so were they. I thought of Lithuania, and fields and the land, when I saw them.' (To the author in May 1954.) [2] *S.S.P.*, p. 69.

place. There would be no failures, no discontented, no brooders. My dream naturally excludes those who can realize themselves through violence only, or even through deliberate mischief-making. The last I should dispatch to far-away islands where they could enjoy each other's activities. The first I should assemble in two armies, and rely on their competitive spirit to develop enough animosity against each other to prevent them from uniting and becoming a danger to the rest of the community.'[1]

In 1916 an essentially professional book for the use of the new collectors in the United States, called *Venetian Painters in America*, appeared with Shermans in New York. In it Berenson reviewed the notable Venetian pictures which had crossed the Atlantic since 1894. But his most important publication in 1916 was the third series of *The Study and Criticism of Italian Art*. It contained seven essays, the first of which faces 'the awful dilemma of not liking a painter and being continually harried by the outpourings of those who say they do'. It is a fascinating essay and a very funny one. One looks at the Virgin of the Rocks with new eyes after reading it. Berenson tries to account for the extraordinary rise in the popularity of his *bête noire*. He suggests that in mediaeval Italy the poets of ancient Rome became wizards who could defy natural laws. Similarly a hundred years ago at the height of the Romantic Movement, just when people were getting disappointed with military heroes and with the epic careers of Napoleonic times, the search for heroes gravitated towards the artist, and the artist, for the first time in history, was to become a demi-god. No one could have been more suitable than Leonardo da Vinci, 'who united many achievements in art and science, was quite conscious of his worth, dressed with origi-nality and distinction, bore himself impressively'. Berenson finds Leonardo 'surrounded so to speak by censor-swinging acolytes' easily filling the place of a modern Empedocles and his 'unmis-takable and manifold genius made him, as it were, the arch-type of the artist as well as the first and worthiest object of the new cult'. For Berenson the real tragedy about Leonardo is that after him 'men could twist the body and the face in all directions'. The new tool of power was a mighty one. Not only form but colour also suffered. Chiaroscuro killed colour. He found plenty of interference with 'the rapture of the aesthetic moment' in Leonardo's painting, and found

[1] *S.S.P.*, p. 70.

these constant interruptions a nuisance. In the drawings he found 'the greatest spontaneity and freedom'. He dislikes Leonardo's theories and finds them false. He finds his instincts true. 'Florentine art tended to be over-intellectual, and of that tendency Leonardo was the fullest exponent.' Leonardo made axioms, problems, doctrines and then concentrated on their fulfilment utterly regardless of obstacles or questions met in the process. Berenson was nothing if not a purist. He found that light and shade and contortions were only permissible when no attention is drawn to them. Leonardo's way was 'full of tactlessness, recklessness, set on pursuing an idea or a formula to the bitter end—in blinkers—never realizing the conflict with another idea'. For him Leonardo has more of the crank than of the genius.[1]

The essay ends with a re-appraisal of Giovanni Morelli, who was of course a great admirer of Leonardo. This passage deserves quotation. He finds Morelli still inspired by the Romantic ideal of genius, the axiom that the greatest artist never declines from his greatness from the cradle to the grave, or conversely that whatever the great artist did was necessarily faultless.

'It was in defence of this that we Morellians fought for authenticity with the uncompromising zeal of Legitimates. It was indeed a brave fight and worthy, although it fortified the glib collector's blind confidence in mere names, and led him to accumulate unpalatable but authentic daubs by Rembrandt and other prolific geniuses. But the very method of establishing authenticity by tests so delicate, so subtle and so complicated has led us on, little by little, to conclusions the exact opposite of the axiom with which we started out. Strict connoisseurship has taken the further and more painful step of recognizing that there are poor things among the autographs of the great artists and that not every Bellini or Botticelli, Raphael or Rubens, Velasquez or Van Dyck is a flawless masterpiece.'

The passage reveals that Berenson as a connoisseur had achieved emancipation from the spell of the great names. The whole essay ends with a vision which seems to be rapidly becoming a reality. He sees the whole art of the world opening up for study and for the exercise

[1] Havelock Ellis joins issue with Berenson over Leonardo da Vinci, in *The Dance of Life*, pp. 103–8. As with Morelli, so with Havelock Ellis, the appreciation of Leonardo is essentially romantic.

of imagination. He sees generations passing before the pictures before they will be all understood. 'The individual's greed for novelty will be able to vent itself without ever coming to the end of the best', although some people he rightly predicted would be attacked by *la nostalgie de la boue* and would 'persist in rummaging among the refuse'.

The essays in this series pay tribute to Cavalcaselle's appreciations: 'I am amazed at the correctness of so many of his attributions.' In the essay on Mr Benson's *Antonello da Messina* Berenson acknowledges the 'artistic personality' which that fine painter had received in 1907 through the discovery by Sicilian scholars of documents relating to him.

Again, on the subject of connoisseurship in this essay, Berenson finds that it is painful to have to confess that so many works of art fail to get active attention unless they have been ascribed to an artist. He quotes a Venus in Dresden which hundreds of thousands of people must have seen and yet not looked at. Then came Morelli and concluded that she was by Giorgione. 'Who has not admired her since?' All these essays are practically unobtainable now and should be reprinted.

*   *   *

The end of the war found the Berensons staying at the Ritz in Paris. Armistice Day was not for them a day of happiness. Berenson was fifty-three and Mary fifty-four, and Mary moreover had had a severe breakdown in her health in the spring of that year, from which she was never to recover. The continued rest which her bladder trouble necessitated made her put on weight and she became, with the years, very stout. Berenson wrote prophetically to Mrs Gardner from Paris in December 1918:

'It is a fearfully fatiguing world that we people who are no longer young are now going to encounter. It will be full of live wires, dynamic personalities, sound propositions and God knows what horrors as yet nameless. Happily we shall not be in it for long, and departing can boast that we are the last of the dodos.'

Mary wrote, too, to Mrs Gardner of 'this awful war, that has destroyed all my instinctive faith in the universe, and somehow with that, happiness has leaked out'.

The First War, the Middle Ages and La Belle Ferronnière

No sooner is the war over and they are back at 'I Tatti' than the visitors begin to come. There are old friends and new faces, especially from England. These are the years in the early and mid-'twenties when Kenneth Clark, then an undergraduate, first comes out from Oxford and takes the habit of coming every year. John Walker (then a very young man) comes from the United States.[1]

Europe after the first war was of course not nearly so shaken as after the second. The 'Russian Menace' was still only a vague danger for defeated Germany. Russia was torn by civil war, of historic importance to the small communist parties forming everywhere in Europe in 1920–22, but as yet hardly causing a ripple on the movement and life of the Continent. In Italy, with his march on Rome in October 1922, Mussolini claimed that he had saved Italy from Communism. Up at Settignano the story was told of how a group of Tuscan peasants waving a red flag had arrived at the front door of nearby Poggio Gherardo, only to be met by Mrs Janet Ross in person, in command of such a stream of Tuscan invective that they all fled, believing that the devil had had a hand in it. No one waved a red flag in front of the high solid iron gates of 'I Tatti'. The household was, if anything, liberal-minded. D'Annunzio had long ago moved away from Settignano to his desired destiny as the conqueror and dictator of Fiume on the Adriatic in 1919, and was now a half-hearted pro-fascist. Italian friends of 'I Tatti' were, with one or two notable exceptions, hardly warm adherents of the new Dictator. As in most cultivated households in Italy, political discussions were too painful to be contemplated. Mary wrote to Mrs Gardner that her illness left her with 'a chastened view of human life'; nevertheless, she recovered sufficiently to accomplish some long journeys to United States, to Egypt and to Greece. In 1917 a young cousin of Count Hermann Keyserling had lunched one day at 'I Tatti'. Her name was Nicky Mariano. Four years later she was to take the place, as secretary to Berenson, which Geoffrey Scott had filled until his marriage with Lady Sybil Cutting.

[1] Both these pupils of Berenson's were to fill the highest posts in the Museum world which their countries had to offer, and were to dedicate some of their books to Berenson. Berenson had hoped that Mr John Walker would become the head of 'I Tatti' after his death, when it would become an outpost of Harvard, but when Mr Walker was offered the Directorship of the National Gallery in Washington in 1956, he asked Berenson to release him from the proposal, and Berenson did so, with regret.

Miss Mariano gradually came to assume more and more responsibility at 'I Tatti', since Mary's health often put her out of action for several weeks on end. Mary appreciated and loved her dearly, as did Berenson. After Mary's death in 1945, and indeed for many years before then, the smooth running of the household, of the library, of the stream of visitors and of Berenson's work itself, rested largely upon her ample shoulders.

* * *

Between 1920 and 1930 Berenson's studies were frequently concerned with mediaeval paintings and manuscripts, upon which he wrote papers in *Art in America*, in the Italian Ministry of Education's Journal, and in the usual French and English art journals to which he had already contributed. All these papers were gathered together into a handsome quarto volume printed by the Yale University Press in 1930 as *Studies in Mediaeval Painting*. In 1921, in a small mountain house which the Berensons now rented every summer at Vallombrosa, Berenson wrote the first of these papers on *Two Twelfth Century Paintings from Constantinople*—small Byzantine panels which opened vistas for him. They had been found in a small town of Calahorra on the borders of Castille and Navarre, and an article in the *Burlington Magazine* in 1918 had attributed one of them to Pietro Cavallini, but Berenson finds that they must be much earlier. The panels are 'gorgeous scarlet, gold, dazzling ultramarine', and have flesh tints 'almost as blond as Giotto's, although warmer'. The medium is tempera. The highlights are like the flare of a reflector; they spurt and splash. 'Colour so gorgeous, so radiant, so pure as we have here, is perhaps never seen in Western painting . . . before the fourteenth century . . . except in illuminations.' To Berenson these panels opened vistas of Byzantine painting before the sack of Constantinople during the last Crusade in 1204. 'By 1200 painting all over Europe was as much Constantinopolitan as for the last hundred years or so it has been Parisian', Berenson wrote. Its condition by 1200 was in fact as though 'all the pictures recently done in Paris by Frenchmen had disappeared, and one could only guess and grope after what this Paris art was like, by Sargent, Zorn, Liebermann, Sickert and Mancini. Then what a revelation it would be to come on a Manet or a Degas!' The two little panels acted as a like revelation.

Others have felt or suspected the existence of a rich school of painting in the Eastern Empire alongside the known mosaics. Berenson recalls that the iconoclast, the native rebel, the Bulgar and the Turk 'participated joyously in nature's destructiveness, so that very little of this art remains'. He was writing before the frescoes were uncovered in Santa Sophia and the mosaics in the great palace at Constantinople, but of Eastern European mediaeval panels (as compared with mosaics) there are still few if any, most having 'in the course of centuries been turned into fetishes to heal or protect the believer . . . injured by crowns and jewels and ornaments nailed on to them, and stained by the sacred oils with which they used to be anointed before being carried in procession'. The two little panels at Calahorra are so exciting that Berenson is indignant with the Doge Enrico Dandolo who, in spite of a pact of friendship with Byzance, persuaded Boniface to turn from Egypt and Syria with his fourth Crusade in 1202 against Constantinople, there to plunder and to sack, in 1204. For Berenson that date is the crucial one in the history of art, and not the capture of Constantinople in 1453 by the Turks. In 1453 the libraries and classical manuscripts of that great city were scattered and so that date became, for the literary-minded people of Northern Europe, the birth of the 'Renaissance'.

In matters of visual art—and they are vital—Europe between 800–1100 has, for Berenson, 'a hole in corner civilization lacking in permanent metropolitan centres'. He recognizes the monasteries' miniature painting on manuscripts, but he cannot accept it 'as an independent achievement'.

In 1925 he was at work on an Italian manuscript of the late fourteenth century, the *Speculum Humanae Salvationis*, of which there were two copies in Paris (Bib. Nat. lat. 9584, and Bib. Arsenal lat. 593) and a third at Chantilly. The long and learned essay by Berenson which follows the preface by Dr M. R. James, the then Provost of Eton, was printed by the Oxford University Press for private circulation in 1925, and reprinted in Berenson's *Mediaeval Studies*. In his preface to that book he apologizes for his 'to the mere layman, rather tedious excursion in illumination'. His essay ranges over many comparisons to arrive at a date and a provenance of the illustrators of the manuscripts. They had drawn his attention to the whole question of provincial and peripheral art, its resemblance to metropolitan art at the very moment when the established forms of art in the big centres are breaking down. Already in 1930 Berenson writes: 'This problem vaguely foreshadows inquiries which I hope to pursue later, in a book on the decline and recovery of form in the arts of visual representation'. Only a fragment of those 'inquiries' were to be published, twenty years later, in a slim little volume, *The Arch of Constantine*. The decline in a period of high art fascinated Ruskin also. Eventually Berenson was to treat the subject from an entirely new angle when he attempted to account in *Aesthetics and History* for what he felt to be the chaos of form in contemporary art.

Meanwhile 'the greatest boon that man can have is to know his Maker and his own state: this the learned can find out from the Scriptures, but the unlearned must be taught by pictures which are the books of the lay people'. In his *Mediaeval Studies* Berenson enjoyed himself as if he were a mediaeval layman being instructed by early frescoes and illuminations, and 1204 remained a great date for him. He came to it with all the freshness of one whose childhood had been devoid of visual art.

In 1927 appeared *Three Essays in Method* dedicated to a French friend, Lucien Henraux, who was a nephew of Carlo Placci, and described by Berenson as 'a freeman of the city of art'. Henraux was a school mate and a great friend of Marcel Proust. Proust was not a visitor at 'I Tatti', but Henraux used to talk to him about Berenson. In the Preface Berenson thanks his 'constant and indispensable collaborators, my wife and my secretary, Miss Nicky Mariano'. Robert Trevelyan, the poet, is also thanked 'for disentangling my over-continentalized English'. Henceforward Trevelyan often read through Berenson's MSS. before they went to the publisher.

The important little book of three essays and an appendix had a fine purpose 'not to show off my own gifts, but to let students into my workshop'. That it did. To some professional art historians it remains their favourite book after the *Florentine Drawings*. It is full of aphorisms.

'In the beginning was the guess.'

'Scholarship necessarily abounds in error.'

'A seeing eye, I mean with all the faculties co-operating . . .' or what he calls, in another place, 'active, not passive eyes'.

'Genius is less ingenious than non-genius.'

'Since 1200 there are almost no works of art worth bothering about which cannot be dated within twenty years; and in Italian painting of the Quattrocento at least the overwhelming majority can be placed within a decade. . . . There is no longer any excuse for treating Connoisseurship as a guessing game or as a field for freak attributions.'

The *Three Essays in Method* were to become a handbook, and a very important one for those who were professionally concerned with attributions. The first essay considers nine small panels which had been attributed to Baldovinetti and must therefore have been painted in the Florentine tradition and before 1450; an attribution which Berenson destroys bit by bit. One roves over the panels inch by inch with him: the churches painted in them are dated, so are the palaces; the shoes are 'court shoes, tipped up, in all the panels', the hats are 'Venetic or Mantuan'; there are turbans 'correctly and tightly wound which betray Venice', because after Bellini's epoch-making visit to Constantinople a romanticism about Eastern costume grew up; and the horses in the panels are all related to the bronze models on St Mark's balcony. And lest anyone should need further explanations, Berenson records that Florentine painting before 1460 'is nostalgic and full of yearnings, romantic in its attitude towards recently departed chivalry, reduced to a pageantry in which every cautious shopkeeper could safely take part, but also towards Antiquity. . . .'

The point of the essay is to 'furnish an example of how to discover when and where a work of art was produced. This had to be done for once in a way, and done in sufficient detail to show the method. . . .' The connoisseur must first identify the time, then the place, and only then the author. Still the panels had no author. At this point the Morellian method is needed to achieve 'the reintegration of an artistic personality from internal evidence' by attaching the series to other works which may be proved to be by the same hand. Then finally, if documents and 'trustworthy literary sources' were luckily available, the connoisseur would have irrefutable proof. The Morellian method was well suited for distinguishing between a Master and his closest followers, but the final decision as to whether the painting is an autograph work or a first-rate studio version 'depends on the critic's sense of quality'. In fact, there are many rules in the method, but there is no rule of thumb. A lifetime of study may never give the sense of quality. That gift Berenson possessed, but here again he disclaims infallibility.

The final decision in this case was aided by the then Keeper of the Ashmolean (Charles Bell) who had referred to twelve panels in the Este Collection in Vienna. Berenson obtained the photographs and found these were by the same hand and the hand is the Venetian's, Domenico Morone. Of course they are unsigned, but 'the tosses and turns taken by certain folds' and 'the relation of the metacarpus to the wrist and fingers . . . are as good as a signature'. It is detective work of a high and patient order, in which the aid of photographs for comparison is essential.

There are interesting observations about photographs of paintings. 'The photograph is an expeditious as well as a painless way of pursuing art criticism, and but for those rare cases where qualitative tests are demanded, it yields satisfactory results.' And again, 'It is pleasant and seemly to be acquainted with original works of art. It is even necessary to know them, if one is required to pronounce on whether a given picture is an autograph, a studio version or a contemporary copy. But for the plainer archaeological purpose of determining when and where and by whom a given design was invented, a good reproduction is enough.'

At that time Berenson can hardly have foreseen what a flood of art books was about to descend upon the world, so that many people began to know paintings only through photographs or through reduced colour reproductions. But he was writing as a professional for professional connoisseurs, and no one ventured to dispute his views until the case of *La Belle Ferronnière* came before the courts. Then he (and other connoisseurs) pronounced upon the authenticity of a painting attributed to Leonardo, without having seen the original, despite the brave words in the first of the Three Essays in Method. More than 'plain archaeology' was involved in this court case.

The other two essays are equally penetrating. The second concerns a disputed altarpiece (in the Uffizi) by Botticelli and the third 'A possible and an impossible Antonello da Messina'. The Botticelli, after careful detective work, is pronounced a Botticelli but 'of second-rate quality'. The 'possible' Antonello is a pure Berenson find, which has not since been disputed: the St Sebastian in the Verona Castle Museum, whereas the Winthrop (New York) Antonello of the Virgin and Child with the infant John (a picture which was changing hands at the time) he rejects after a long and interesting discourse on the arrival of two infants in these Madonna pictures, and a vivid appreciation of the qualities of Antonello which is now shared by all lovers of Italian painting.

One is perfectly aware that it would be easy to arraign Berenson

PLATE XVIII Bernard Berenson and his assistant, William Mostyn Owen, Miss
Mariano behind, in 1955

PLATE XIX   Miss Mariano and Bernard Berenson at 'I Tatti' (1955)

on the disharmony of his *Essay in Method* with his evidence on *La Belle Ferronnière* (to which we shall come). But the Essays remain a handbook and a statement, such as no one had made before or since, of how the connoisseur should proceed in ideal conditions of work, in order to arrive at a just attribution, or as near to one as possible.

In the Essays he called Connoisseurship 'a sport' which 'one must enjoy for no utilitarian or pretentious reason'. Was this self-deception? After all, 'the sport' brought in a handsome income. By the age of sixty the fact that one is paid handsomely for one's skill, the happy marriage of income and capacity can hardly be questioned every morning. Yet there were qualms from time to time.[1] In the case of the Duveen brothers, from all the accounts which have appeared to date, and will doubtless continue to appear, a great part of this energy seems to have found its way into legal squabbles of one brother against another, cousins, brothers and uncles at sixes and sevens, with few, and least of all the man who was to become Lord Duveen of Millbank, enjoying leisure or the delights of a settled home. In the case of Berenson, he had taken immense and successful measures, after his first practical and daily experience of the dealers' world when buying for Mrs Gardner, to withdraw into an oasis of his own making on the hillsides above Florence, so that there were long hours of the day in which he knew how to be completely solitary. That was the self-mastery which his employer seems never to have achieved.

For many years already Mary had taken over most of the correspondence with Joseph Duveen, Berenson finding it more and more difficult to communicate with the man who was now head of the firm.[2]

*   *   *

Human nature being what it is there will undoubtedly, from time

---

[1] This was the between-war period when he wrote that disenchanted passage in an enlarged edition of the first series of *The Study and Criticism of Italian Art*, published in 1920 (p. vi): 'I see now how fruitless an interest is the history of art, and how worthless an undertaking is that of determining who painted or carved or built whatsoever it be. I see now how valueless all such matters are in the life of the spirit.' He hastens to add that without connoisseurship, the idea of a history of art is impossible. His dream was to see the world's art studied like flora and fauna, without chronologies.

[2] A member of the Duveen family complained to the author with some annoyance that 'Berenson always refused to visit the Duveen shop when he was in London'.

to time, arise ambitious 'connoisseurs', anxious to destroy Berenson's work and to set themselves up as infallible authorities. At their disposal will be a host of new scientific aids, chemical analyses and X-rays, and even the latest medical data on artists' eye diseases. Such a tussle, between science and instinct, a tussle of a very inconclusive nature, occurred in 1920. The tussle involved Berenson when the case came up in April 1929 for its first hearing.

A picture called *La Belle Ferronnière,* belonging to a Mrs Andrée Hahn and held by her to have been painted by Leonardo da Vinci, was for sale. The Kansas City Art Gallery was about to buy it when Sir Joseph Duveen gave a statement to the *New York World,* saying that the Hahn picture was a copy of the real *Belle Ferronnière* in the Louvre. The Hahn family sued Duveen, who had never seen their picture. We know that by the 1920s, after fifteen years as head of this firm of dealers, Sir Joseph Duveen hoped to achieve by any and every means a complete monopoly in the world's sales of Italian masterpieces. People were to sell and buy them through him, or not at all. The arrival on the market of a 'non-Duveen' Leonardo caught him unawares. A furious account of the various hearings of the case, for those who are interested, is to be found in a book written by Mr Harry Hahn called *The Rape of La Belle,* published in 1946 by Frank Glenn Publishing Co., in Kansas City, Missouri.

An example of the style of this book and the anger with which it is written is a suggestion in the first few pages that Berenson's 10 per cent commission on the sales price of all the paintings which he authenticated for Duveen 'may possibly be . . . the prime reason for some of the attribution bunglings of Mr Berenson'. The book is a violent attack upon Berenson's work and methods by a party to the dispute which feels itself to have been deeply injured in being deprived of a sale, which was on the point of being completed.

Opinion is still divided about the authenticity of the Hahn or the Louvre Leonardos. Berenson was one of the ten experts who appeared in court when the case came up. Together with Sir Martin Conway, then Director of the Imperial War Museum in London, Sir Herbert Cook of Doughty House, Robert Langton Douglas, one time director of the National Gallery of Dublin and editor of the later editions of Crowe and Cavalcaselle, Roger Fry, Sir Charles Holmes, then Director of the National Gallery in London, Professor Schmidt-Degener, Head of the Rijksmuseum in Amsterdam, Maurice Brockwell, art critic, M. Leonce Marie Nicolle, formerly of the Louvre, and A. P. Laurie, an Edinburgh Professor of Chemistry who had specialized in colour pigments—Berenson was called to the defence of Sir Joseph Duveen. Like most people who had compared the two photographs of the alleged Leonardos, Berenson testified that the Louvre one, if it had a fault, was too hard and too firm, and that the Hahn picture lacked the severity and the hardness 'of the Louvre original'. By using the word 'original' he committed himself to the Duveen case.[1] He admitted that he had never seen the Hahn picture.

We know that as long ago as 1888 Berenson and Leonardo da Vinci, facing each other in the Louvre, failed to get on. His essay on Leonardo in 1916, long before the Hahn case, confirmed his aversion for Leonardo as a painter, the absence of 'the rapture of the aesthetic moment', the departure of the poetry, of the excitement in da Vinci's work. The essay confirmed his appreciation of Leonardo's drawings, but it exposed his profound distrust of Leonardo's theories. In the *Drawings of the Florentine Painters* Leonardo's disciples, the pretty Milanese painters, are likewise exposed.

By now it must be evident to the reader that Berenson cared most and always for the effect of the work of art upon the person looking at it. Nevertheless, that was not his job as Duveen's authenticator. The tension between what he was aiming at in all his writing and the job he had to do must at times have been intolerable. Ultimately he resolved the tension in the only possible way by breaking with Duveen.

In the Hahn case, for the first time, X-ray evidence was admitted. Mr Justice William Harman Black of the Supreme Court of New York heard the case with a jury in New York. But in his final summing up after the case had been running for four weeks and in spite of 'much X-ray evidence' he announced that the jury, having sat for fourteen hours, had decided finally at 5.13 a.m. on April 13, 1929, 'that it would be impossible for them to come to the unanimous decision that the law requires before there could be a verdict'. So there was no verdict, and the case may come up again. The jury were thereupon dismissed and the judge reviewed some of the evidence he had heard. No judge in modern times, or perhaps at any time, had had to listen to so many eminent art critics. It must have been an ordeal for a man with a legal mind. Mr Justice Black stated that

[1] In the Berenson Lists of Renaissance Paintings published in 1932, the Louvre *Ferronnière* is listed as Leonardo's. The Hahn picture is not listed.

he had a profound respect for the critics whose conclusions rested upon facts—a rational enough view.

He said that there was much X-ray evidence regarding both the Hahn and the Louvre version of *La Belle Ferronnière*. Regarding the experts he said:

'There are two ways that experts can help in this case with their opinions. One is by their study of the authentic history of a painting. The other is by their study of the methods used or materials employed by the painters or schools of painting of the period in which it is claimed the pictures were painted.'

But the eminent judge had found himself listening to a great many other opinions, without which the appreciation of a work of art could hardly be called appreciation. The judge was in a quandary about such experts, just as logical, mathematical and business people would be in a similar quandary. But he struggled on to absolve the jury who had failed to agree. After stating his profound respect for critics whose conclusions rested upon the facts he said,

'What they say should be carefully considered by a jury. The opinions of any other kinds of experts are as "sounding brass and tinkling cymbals". Some of them expound their theories largely by vocal expression and gesture; others wander into a zone of speculation founded upon nothing more tangible than "psychological correlation". I do not say this is as absurd as it sounds to a layman, but it is too introspective and subjective to be the basis of any opinion a jury can pin its faith upon. There are also experts who admit that they have no formulas, rules, or ability to produce any artistic thing, but who claim to have a sixth sense which enables some of them after they have seen a picture even for five minutes to definitely determine whether it is genuine or not. I do not say that this faculty may not be possessed by some men, but it is not based upon enough objectiveness to convey definite meaning to a jury. It does happen, though, that some or all of these experts are today counselling the purchase or rejection of art objects of great value.'[1]

The judge called it 'a sixth sense'. In the case of Berenson, as we know,

[1] Reproduced in *The Rape of La Belle*, pp. 223–36.

'those who are capable of receiving direct pleasure from a work of art, are generally led on to the further pleasures of self-consciousness.'[1]

A heightening of all the senses rather than a sixth sense cannot of course 'convey definite meaning to a jury'. If it could this book would have a very different shape and form.

Berenson gave his evidence almost monosyllabically and when asked the vital question about whether those pictures which Leonardo da Vinci had painted did *not* include the Louvre *Ferronnière* he answered 'Apparently not'. Except for the one reference, which most of Duveen's witnesses seem to have made in this unsatisfactory case, to the Louvre picture as the 'original', Berenson's view of this picture fluctuates with the years. In the 1907 edition of the *North Italian Painters of the Renaissance* he is unwilling to accept the Louvre picture as Leonardo's. In his 1932 lists it appears as a Leonardo.

In the 1952 edition of the three little volumes, the passage in the North Italian Painters of the Renaissance about *La Belle Ferronnière* is deleted. From the early days, back in 1888, when Berenson had rejected his beloved Walter Pater's effusion on the subject of the Mona Lisa, that painter's work never again ranked for him as more than a great labour 'to render the significance he felt but which his hand could not reproduce'.[2]

A. E. Housman, the poet, suggested in a lecture that, when he came upon true poetry while shaving, his reaction was such that the operation became a fraction more difficult. He too (in court) would have presented a jury of twelve good men with a fearful problem. How could they have assessed him as a competent critic whose conclusions rested upon facts? Housman claimed that his hair bristled. Berenson said his self-consciousness was heightened: we know what each means. But judge and jury could not pursue the matter, and there, for the time being it must rest.

[1] *I.P.R.*, p. 42.   [2] *I.P.R.*, p. 56.

CHAPTER XIV

Into the Second War

Dowel, Dobet and Dobest.

PIERS PLOWMAN

IN 1925 Berenson was sixty. He says he suddenly became haunted by the feeling of hurry. He had always been able to find time for work, but now he would have to husband his hours:

'No more browsing on books in out of the way fields and remote corners, no more free-hearted conning of the classics for hours together if the mood seized me. I had planted a garden with nooks where I was going to sit and take pleasure in my favourite *Dichter* . . . by the time it had grown and could be enjoyed, hurry seized me; and for the arbours and fountain curbs where I was to sit and listen to the nightingales, blackbirds, thrushes and larks, and draw in the fragrance of roses, lotuses and lime blossoms I never found the leisure. I could only glance and pass on.'[1]

Time goes faster as people grow older. He imagined that if one could only live long enough, say to one hundred and fifty, one would lose the sense of the lapse of time altogether. 'The psalmist who tells us that to the Eternal a thousand years is but a minute does not poetise. He may understate a fact.'[2]

Work on the three *Essays in Method* (1927), the catalogues of the Carl Hamilton Collection (1929) and the Michael Friedsam Collection (1930) filled these years with daily research and writing. The catalogues were of the kind which Duveen 'allowed' his clients to possess, when their collections had reached a certain size. The flow of visitors to 'I Tatti' was uninterrupted, likewise the arrival of photographs for authentication.

In 1930 Berenson's *Studies in Mediaeval Painting* appeared. He dedicated it to a French friend, Emile Bertaux, who had been Pro-

---

[1] *S.S.P.*, pp. 103–4.   [2] *S.S.P.*, *idem.*

fessor of Modern Art at Lyons University (Modern as opposed to Ancient), and who had published original work on relations between Spanish and Italian Renaissance art. American collectors were interested in the book since it discussed some of their newly acquired panels. Berenson calls the pursuit of authorship in these early fourteenth-century panels 'an infantile pursuit' and unlikely to yield convincing attributions. He writes that he would follow one colleague, Professor Richard Offner, 'blindfold' in the matter of Jacopo da Casentino. He writes of 'Meo da Siena's tiny personality', and finds in both Meo and Jacopo 'the same Bolognese smudginess of contour and hotness of colour'. Merely historical works of art devoid of beauty, such as abound in mediaeval painting, could not hold his attention for long. He, the faithful, the first, and so far, the only follower of Pater, would never compromise on this matter. Pater, and the constant re-reading of Pater, refreshed and liberated him in his criticism.

In the essay (No. 7) on the Tuscan Painters of the Trecento in the Staedel Museum in Frankfurt-am-Main Berenson finds 'themes worthy of a great Sung painter', but often 'the physiognomy of the figures is amiably imbecile', 'the action and gestures remind one of marionettes fashioned by a ploughman in rare moments of leisure'. No one had ever spoken so frankly, many would have liked to, one imagines: Berenson finds a Christ Child 'distinguished by a pose as affected and silly as in most of the Southern Indian bronzes', and as for Barnaba da Siena, who signs and dates his panels, and leaves nothing for the art critic to do except criticize, Berenson hands him over to 'silence and oblivion'. His interest really begins to revive with Bernardo Daddi 'the ablest of Giotto's disciples, endowed with an almost Raphaelesque facility as well as felicity'. The Orcagnas, he thinks, probably belong to Daddi's studio. One is given a vision of hundreds of small triptychs, gem-like in colour, exquisite in line, redolent of chivalry, refined in feeling, coming out of Daddi's workshop, and sold at the fairs of Champagne, thus spreading a knowledge of Tuscan art all over Northern Europe. Barna's *Crucifixion* in San Gemignano Cathedral, its 'prophetic zest and ecstasy', make Berenson mourn the early death of this painter as 'among the disasters that have beset Humanism'. The lightning sketches continue with the already familiar Sassetta, 'one of the most spiritually minded and most delicate geniuses that Siena ever had', with Paolo di Giovanni Fei: 'this usually awkward, vulgar practitioner had, early in his career, moments of quaint daintiness, and later an occasional heartiness that is winning'. But the two artists who alone never deteriorate for Berenson are Duccio and Simone Martini.

Berenson confesses that he is 'not a bit of an epigraphist and as little of an hagiologist'. He finds that many of the best mediaeval artists in France, Spain and Germany 'twirled away' calligraphically, making 'little better than dancing dervishes in paint'. Anyone who has seen twelfth- and thirteenth-century frescoes in Northern Germany and in England, and has not been overawed and benumbed, as so many tourists are by mere antiquity, would be delighted with this essay.

For Berenson the Renaissance did not suddenly burst upon the Italian scene. 'On the contrary, even in Florence, most people were cheerfully unaware of it well on to the middle of the fifteenth century, and ordered more and more elaborately gorgeous, refulgent, twirling, blinking creations of the sunset of gothic design.'[1]

In 1930 there appeared a volume called *Pictures and People* (Gollancz) a correspondence between Roger Hinks of the British Museum and Naomi Royde-Smith. It was the year of the great Italian Renaissance Exhibition in London, the first and probably the only time (if the Florentines get their way) that the greatest masterpieces of the Italian galleries travelled by cruiser overseas, and faced a perilous storm on their return journey. Bernard and Mary came to England and stayed with Mr and Mrs Robert Trevelyan at Holmbury St Mary, near Dorking. Now people were re-reading Berenson's four essays on the painters of the Italian Renaissance which the Oxford University Press had brought out in one volume for the occasion. Roger Hinks wrote:

'I was surprised how well they had lasted. At first one sees nothing but "tactile values", "life enhancing" and all those other bits of B.B. talk . . . and one thinks of all the priggest aspects of that paradise of prigs, Firenze. But having dispelled these unworthy associations one returns with delight to Mr Berenson and relishes his subtle historical sense . . . how good he is on impersonality in art. He says that real artists never worry about self-expression knowing that the self will get expressed anyhow: what a brave doctrine in 1897. I wonder that the cultivated Florentines didn't sally forth in their carozzas and storm "I Tatti" and rend B.B.

[1] Bernard Berenson, *Mediaeval Studies*.

limb from limb, as the Bacchantes did to poor Pentheus. What a smack in the eye for his neighbour, Vernon Lee! and how sensible he is about Humanism, and the antique being dangerous rather than helpful to the artists of the early quattrocento. . . . I do think there is more relevant information in that little book than in all the colossi and pyramids and mausolea that pedantry has dedicated to Italian art in the last fifty years.'[1]

* * *

If Berenson's writing of forty years before was coming into its own among a growing public with the great Italian Exhibition in London of 1930, his authority amongst historians was greatly enhanced by the publication in 1932, at the Clarendon Press, Oxford, of an index (or rather two indexes) of painters and places, with no text (except for a brief preface) in a volume of 723 pages, in which the layman or the expert could for the first time look up any Italian picture of importance painted in the thirteenth, fourteenth, fifteenth and sixteenth centuries. No such comprehensive alphabetical list had ever been made, even by Berenson himself. Over 12,000 pictures were listed. He had appended lists to each of the slender volumes of his *Renaissance Painters*, but the lists in these editions were based on autograph paintings, and were therefore limited. Berenson, in the preface to the handy little volume on India paper, called his previous lists the fruit of 'an adolescent attitude'. Now, as a connoisseur, he is led to include not only the works which artists painted 'with more or less assistance, but such as were turned out in their studies from their designs, and even copies as well, providing they faithfully transcribe lost works'. He says he rejects without mercy those attributions which are merely happy thoughts or bright guesses.

'None of my lists give me complete satisfaction. More and more work will be required for two or even three generations before this task will be adequately accomplished. And when it is, let us hope that our successors will show their gratitude by using the material gathered by their forerunners as a foundation for their finished structure.'[2]

[1] Roger Hinks and Naomi Royde-Smith, *Pictures and People*, p. 113, Victor Gollancz, 1930.

[2] Bernard Berenson, *Italian Pictures of the Renaissance*. A list of the principal artists and their works with an index of places, p. vi. Oxford, at the Clarendon Press, 1932.

Of course the numbers of pictures were very greatly increased in these lists, when compared with the earlier lists, partly owing to the new method which Berenson describes, and partly owing to ever-increasing discoveries.[1] These arrived sometimes in the form of a photograph, from an owner who wanted to know whether he possessed a masterpiece; sometimes in the form of more photographs or of the picture itself, sent by Duveen Brothers to 'I Tatti' for comment; and sometimes through observation by Berenson on his travels in Italy, and on his visits to public and private collections in the peninsula and abroad.

'As to the sources upon which I have based my views of the influences that formed the painters, I need scarcely say that we have next to no information in the matter, and little reliable tradition, so that influences given in these lists are derived almost entirely from observed resemblances between the works of a given painter and those of his predecessors. Personal contact is not necessarily implied. A man may owe almost everything to another without ever having seen him.'[2]

It was the work of a lifetime. The acknowledgements alone cover three pages and name almost every great authority from Milanesi, Cavalcaselle and Morelli to the founder of the Warburg Institute, and among the living to the heads of every great gallery in Europe and the United States and to wellnigh every living writer on art from Dr Yashiro in Tokyo to Van Marle, Louis Gillet and younger men like Benedict Nicolson and Kenneth Clark. But the last word, despite or with the help of all these works, lay with Berenson's own 'observed resemblances'. Nearer home, within the walls of 'I Tatti', five women are especially thanked for their research and for compiling the place index, and among them Mary and Miss Nicky Mariano, without whose devoted collaboration the great task could not have been finished.

'What meagre results for the task of a lifetime! Yes, had it been a task. But it has been a way of living. Few are the items in these

---

[1] Thus to take Lorenzo Lotto alone, as an example. In Berenson's 1894 edition of the Lotto, 96 Lotto paintings are listed; in the great 1932 lists, 154 are listed; in the 1957 edition, 218 are listed. In 1896 none were in the United States of America; by 1932, 11 Lottos had emigrated. Today the number of Lotto emigrants has vastly increased.   [2] *Ibid.*, Preface.

lists which do not call up, as my eye glances over them, moments of eager discovery, of happy enjoyment, recollection of enchanting landscapes into which they took me, of interesting personalities they led me to meet.'[1]

These famous lists with their brief, succinct, telegraphic, three-line biographies beneath the name of each artist were henceforth to be the foundation upon which every student of Italian art would build his knowledge. For the next twenty-five years the little book accompanied many an ordinary tourist on his journey to Italy or to any gallery of importance. No work on Renaissance painting is so frequently consulted in the great museums of the world. Then, when Berenson was ninety, he began revising and completing the lists, for a grand six-volume edition (for the four main schools), each of which was to have eight hundred illustrations. This was made possible by a generous grant from the Kress Foundation in the United States of America. The first two volumes devoted to the Venetian School appeared in 1957. This time he was assisted again by Miss Nicky Mariano, and two resident assistants, Luisa Vertova and William Mostyn Owen,[2] and the Librarian Baroness Anrep and her young assistant, the daughter of the bailiff at 'I Tatti', Signorina Gioffredi.

Such a large and profusely illustrated edition was intended to give the museums of the world their own photographic reference book to the Italian Renaissance painters. The revision involved the study of thousands of photographs—a task that could not but be fearfully strenuous for a man of over ninety. There were days when the chores seemed overwhelming. 'I don't know why I wade through all this filth', he would sometimes cry in despair, when surrounded by photographs all over his bed in the usual early morning work hours, and then he would quote from Jeremiah:

'For I heard the defaming of many, fear on every side. Report, say they, and we will report it. All my familiars watched for my halting, saying, Peradventure he will be enticed, and we shall prevail against him, and we shall take our revenge on him.'[3]

[1] Bernard Berenson, *Italian Pictures of the Renaissance*. Preface.
[2] See Plate XVIII.
[3] Jeremiah xx. 10. The Bible, as often, lay open that morning on his bedside table, and he bid his visitor read the verses to him.

237

One effect of these lists might be that, at one fell blow, a man far away from the scene of these labours who thought he was the proud (and wealthy) possessor of a masterpiece might find that he was the possessor of nothing at all that was marketable, for every known private owner of Italian masterpieces was included in the lists. Private owners, and museums also, might wake up on the morning of publication with heartburning about their most treasured attributions, or surprise about others they had not considered of such value. But Berenson was nothing if not free and disinterested, and even more so, if that were possible, by the age of ninety, at the time of the great revision.[1] He had so often been confirmed in his attributions that American collectors refused to buy Renaissance pictures without his 'passport'. His detachment had come early, as it usually does with genius. Something of his early Old Testament training fortified him here. If there is one strong desire which runs through the great Hebrew prophets, it is the desire for the liberation of the self for the purpose of uniting it with God, or with what Marcus Aurelius, a philosopher very near to Berenson, called 'the God-like symphony of the whole'.

'This feeling, that one must strive for the enduring, this promotion of the permanent, the surviving, the eternal, to aesthetic and even moral value, has tended to inhibit and even to disperse my

[1] When the first two volumes of the Venetian School revised lists with 1,333 illustrations appeared, *The Times Literary Supplement*, in a three-column article, said that the use of the Lists, as an aid to travelling, would soon be at an end, for a single volume of pocket size would have become eight massive illustrated volumes, 'in every other respect, however, its use has been enormously enhanced'. The vast number of secondary artists now included resulted in a more truthful picture of Venetian painting than did any of the previous lists. 'Indeed it seems that no signed altarpiece in a hill-town in Friuli, no modest piece of carpentry in a village in the Bergamasque has eluded Mr Berenson's penetrating glance'. Of the illustrations, the reviewer said: 'No visual survey of any local school on such a scale has ever previously been attempted, and in conjunction with the lists, it transforms an invaluable *vademecum* into one of the most remarkable volumes on the history of painting that has ever been produced.' Perhaps the most remarkable of the many newly attributed pictures occurred in the hitherto meagre Giorgione lists. Four pages of autograph paintings, copies, school and furniture paintings made Giorgione take 'his place among the most formidable painters of his or any other time'. (*T.L.S.*, February 14, 1958, p. 89.) M. André Chastel wrote in *Le Monde* appreciatively. Reviewers everywhere received the two volumes with high praise.

energies. . . . Unless I could acquire the illusion that I had something to offer that would be lasting, it seemed only decent to do nothing.'[1]

One has heard it said that he had undertaken more than one man can do, and that 'it was the American slump of 1929 that saved him from over-attributing, as it slowed down the vast purchases'. People will say anything. The more serious view is that the Lists, in these young days of the history of art, were one of Berenson's most lasting contributions to its future course, at least in the world of Italian Renaissance art.

Mary published two books of her own in her lifetime, and collaborated with Mason Perkins on another. The second of her own books was a re-writing of the first. In 1935, several years after she and Berenson had made a journey in Tunisia and Algiers, she wrote an account from memory of that journey, as solace for 'a year of serious illness'. Their travels took them on visits to Carthage, Tunis, Kairouan, Sfax, Gabea, Tozeur, Sbeitla, Tebessa, Timgad, Lambessa, Kantara, Biskra, Sétif and Algiers, and then through Philippeville and the towns of Kabylia. Everywhere they visited the remains of Rome, of Byzantium and of Moslem and Phoenician rule. It is not a learned account: just a travel book of contemporary experience such as have abounded since the second war. It was printed in Italy (by Giachetti at Prato, in 1935), and she called it *Across the Mediterranean*. There is one moment in Tunis in the Musée Alaoui where she was much discouraged by the pre-Roman sculptures and by the early Christian art 'which one can study to one's heart's disgust in this museum'.

'My husband, however, was like a war horse scenting the battle. He loves to see art gradually decaying to its lowest and most degraded form. His remorseless energy and curiosity invest every step of art history with fascination, whereas I often feel myself in a museum like a hen scratching round to find a grain of corn in a dust heap.'[2]

Like a hen . . . to find a grain of corn in a dust heap. She had travelled a long, long way from the days when only that which enchanted seemed worth recording. Three years later, when her health prevented a second journey to North Africa, Berenson and

[1] *S.S.P.*, p. 53.   [2] *Across the Mediterranean*, p. 27.

Miss Mariano, accompanied part of the way by Mr and Mrs Henry Coster, visited many of the same and some new places. Mary then wrote *A Vicarious Trip to the Barbary Coast* (Constable). The book is compiled largely from letters from the travellers. Again it is not a learned or historical work, but simply records the enjoyments of four intelligent travellers wandering in a period of time and of art not strictly their own. That journey ends in Naples with a visit to the excavations of Umberto Zanotti Bianco and his assistant Dr Zancane at the mouth of the Sele near Paestum. Mary quotes a remark pregnant with *Weltanschauung* in a letter from Berenson: 'To the profane eye, i.e. the aesthetic one, the excavations offered small interest.' Mary records how they unpacked some of the finds and 'the only interesting objects were one or two metopes with good Ionian reliefs of the seventh century (B.C.) perhaps'.[1] Berenson's letter goes on:

'We then sat down to eat and I discovered that the assistant was extremely intelligent, knew her job well, loved it so much that it glorified her little face as she talked.'

As often happens, the human factor compensated for what was (to him) the boredom of the artefact. Good spirits return in the letter when the sun sets on the nearby columns of Paestum and on the roses which blossomed about their bases. The vitality of the excavator, the glow of the sun, revived the spirit, which the turned-up earth and the broken bits of marble had sorely depressed. Berenson was like that—never indifferent to his surroundings.

Mary's book was appreciatively reviewed in *The Times Literary Supplement* and in the American *Geographical Journal*.

* * *

All these activities, between the wars, took place in a world which was revelling in psychoanalysis under the inspiration of Freud and Jung, in a recurrent anti-Semitism, soon to assume gigantic proportions involving the mass murder of five million Jews by Hitler; in a world in which painting, led by Picasso, had been distorting the human figure beyond recognition, and in a world where English 'literature' was distorting language beyond the pales of grammar or

[1] All these metopes have now been displayed on a model of a temple in the new museum at Paestum.

syntax under Gertrude Stein and James Joyce. Berenson was accused by those who did not know him of turning his back upon contemporary arts, but nothing could be further from the truth. He was quite aware of what was going on around him in all the arts. 'I Tatti' was full of contemporary literary and art magazines. They arrived regularly from the chief capitals of Europe and from the United States of America. Visitors spoke of the Picasso and Matisse rage.

Already in 1908 he had taken offence at a review in the New York *Nation* of the paintings of Matisse in the *Salon* in Paris that autumn. The reviewer had complained that Matisse forgets 'that beholders are not all fools, and that it is not necessary to do differently from all other artists'. Berenson wrote to the New York *Nation*[1] identifying himself with 'the fools' and complaining that the critic was using the most hackneyed phrases: 'Of what great painter or sculptor or musician of the last century has it not been said in the cant phrase of the boulevard *"C'est un fumiste. Il cherche à épâter le monde"*?' Berenson stated his conviction that Matisse had 'after twenty years of very earnest searching at last found the great high road travelled by all the best masters of the visual arts for the last sixty centuries at least'. Matisse was for him 'a magnificent draughtsman and a great designer' (at least in 1908). Berenson would not commit himself about Matisse's colour. His letter appreciated Corot, Rousseau and Millet as 'those mighty ones'.

Many years later Berenson recalled how he had met the young Picasso and the more mature Matisse at Michael and Sally Stein's house in Paris in the first years of the century, when Matisse was so poor that he would have taken any job, as a porter even, in order to live.[2] Berenson added:

'The attention aroused by these few lines of print [in the *Nation*] made me aware of the authority I could wield as a critic of modern art. The entire Stein family, Michael, Sally, Leo, Gertrude, who at the time arrogated to themselves the office of High Protectors of newness in painting, began to prod me to leave all I had and to dedi-

[1] New York *Nation*, November 12, 1908.

[2] Berenson, *Valutazioni*, 1945–1956, p. 161, Electa, Milan, 1957. Berenson recalls his first visit to Matisse's studio and a drawing of dancing nudes there which, even fifty years later, he deemed to be the nearest Matisse ever reached to a great work of art. It reminded him of Pollaiuolo's dancing nudes which had been discovered in the Torre del Gallo in Florence in 1897. In 1908 the letter to the *Nation* had an immediate effect in Paris.

cate myself to the merits of the new school. . . . I dreaded the personal element in my job, and that was a contributing, and perhaps the chief reason why I would not write on contemporary art. My standards were based on what survived of the greatest and best in fifty centuries of creative genius. It would not be fair to measure up against it the product of any single day, not even this day.'[1]

Berenson revisited Matisse's studio just before the first war with J. Pierpont Morgan's daughter. He found it hung with casts of Cambodian sculptures, and told Matisse that there was too much resemblance between his work and that art. Matisse firmly denied any Cambodian influence. Berenson insisted, pointing to the casts, but in vain, and decided that either Matisse did not know that the casts were Cambodian, or 'more likely' (in his experience of artists) that Matisse was unaware of what was influencing him.[2]

On that occasion Berenson purchased a rough painting of a wood for '500 good gold francs'. For thirty-five years they did not meet again. Berenson says his own interest in Matisse flagged completely when he found Matisse falling under the fascination of 'the Catalan wizard' (Picasso) just as every other painter was doing. One night in 1950 Berenson drove home from Pau via Nice, and he called on the old painter and found the walls covered in 'heavily painted' sketches for the Vence chapel, and the master surrounded by shelves of books about himself and inquiring only whether Berenson still possessed the painting of the forest. On the walls now were Polynesian sculptures.

Among the artists whom the Steins took up, 'the most indigent and most unappreciated' was Picasso. The fascination of Picasso's vitality through the years upon contemporary painters was noted by Berenson as a fact, if an unfortunate one. He describes their meeting:

'This most protean and acrobatic of painters, the most ready to take any jump, to put on any motley or mask, to twist himself into any shape and always with dazzling dexterity. Meeting him after he had become the sovereign idol of the public that writes, that turtle-eats, that buys, he condescended to recall that he had known me at the Steins and added: "Ah, those Steins, how they did exploit me!" '[3]

[1] *S.S.P.*, pp. 40–1.
[2] Berenson, *Valutazioni, ed. cit.*, p. 162.   [3] *S.S.P.*, p. 41.

In conversation Berenson once or twice put forward the theory
that Picasso would probably not have so radically deformed and
doodled the human face and figure unless he had found that the
process paid. With the dealers, the writers and the purchasers, the
men who had turned patronage into a profitable gamble, Berenson
had no patience. He thought Picasso himself lost no opportunity to
hide his true gifts.

'Perhaps in deepest secret he draws in orthodox fashion everything he bedevils while painting, as I have been assured Joyce wrote
out in plain King's English what he fricasséd for his printed prose.'[1]

Picasso and Joyce are paired often by Berenson in what he calls
'the chopping and juggling, distorting and fooling with shapes'. He
thinks that something of the kind had occurred before in human
history, at the end of the Gothic period, 'with its spidery architecture, recklessly calligraphic draperies and affected smiles', but
then came the great reaction which produced the Van Eycks and
eventually Masaccio and all the others. It had happened before that
the search for novelty began in a classical past, but never 'in
deliberate opposition to it'.

'It is in our own day that for the first time in history a long-
accepted classical tradition with all its invaluable conventions has
been wantonly, jeeringly thrown away. . . . In the figure arts it has
meant throwing away composition, for which already a Degas had
shown a distaste that in the long run will count against him. It was
accompanied by the conclusion not based on seeing, on observing,
but on exasperation and on the preconceived assumption that the
squalid, the sordid, the violent, the bestial, the misshapen, in short
that low life was the only "reality".'[2]

---

[1] *Seeing and Knowing*, p. 24.
Further light on Joyce's composition was thrown, for the author, in Trieste,
by a great antiquarian, and the owner of the largest bookshop in Trieste, a
friend of James Joyce's, who maintained that Joyce often told him of the fantastic mispronunciations of English made by his Austrian, Greek, Italian,
Turkish and other pupils at the Berlitz School in Trieste where he taught.
This cultivated Italian claimed to have recognized all these distortions in
Joyce's later writings. First they drove Joyce mad, then after years of repetition
by every new foreign pupil (said the famous bookseller) he began to laugh at
them and use them himself.   [2] *S. and K.*, pp. 22–3.

Deformations in art there have always been. Few have survived. They easily join the dust heap in every age. It is after the First War that the deformity grows with the despair about the future and the contempt 'for everything in the social order, in politics, and in all the arts' which had led to such a horrible massacre. Compromise is always killed by violence, and even the revolt in 'abstract' art against all the violence of war is another and a new failure to compromise.

'For many thousands of years visual art has been based on ideated sensations, on a compromise between what one knows and what one sees and between what one sees and what one can reproduce for others. It therefore would seem to correspond to a continuous need or desire or demand of human nature, of man who is matter and spirit, body as well as mind. . . . So there is but one way out of the brambly maze in which we are blindly beating about: follow the tenuous beam of reason that will lead us back to the compromise between "seeing" and "knowing", between retinal vision and conceptual looking, on which rests visual art as an eternal function of human nature.'[1]

Freudians might be busy psychoanalizing incomprehensible paintings in search of the painter's private 'complexes' and 'inhibitions'. Jung might scrap all that and claim that age-old myths and symbols far transcending the individual's experiences feed the creative imagination. Berenson is urgent and practical.

He believed that the visual arts would revive, but only when the artist based his skill and his creation on the human nude.[2] That alone could bring new vision and re-create true proportion. Berenson had no fear that the camera in all its various productions in illustrated papers, cinemas or television would ever quench the 'psychophysiological' urge to create which belongs to human beings. His faith in the past achievements of art and in its future revivals was unquenchable, regardless of all the mechanical and electronic devices which might be enlisted for making likenesses.

The general subject of the decline in periods of great art also interested Burckhardt and Ruskin. For Berenson the subject was

[1] *S. and K.*, pp. 26 and 28.
[2] Any artist knows how his line drawing improves and develops after each life-class. Drawing from the nude seems to occupy the place of preludes and fugues in the life of a pianist.

actual and contemporary. In mid-twentieth century art he found one type of decline from 'all values except those that arise from the part of us that is below the belt'.[1] Berenson found another contribution to the decline in the sudden unloading in Europe of vast quantities of primitive art objects and replicas from all the four corners of the earth. He had seen them in Matisse's and in other studios. He elaborated these ideas on the decline of art (after the second war) in an essay dedicated to The Arch of Constantine.[2]

That essay was intended as a first chapter to a big work on 'Decline and Recovery in the Figure Arts', a work which never came to be written. The keeping of the diary, the seeing of many paintings and photographs, the visits of many people, the re-issue of early books with vastly increased illustrations each one of which was personally chosen, and each caption read and re-read in proof—all this took up the hours available for creative writing. Those hours decreased inevitably with age and diminishing strength, from the daily allotment of five to three hours after the Second War, and then by 1950 to two and one and a half hours a day. There was a further complication of long standing, sometimes attributed to the inadequate literary disciplines of Harvard teaching in the 1880s: the immense difficulty of organizing a book at all. Berenson in this matter faced the problem of all writers. Nor would he use any of the modern aids. He wrote his books, like his letters, by hand. He says he had 'to fish them out of myself'. Dictation or recording tapes he spurned.[3]

But to return to the shattered fragmentary production which lay all around him under the title of 'Modern Art' in the twentieth century. He searched and searched for a reason. He could not blame governments. 'Never has the State done more for the individual painter and sculptor than between the last two wars.'[4] He decided that both the artist and the public had become thoroughly confused, had had their 'visual convictions' destroyed by this vast arrival of queer

---

[1] *S. and K.*, p. 38.

[2] Bernard Berenson, *The Arch of Constantine*, Chapman and Hall, London, 1954.

[3] I remember once saying to B.B. in Rome in 1948 that I had to give a little talk in Italian at the British Council on the poet Gerard Manley Hopkins. 'How long?' he asked. 'Oh, about fifty minutes.' 'Good heavens—how do you do it? I have never been able to talk about anything for more than five minutes. I couldn't prepare a talk about anyone.'

[4] *Arch of Constantine, ed. cit.*, p. 62.

outlandish primitive art, 'written up by the critics of the day as being so good as, if not better than the masterpieces we Western peoples had been admiring for centuries, nay for thousands of years'. The infantilism in everyone was appealed to and the young artist thought he could do without the sweat and toil of years of traditional training, and he scratched, daubed and smeared while the critics praised and alleged they found deep meaning, strange beauty, revealing newness.

In the essay on *Seeing and Knowing* Berenson most roundly states the belief that merely mental or geometric conceptions can never replace 'the bread of art'. However carefully globes in wood or stone might be polished so as to suggest 'broad bottomed, deep-breasted females', they would never replace great sculpture.[1] He was un-interested in advertisements and shop decoration or dress materials where some of these productions have found a home.

Knowing nothing of the peculiar and non-natural diversions of the great city dwellers of old and new towns in the old and new world, where 'seeing' is often an activity to be avoided, Berenson could only hope that his readers would somehow make the effort and learn 'to see' again. Those who read him carefully, succeeded. Within the decade other writers on art like Eric Newton and Sir Kenneth Clark began to devote much time to 're-educating' the public's eye from the ravages of the ugliness and horror patronized by the dealers.

For one so discriminating and so appreciative in matters of beauty and taste as Berenson, the subject of contemporary distortion and incompetence was inevitably a distressing one. He would rejoice greatly at any newspaper art critics who upheld the human and classic standards of high art, but when they did not (as more frequently happened) he found that the style 'sweated conviction' and was 'so elaborate, so complicated, so subtle, that one wonders whether they as much as expect readers to follow them'.[2]

After the First War he was once taken to Berlin to see all the fierce German daubs of the 'twenties, the Nolde's and the rest, and found that 'their pigment, seemingly not yet dry, suggested syrups and jams of raspberry, strawberry, greengage, plum, blackberry'.[3]

*   *   *

[1] Bernard Berenson, *Seeing and Knowing, ed. cit.*, p. 27.
[2] Bernard Berenson, *Caravaggio, His Incongruity and His Fame*, p. 93, Chapman and Hall, London, 1953.   [3] *Idem.*, p. 92.

Berenson's attitude to psychology was quite rational. For him psychology was a 'branch of biology' and intended for the sick. Not a few transatlantic visitors, practised psychologists, tried to put him through their paces, but they gave up in face of his amused tolerance. The kind of things they wanted to find out he would not betray, and for the rest he was far more uninhibited than they were. Many elderly men seem to read or to write some pornography. Berenson limited himself to enjoying Henry Miller's books—for a year or two. Berenson's analysis of the psychology of the Nazis is certainly uninhibited. He thinks that the Nazis are curiously 'faithful to the Israelitish pattern' with their claim to be the chosen people with an exclusive right to dispossess others 'in good Hexateuch fashion', their ban on intermarriage with any other race, and on reading anything written by a Jew.[1]

Before the Nazis came to power he had never been in favour of the Zionist movement or of the return of Israel to the Jews. But once the persecution started in earnest, he believed that no other course was possible. But he did not financially support this or any other 'movement', for all his expenditure, apart from the running of the house, books, photos and travel would now be cut down to form the endowment fund, without which Harvard did not feel it could accept the gift of 'I Tatti'. Mr Paul Sachs, who helped to create the Fogg Museum in Cambridge, Mass., and the grandson of Emerson, Mr Edward Forbes, had put Berenson's gift before the Harvard trustees in October 1933, and it was acknowledged with gratitude by President Conant, providing that a suitable endowment should accompany the estate. This condition, which the University also attached to another great legacy, Dumbarton Oaks, gave rise to unwarranted rumours that the gift was not welcome.[2] Mr Sachs maintained that the only hesitation concerned income from the endowment. In June 1939 a meeting of the President and the Fellows voted to conclude negotiations with Berenson at a certain figure. Then negotiations were suspended owing to the war. An offer came from Harvard to take over 'I Tatti' immediately in

[1] *R. and R.*, p. 113.

[2] Mr Paul Sachs to the author in Boston in June 1955. He quoted from President Conant's letter to Berenson of December 13, 1933, which said that 'the Corporation . . . is enthusiastically receptive to the general idea' of 'your extremely generous offer'. It was 'completely in sympathy with your plan that the Fine Arts Department of Harvard University might have the opportunity of establishing this important outpost in the home of Italian art'.

September 1939, in case Berenson wished to leave it. But, as we shall see, he stayed. Not until after the Second War was the gift fully accepted, when it was accompanied by Berenson's endowment of a million dollars. It was Berenson's keen hope that further endowments would follow so as to enable more than five students to be in residence. He stipulated that the scholarships should be open for a proportion of British and European students also. Harvard is one of the most well endowed of universities, but extremely cautious. It knew how costly such an establishment as 'I Tatti' could be to run. President Pusey signed the final agreements in 1955.

*   *   *

Three years before the outbreak of the Second World War, just after Berenson had reached his seventieth year, 'all ambition spent and passion of sense, heart or mind stilled',[1] the final break with Duveen occurred. Berenson could now afford the break, and he much desired it. To Mary and to Nicky Mariano it came as a great relief. The immediate cause, as we know, was an attribution which he would not give.

Mr S. N. Behrman maintains that Duveen never recovered from the separation and that Berenson never recovered from the association. Duveen died two years later. Berenson still assisted several collectors like Count Contini Bonacossi, who sold numbers of pictures every year, and worked for Mr Paul Getty and the art firm of Georges Wildenstein in Paris, but the pace was a far slower one now. For the first time he felt free to enjoy 'my long interrupted It-ness'. 'It' meaning the kind of Arcady which he had wonderfully enjoyed until the age of thirty.

' "It" is every experience that is ultimate, valued for its own sake and in our own intention. . . . "It" accepts what is as if what is were a Work of art in which the qualities so outweighed the faults that these could be ignored. "It" is incapable of analysis, requires no explanations and no apology, is self-evident and right. One may sing about it but not discuss it. "It" is the most immediate and mystical way.'[2]

Another expression which he liked to use about the way in which he could enjoy certain moments of his life was culled probably from

[1] *S.S.P.*, p. 122.   [2] *S.S.P.*, p. 120.

the sonnet sequence by Dante Gabriel Rossetti called *The House of Life*.

'The more humanized we get the more storeys has our House of Life. At the bottom live those who rise little above other domesticated animals. It is well with them and they should be properly fed, kept clean and healthy in body and mind, and treated as the androplasm out of which will spring more humanized men and women. These progressively occupy the mounting storeys to the top, where abide the few who come nearest to a humanly conceivable perfection.'[1]

Inevitably such a view of life could not allow for the dreams and plans, already taking shape, of a welfare state in England, in Austria or in any other country. Berenson was consistent. He thought such a state would be expensive and economically unsound. People would sponge on it and ruin it.

He had little patience with optimistic idealists who would forget 'the animal basis of our nature', and would 'lose the sense of things'. Pessimistic authoritarian totalitarians, political or religious, he put in this category. He wished that Sir Christopher Wren had been allowed to rebuild London after the Great Fire 'or Ledoux,[2] at the dawn of the industrial age, had been able to realize his plan for a noble manufacturing town'. It was not to be, but Berenson believed that it would nevertheless happen one day.

*　　*　　*

The garden, the five gardens, which provided enchanting and varying daily walks, had grown to full and rich maturity. Those walks, and the walks in the hillsides above 'I Tatti', provided Berenson every morning and every afternoon with 'enough newness to suffice for the day'. He claimed—and the claim was a real one—that each day as he looked, he wondered where his eyes had been the day before. New colours, new lights, new beauties in that transparent

[1] *S.S.P.*, p. 118.
[2] Claude-Nicolas Ledoux, 1736–1802, who built the Pavillon at Besançon, Madame Dubarry's house at Versailles, and a score of private houses in Paris and the Provinces, all based on the architecture of Palladio. He built a salt works at Chaux in Lorraine, part of which still stands, and planned a military forge with pyramidal furnaces and a 'social town' with pleasure palaces, Temples of Reconciliation and Schools of Ethics. See Marcel Raval, *Ledoux*, Arts et Métiers Graphiques, Paris, 1945.

Tuscan hillscape seemed inexhaustible. He wrote about them in his diary, and to his friends. He would interrupt a walk to speak about them, and rarely with the words of yesterday. In those hillsides he felt *inside* the landscape of the Florentine painters, walking about in their backgrounds, even if they, as artists, rarely painted from nature. Of sculpture he had no need 'because my imagination has become so moulding that having about me such models as the Tuscan peasantry I can visualize them as statues in movement'.[1] Yet he possessed many Oriental bronzes, and the green gardens were dotted with agreeable statuary.

The grace of the Italian race in its movements, whether in town or country, is familiar now all over the world through Italian films. Berenson still marvelled at it after nearly seventy years of familiarity with it.

Into this world, in which he had created and achieved a high degree of personal happiness and a wonderful intimacy with those aspects of the past which most appealed to him, fewer friends now came. English friends had nearly all left Italy by the summer of 1939.

'Friends were urging me to go, because foes were suspecting and accusing me of carrying on propaganda and even spying. We were avoided by all but the fewest. An atmosphere increasingly hostile thickened around us . . . so humble have we got, so modest in our expectations, that all I venture to hope for in this new year is that it shall not be worse than the last; and that a year hence we may still be here, all of us, that I may still be enjoying my library, my walks, my few faithful friends, my meditations, my daydreams.'[2]

So he wrote in his diary on January 1, 1941, when Italy was not yet at war with the United States, and indeed the United States had not yet been driven into the war by the Japanese attack on Pearl Harbor which was still eleven months ahead. Mary was far from well. Should he try to take her to America? The whole question of whether to stay or to go had really arisen on September 3, 1939. The Harvard offer to take over 'I Tatti' was there. Berenson does not seem to have had much faith in the possibility of Mussolini's neutrality. Any such belief in any case was shattered by the choice moment—June 10, 1940—immediately after the fall of France, which Mussolini picked for entering the war on the side of the one he

[1] *S.S.P.*, p. 134.   [2] *R. and R.*, p. 16.

believed to be the imminent victor, Hitler. The outbreak of the war and Italy's entry into it against England and France filled Bernard and Mary with horror and indignation, but also, as such events do, with the power of decision. They would stay with the art treasures, the books and the photographs collected during the long years and bequeathed to Harvard. If these were doomed to destruction, then the Berensons would face the storm, always hoping to save what could be saved.

*   *   *

After the attack on Pearl Harbor in 1941 Mussolini declared war on the United States from his balcony in Piazza Venezia. Mr Wendell Phillips, the United States Ambassador, was asked by Mussolini's son-in-law, Galeazzo Ciano, with whom he was on good terms, whether there was anything Ciano could do for him after he had left Italy with the Embassy staff, 'Yes, look after the Berensons.'[1]

Ciano succeeded in getting Mussolini to sign an order that the inhabitants of 'I Tatti' should not be molested. The telephone, but nothing else, was cut off. All was well until the tide began to turn against Germany and Italy in 1943, a few months before the Italian collapse. Ciano then wrote to the Berensons to say that he could control matters in Rome, but not necessarily in Florence. There, however, fortunately for the Berensons and for others, the representative of Hitler was a 'good German' and advised Berenson to leave 'I Tatti'. Then, in the famous July session of the Grand Fascist Council in 1943, Ciano and many others revolted against Mussolini. The September 8th Armistice followed. The Fascists fled to the north, where Mussolini set up a puppet republic at Salò on Lake Garda. It was supposed to rule all Italy, but soon lost half of it. Ciano was shot in the back as a traitor in Verona in February 1944 after a brief trial. For the Berensons all now depended on Dr Gerhard Wolf, the German Consul. By then the German army had descended in force into Tuscany, and Berenson was already in hiding two miles away as the crow flies from 'I Tatti'.

Mr Wendell Phillips' intervention led to awful rumours that Berenson was an 'agent' working on both sides during the war. This ridiculous misunderstanding caused some passport difficulties, but not for long. His American passport was restored soon after the war.

[1] Berenson to the author in November 1955.

251

CHAPTER XV

The Second War

A man of real taste is always a man of judgment in
other respects.

SIR JOSHUA REYNOLDS

RUMOUR AND REFLECTION is an exhilarating war diary, of
earliest morning ideas and jottings, influenced maybe by
André Gide's *Journal* which came out in 1939. Unlike Gide,
Berenson does not oscillate between anarchy and order, hell and
heaven. Berenson comes down on the side of heaven and of order, after
roving far and wide like the Tory anarchist he is. It contains in its
far more complete Italian edition (*Ecchi e Riflessioni*, Mondadori,
1950) and in its abbreviated English edition (Constable, 1952)
extracts from Berenson's war diary between 1941 and 1944, on every
conceivable subject, from his reading in all its immense range; his
memories of friends of a lifetime, of collectors, of art historians;
memories of his travels; his ideas about the Jews, anti-Semitism,
Fascism, religion, politics, or just to take a few of the 'S's' in the
index, about Salvemini, Sex, Shelley, Siena, Sincerity, Sitwells,
Slang, Slavery and Snowfalls. There is no end to the wide range of
Berenson's mind, Jewish in its universality, prophetic often, sceptical
because well informed, with a rich and magnificent sense of the past
and no simple Emersonian optimism about the future. It is no art
book but the book of an artist who, suddenly finding himself cut off
from the world, with no telephone, no foreign post and very few
visitors, in a country at war with his own, surrounded by incredible
rumours, wakes up every morning and lets his well-stocked mind
spin. It sketches a score of books he will not live to write, and scores
of ideas which he would live to speak or to elaborate—if he could
survive the war. That was never a certainty. On July 25, 1943 (when
Mussolini called on King Victor Emmanuel III at the Quirinal to
tender his resignation, after the rebellious Grand Fascist Council
meeting, and the King had the Dictator removed from the Palace in

an ambulance), Berenson's faithful barber came up with the news of how people in Florence had embraced in the streets without knowing each other and had hung out the gayest flags in token of gladness. All over Italy millions rejoiced like children waking from a nightmare of war into what they hoped was an outbreak of peace.

Then came the armistice on September 8, 1943, and the beginning of Italy's long *via crucis*, with the descent over the Alps of thirty German divisions and, in their rear, a revived Fascist government and police harassed by partisans—in a word, Civil War. The Tuscan hills were full of anti-Fascist refugees, escaping British prisoners of war, Jews in hiding and young men avoiding the great nightly swoops by the Germans to collect anyone they could find to work in their factories at home.

Two days after the armistice a kindly *deus ex machina*, in the shape of the diplomatic representative of a very small State to a geographically even smaller State, the Marchese Filippo Serlupi, Minister to the Holy See of the Republic of San Marino, appeared at 'I Tatti' to offer the Berensons and Miss Mariano asylum in his nearby house above Carreggi. There the Marquis flew the yellow and white Papal flag proclaiming his diplomatic immunity, which the Germans, who like this sort of thing, miraculously respected. Mary was too ill to be moved. Within a few months the Germans had occupied the first and second floors of 'I Tatti', obliging her, though bed-ridden, to move up to the top floor. After Sicily, Naples; after Cassino, Rome. The Allies were now approaching Florence, fighting all the way up the peninsula. In July 1944 Berenson hears from the runners who passed between Carreggi and Settignano that the Germans have urged Mary to leave because 'they believe it likely that "I Tatti" will be under heavy fire and may suffer destruction or at least serious damage'. The Germans offer transport to take her down to the best hotel in town. News comes up from Florence that this very hotel has been entirely evacuated along with every other building in the area, and Berenson hopes that they have not carried out their plan, but is powerless to interfere.

Until the moment when Berenson and Miss Mariano moved to the Serlupi's, the diary often refers to the happy preparation of a book on Aesthetics. (Only the preliminary essay was ever written, and published under the title of *Aesthetics and History*.) After the move very many of the entries are concerned with what was after all the main reason for taking refuge—anti-Semitism, and there are many penetrating excursions into the relations between Judaism and Christianity. These are too lengthy to be quoted here. They end with the view that 'insulators or ghettoes' cannot be re-established in Western lands, even if the alternatives still remain: 'complete isolation or assimilation'.

But events were moving very fast and dangerously. The household at the Serlupi's were reading aloud, mostly classic plays in English, French and German. The villa gradually moves into a no-man's land between the retreating German army and the advancing Allied armies, and there is 'booming, banging, crashing, whistling, hissing and the house creaking and shaking, threatening to crack open'. Goethe's *Iphigenia* has to be laid aside. Where educated people had to live for months and years under bombings, in England and elsewhere, they found similar solace in the great classics. But there are moments when even these mighty comforts failed to keep out fear.

The Germans now wanted to place their machine-guns on the terrace of the Serlupi's house.

'Nicky rushed to their camps to mollify them. They would do their best to put the guns not on our ground—which they would try to repect as neutral territory—but to right and left just outside. More than that they could not do, because they must defend the hillside, as it commands an important line of retreat.'[1]

Berenson notes in his diary, as the shells burst almost overhead, that he had never felt so isolated from the rest of the world. 'It is like being on a whaler in the good old days, which did not touch port for many months together.' There was now no news of Mary. He did not know whether she was still alive or whether 'I Tatti' was still standing. Rome had been declared an 'open city'. The Germans abandoned it on June 4th. Barely two weeks later all attempts to declare Florence an 'open city' failed. A sound of explosion after explosion, of all the Arno bridges being blown up, reached the villa in early August, but no one yet knew what exactly was being blown up. Sleep became impossible, and reading was limited to daylight hours, since electricity had long been cut off.

'Strange how quickly one settles down to getting on with the least of everything! As oil for lamps is strictly limited and candles even

[1] *R. and R.*, p. 340.

more, one thinks twice before using them. One shrinks from using more than the smallest quantity of cistern water for washing, and of spring water for drinking.'[1]

The encamped German soldiers nearby sing to a concertina in the evening, 'manifestly enjoying life, saying "yes" to it'. They would drop in and ask for wine, milk, coffee and cigarettes, and get them. Then on August 16th, 'as we were finishing luncheon, a missile came through the window, passed between me and my hostess and hit the wall opposite. It was the splinter of a shell which had burst near the kitchen door.'

Others followed, breaking windows. Fragments of the ceiling in Berenson's bedroom came down. Most of the days and nights were now spent in such shelter as the cellars could offer. Then at last, on August 17th, a little outside news arrived. Florence, abandoned, had been taken by the partisans. The vanguards of the Eighth Army were entering. A new mayor had been appointed, 'Dr Pieraccini, a Socialist deputy before Fascism, a saintly physician, and great scholar, whose life at Mussolini's order, to use Mussolini's own words, had been made "difficult for him".'[2] The visitor who had got through with this news also brought news of the terrible and wilfully slow Russian attack on Warsaw, awaiting (as one later knew) the annihilation by the Germans of the Polish resistance in the Warsaw rising. And he brought news that 'I Tatti', still occupied by the Germans 'who are behaving correctly', was standing, and Mary alive, with the Anreps[3] looking after her.

'The Anreps are the sister, the brother-in-law and the nephew of Nicky . . . they have done through an entire year for my wife and my place what Nicky has done here for the last three weeks.'[4]

For a whole month the battle raged and a live shell landed, without exploding, in a room on the first floor of the Serlupi's villa. It was removed by a German parachutist. The household was now living like moles in the dark, which was 'depressing, stupefying and hypnotizing'. Berenson did Swedish gymnastics twice a day (at the age of

[1] *R. and R.*, p. 345.
[2] Dr Pieraccini died in 1957 in Florence. *The Times* gave him a long and appreciative obituary.
[3] References to the Anreps are frequent and grateful.   [4] *R. and R.*, p. 347.

seventy-nine) to replace his daily walk, but a day was not a day without those walks. The household was getting bored and 'confess that they can turn to no activity'.

'That is not my case, because my dominant interests are unactual. Theirs depend on the events and contrasts of the day. Mine do not. Mine go on despite alarms and excursions. . . . Even if deprived of everything but one's mind one could still carry on for a good while, and bridge over an interlude like this.'[1]

In fact he had discovered anew something which he had known all his life, that there was no guarantee against boredom so good as historical pursuits of any kind, 'history not only of events but of ideas, of literature, of the fine arts, of the sciences'. He believed that individuals 'armed with these hobbies' would never come to the end of their tether, whereas mathematicians and 'philosophizers' might. He was mercifully in good health or he would have suffered far more.

The cattle belonging to his host were brought in under the shelter of the house walls. A cow and a calf were killed by shellfire. Another day one of the peasants trod on an unexploded shell in the garden. August 31st was the worst day yet. 'The house trembled, shook and rattled. It was not easy to keep one's heart from quaking.' Then at last, on September 1st, the noise grew less and young friends from Florence trooped up: Giovanni Colacicchi, the painter; Arturo Loria, Berenson's translator and himself a fine writer; Igor Markevich, the composer and conductor, who had been living with his wife (Nijinsky's daughter) and their son in the *villino* of 'I Tatti', all good friends and true, and led by the Swiss Consul, Steinhauslin, and his wife, coming up to see how the American in hiding and Nicky Mariano had survived the month's fighting. Berenson drove over to 'I Tatti', only to find to his distress that Mary was very ill and 'her speech was clogged'. Much of the glass in the house was broken, and Berenson carried away 'a disastrous impression' of the squalor and disorder on the farmlands of his estate. One of his very first visitors was an American soldier, his cousin Robert Berenson, now the son-in-law of the famous Paris dressmaker, Madame Schiaparelli. Many others in uniform, from the British and American armies, followed: anyone who had read an 'art course' at an American University came up to call, but it was the British rather than the Americans at this

[1] *R. and R.*, p. 346.

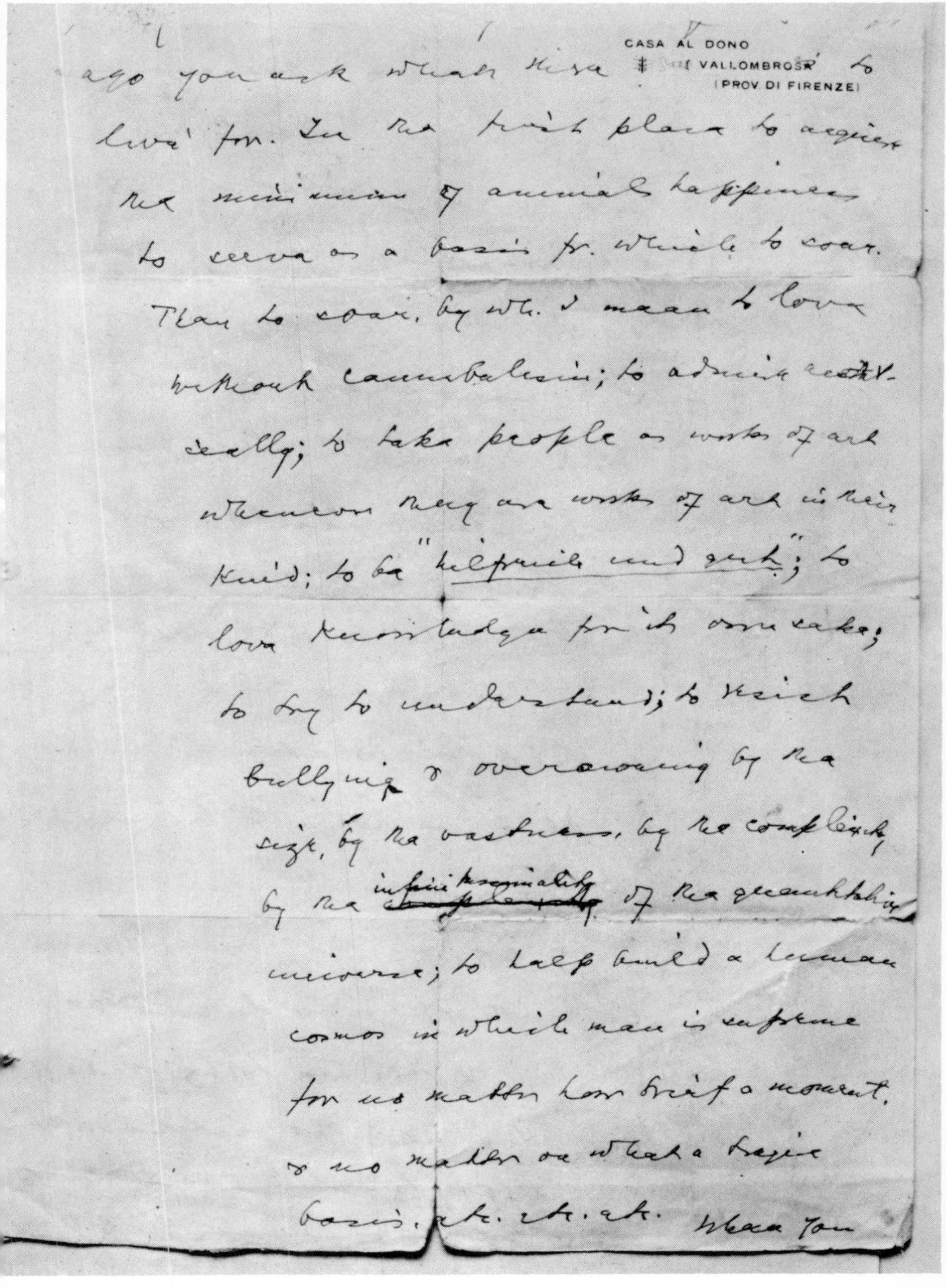

CASA AL DONO
VALLOMBROSA
(PROV. DI FIRENZE)

ago you ask what is a [illegible] to live for. In the first place to acquire the minimum of animal happiness to serve as a basis fr. which to soar. Then to soar, by wh. I mean to love without cannibalism; to admire ecstatically; to take people as works of art whenever they are works of art in their kind; to be "hilfreich und gut"; to love knowledge for its own sake; to try to understand; to resist bullying & overawing by the size, by the vastness, by the complexity, by the infinite inscrutability ~~complexity~~ of the quantitative universe; to help build a human cosmos in which man is supreme for no matter how brief a moment. & no matter on what a tragic basis. etc. etc. etc. When you

PLATE XX A letter from Bernard Berenson written to the author in 1951

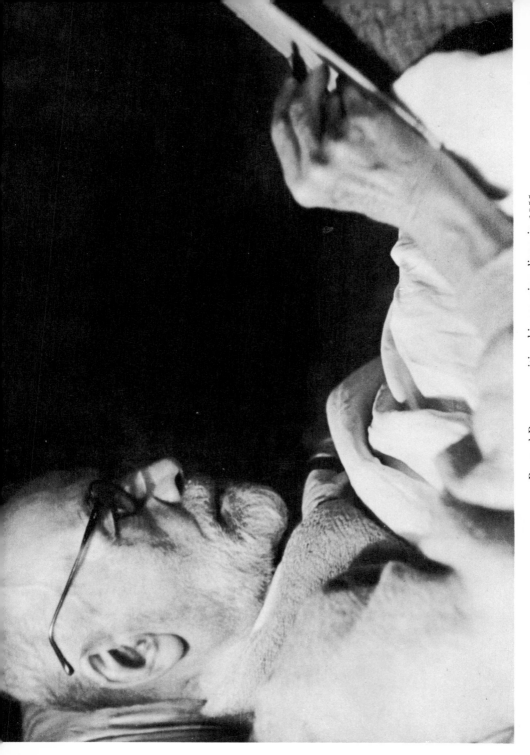

PLATE XXI   Bernard Berenson writing his morning diary, in 1955

stage who were helpful and friendly. Later Berenson especially remembered two English Yeomanry regiments who assisted the household.

Finally, on September 24th, he returned to 'I Tatti' with Nicky Mariano to meals of 'thin vegetable soup, boiled potatoes, salad and fruit', and smoky kerosene lamps. Friendly allied officers brought food, medicines, cigarettes, candles, matches and most welcome of all, new books and English and American newspapers and magazines.

'I am devoured with curiosity to learn what people who enjoy a free press think, and what they plan for the future not only at home but abroad.'[1]

But he adds that he would have lacked the courage to write down all his reflections and meditations (in *Rumour and Reflection*) if he had had access to these books and reviews earlier. Politically, *Rumour and Reflection* is a mine of insight into the flimsy foundations of Italian Imperialism, into likely developments in Russia, in China, in England, Germany, Europe, into the likely revival of Liberalism and Rationalism, and into Judeo-Christian relations. A book to read still, prophetic and provocative.

His treasures at 'I Tatti', most of the paintings and sculptures, all the photographs and some 20,000 of the rarer volumes had been removed on September 10, 1943, to places of hiding. In June 1944 Dr Ludwig Heydenreich, the Director of the German Institute in Florence, had been ordered to send all Berenson's works of art northwards, but he 'managed to create so many difficulties' that nothing had been done about it. Dr Gerhard Wolf, together with the reigning assistant chief of police (Signor Virgilio Benzi), had known where Berenson was hiding 'but spread the semi-official declaration' that he had gone to Portugal. Many were his friends among the Italians whom nothing would have induced to give him or his hiding-place away, and he names some of the loyal friends of those years in gratitude: his neighbour at Vallombrosa, Vittorio Emanuele Orlando, the ex-Prime Minister, and all his family, especially his daughter Carla Garabelli; Countess Marina Volpi (to whom Miss Freya Stark also pays high tribute for her friendship to Mrs Stark at Asolo during the war); Count Vittorio Cini, the Venetian, who later bought

[1] *R. and R.*, p. 380.

a long lease of the Island of St George to make of it a naval school and an art centre; and many others.[1]

Looking back upon the whole strange experience of thus living in a country at war with his own in the twentieth century, Berenson has this to say:

'I am glad I withstood persuasion and pressure to return home, and that I stuck it through in Italy.

'The six years of the war went a good way to complete and perfect my acquaintance with Italian mankind. It has been worth while: for, when their material interests, their personal dignity, and their national vanity are not put in question, they are the most understanding, the most easy-going, the least censorious, the least "I-am-holier-than-thou" of peoples. Their sympathies for suffering, whether physical or moral, are wide and warm. No other society is so indulgent to the frailties flesh is heir to, or expects less by way of heroics.'[2]

The provisos he makes in that paragraph embrace a good deal: yet his experience was endorsed by many a British soldier who escaped from prisoners' camps during those last two years of war.

* * *

If he loved the Italians more after this experience, they in turn were immensely appreciative of his decision to stay. The complaints that Italian pictures were leaving Italy in vast numbers (first, as we know, for the Gardner and other collections, and then, under the aegis of Duveen and therefore indirectly of Berenson)—these complaints had come from the correspondence columns of the London *Times* and from various British magazines. Some were crocodile tears. The Italian Press had never complained. A few deputies had worked hard to tighten the laws on exports of works of art and to replace the inadequate Pacca law with a list of classic painters whose works could not be exported without a Government permit. But so vast were the treasures of art in Italy that the exports, at least in the twentieth century, never seemed to the Italians more than an infinitesimal fraction of the national heritage. The Italians and especially the Florentines, liberated from Fascism, began to treasure their surviving sages, and high on the list they placed the Sage of

[1] Count Cini: see Plate XVII.   [2] *R. and R.*, p. 387.

Settignano, who had lived among them since 1888. For this they were grateful. He had weathered two wars with them. And he was not politically compromised—rather was it they who felt compromised by the ridiculously un-Italian anti-Semitic campaign in 1938 and the bombastic Fascist declaration of war against America in 1941. Their distinguished guest had brought Italy and Italian art nothing but honour and renown. They would make amends as best they could. That was how Florence and how Italy looked upon Berenson in 1945. First a few friends, mostly Italian Fine Arts professors and officials, clubbed together to present him with a token of respect in the shape of two bronze medals, one a fine Malatesta medal of the fifteenth century, which had been found in the debris of heavily bombed Rimini and was released by the Government for the very purpose of presenting it to Berenson; the other a medal of the same size but of not remotely similar workmanship inscribed with his name and the date of the presentation. That was in 1947.

But when Berenson returned to 'I Tatti' on September 23, 1944, his companion of a lifetime had but a few months to live. It was a lonely and bewildered woman who awaited his return, and who had spent the year trying, in the intervals of pain, to jot down some notes for an autobiography, which ends with a quotation from Coventry Patmore:

> When that night I prayed to God, I wept and said
> O Thou who seest of what toys we make our joys
> How little understood Thy great commanded good,
> Then fatherly, not less
> Than I whom Thou hast moulded from the clay,
> Thou'lt leave Thy wrath and say,
> 'I will be sorry for their childishness.'[1]

She wrote the last line, in what may well be an earlier reading:

> I will be tender with their childishness.

The year's absence had made her look back to the earliest days of her life with Berenson in the 'nineties and to the great host of visitors that had passed through the portals of 'I Tatti' from every corner of the world. That procession of visitors and friends formed a

[1] Coventry Patmore, *The Unknown Eros*, Book X.

pageant which might be worth recording, but they were like ships that pass too swiftly for a real record. She no longer had the strength to do more than jot down names. Her mother had once written to her:

'I must confess that the sort of life you lead, with such a continual procession of visitors, would be weariness beyond words to me, and it is a continual amazement to me that you stand it . . . but I suppose that you could not easily get out of it, so you must try and make it profitable somehow, either to yourselves or to your friends.'[1]

All who remember Mary Berenson remember her as a hostess who entered heart and soul into the business of entertaining new and old comers to 'I Tatti', and most would say, as she herself wrote, that she loved her husband even to 'the very things in the other that are not congenial to you, because they belong to the person you love'. At moments until the First War she was deeply in love with him, and would write to her own mother to say so. The Pearsall Smiths often 'thee'd' each other, as was the custom in Quaker families, and Mrs Whittall Smith would write back:

'I should be only too delighted if I could believe thee really did adore B.B. It is such a rare trait in a wife that I could hardly believe it; but, if it is true, thee could not have a more secure foundation for happiness.'[2]

To this observation, Logan Pearsall Smith, who edited the letters, adds the footnote that it had no bearing on Berenson's character 'or on his mother-in-law's opinion of him (they got on well together); it was merely the result of a constitutional disbelief that any woman could become happy because of marriage'.

I never knew Mary, and my portrait of her is necessarily inadequate. From Berenson I received very little help except in the matter of their radiant early love, which was as genuine and as mutual as it could possibly be. Their joint capacity for enjoying life and travel until the First War seems to have been altogether engaging. Already then she fascinated children. Harold Acton recalled in a broadcast talk on Berenson's ninetieth birthday year in 1955 that to himself and his brother as small boys Mary seemed 'a jolly Juno of American Quaker origin' who entertained them magnificently and imagina-

---

[1] *A Religious Rebel*, ed. cit., p. 197.　　　　　　　　　[2] *Ibid.*

tively. She knew Lewis Carroll and Edward Lear by heart, to their great delight, and 'her twinkling eye was an invitation to mischief'. People go their own ways in marriage for so many diverse reasons that it is difficult to attempt any account of such a long joint journey as that of the Berensons. Undoubtedly Mary returned to a very strong, and in Berenson's eyes, an overwhelming interest in her own children, as their grandmother, Mrs Hannah Whittall Smith, grew more immobile and then died in 1911. Berenson had, all his life, a slight horror about families. He dreaded visiting his own, on the rare occasions when he went to the United States. He settled a handsome annual sum on each of Mary's daughters, and seems to have had a growing irritation with her intense interest in them. If he and Mary drifted apart other reasons may have been her extravagance, his loves, her loves, and the fiery temperaments of both, which only mellowed with the years. But they did not let the world see it, and the brunt of running the great household, albeit extravagantly, fell on her shoulders until Nicky Mariano, to the enormous relief of both Mary and her husband, took over the household reins after the First War. Mary's help to Berenson in the early years, in pressing him to write and in revising his manuscripts and correcting proofs, was enormous.

She seems to have had a great capacity for idealizing people, and the journey back to normal relations was fraught with difficult and depressing moments. That is the price women pay for spontaneity. All these things were put into fiercer and sharper words by Berenson. He believed her, years after she was no longer alive, to have been full of 'the dread which most people have of how to get through the day without anguish and boredom'.[1]

To achieve a 'diversion' he thought that Mary would use any means, but was not this a joint problem, a problem which whoever ran the household would have had to face? People who 'go out to work' can hardly imagine what the organization of a lifetime is like, in which all the members of a household perform their duties inside the walls of the house and, in the case of 'I Tatti', enjoy all their leisure and their distractions also within its walls. Such a way of life required its own disciplines in the large, patriarchal and isolated country houses of England, until the Industrial Revolution at the end of the eighteenth century came to alter the ways of English life, and the impoverishment of whole classes through death duties and

[1] Berenson to the author in 1954.

taxation to pay for the welfare services, severed the tradition of hospitality in many a home. In Italy the ancient tradition became the subject of a famous book on civilized behaviour, conversation and pastimes in the castle of Urbino under the Montefeltro's—*The Courtier*—written in 1514, by Baldassare Castiglione. But it remained a literary memory rather than a practical way of life after the Risorgimento.

Here and there in England and far more in Europe, the way of life still goes on in some great houses, and in the few remaining Courts, but by and large great confusion has set in with the destruction of ancient wealth and much moving about. The newly enriched classes have looked in vain for an Art of Living, and have largely fallen into the hands of advertisers offering 'gracious living' in the form of frequently ignoble furniture and imitation marble and mosaic, embroidery and weaving, carried out in every kind of artificial fibre and plastic.

No life is civilized without taste, habits, disciplines—but *which* tastes, habits and disciplines? This problem of self-government was solved at 'I Tatti' year by year in a rhythm not very dissimilar from the terms and vacations of a university. Of the year's twelve months, two to three long summer months came to be spent high up on the hillside of the Casentino near Vallombrosa, where the remoteness allowed more time to study, and time for long walks. At least six weeks every year were spent in travel in Italy and abroad on voyages of discovery and study. And could one then still fear anguish and boredom? Of course one could. Berenson himself was never quite immune from the dread of them. They are ancient and eternal human burdens. In the Middle Ages they were called Accidie, in the late nineteenth century in Paris *spleen*, in the twentieth century in England *Angst*. The National Health Service in the mid-twentieth century in England found that by far the largest number of the nation's patients had fallen victim to their 'nerves', and had to be cared for in crowded mental homes. It was a new name for an ancient sickness.

High intelligence increases the burden, but likewise devises and discovers many more new ways of carrying it, than does low intelligence—new ways of service, new contributions towards resolving the dilemmas, the confusion and the chaos. Such problems always assume a religious or a highly philosophic nature.

Mary, in the early days, in her love and devotion to her husband,

262

thought that she could travel along his road and contribute her share of study and discovery to Berenson's work. And so she did. His last reference to her work, however, occurs in the *Drawings of the Florentine Painters*, which had appeared in 1903. The impetus was an impetus: it was not founded upon enough study and insight to carry her on alone, once his main work was accomplished. So she threw herself into less exacting and more consoling activities. Then came that failure in health which clouded her horizons, intermittently to the end.

Mary died in May 1945 knowing only that her husband was back, her children and grandchildren alive, 'I Tatti' safe, and its way of life in the hands of a devoted friend—Nicky Mariano—to whom she was deeply attached.[1]

---

[1] She is referred to under her pen name, Mary Logan, as having 'recently reconstructed Pesellino's artistic personality' in articles in the *Gazette des Beaux Arts*, of July and October 1901. (*Drawings of the Florentine Painters*, p. 59.)

CHAPTER XVI

Old Age

> *Socrates* . . . I fancy, Cephalus, that people do not generally acquiesce in these views of yours, because they think that it is not your character, but your great wealth, that enables you to bear with old age. For the rich, it is said, have many consolations.
>
> *Cephalus* . . . to those who, not being rich, are impatient under old age, it may be said with equal justice that while on the one hand a good man cannot be altogether cheerful under old age and poverty combined, so on the other, no wealth can ever make a bad man at peace with himself.
>
> PLATO'S *Republic*, Bk. I

SANTAYANA, Berenson's contemporary and fellow-student at Harvard, thought that the point about old age was 'to have expressed and discharged all that was latent in us, and to this perfect relief various temperaments and various traditions assign different names, calling it having one's day, or doing one's duty, or realizing one's ideal, or saving one's soul'.

Santayana had wandered and written much before he came to rest as a guest in the Convent of Santo Stefano Rotondo in Rome, for the last decade of his life. He died there on September 26, 1952. With the years he had drifted far from Berenson, drifted into downright misunderstanding, as we know from his letter to Mrs Toy about Berenson.[1]

Berenson often spoke of Santayana in the last years of his life. He was the Harvard contemporary who most interested him. It is therefore natural to return to Santayana for a moment. Santayana was a realist; he expressed his boredom or *ennui*, or 'unspirit' or 'infinite annoyance' as he sometimes called it. Berenson acknowledged *ennui*, but decided very early in life that the art of living was the art of transforming 'unspirit'.

[1] See p. 71 above, footnote.

During his twenty-three years of teaching philosophy at Harvard, Santayana had a string of famous pupils and fellow-teachers, William James, Royce, Conrad Aiken, T. S. Eliot, Van Wyck Brooks. He had come into money in 1912 and spent the rest of his life as a Spanish citizen writing some twenty-three books, in English, travelling between European cities. The most remembered and read of his books is *The Life of Reason*.

He left a remarkable manuscript, written in Rome during the Second World War, for posthumous publication, entitled *The Idler and his Works*.[1] It is more testamentary than Berenson's *Sketch for a Self-Portrait*, and much briefer. Santayana maintains that 'what is called experience, the obvious and inescapable pressure of sensation, is intrinsically a dream, something arbitrary, fugitive, unsubstantial, coming out of nothing and ending in nothing'. It is a whimsical testament. It records the 'two love affairs' of his 'political fancy', with Greece and with England, in which he allowed, he says, his mind to float lazily in casual enthusiasms. 'Soon experience in the case of England and a little more reading in the case of Greece brought my two political love affairs to an end.' He says he was as a man too self-indulgent, as a writer too miscellaneous, as a thinker, born at the wrong time and bred in the wrong way, to be a Sage: 'I can identify myself heartily with nothing in me except with the flame of spirit itself. Therefore the truest picture of my inmost being would show none of the features of my person, and nothing of the background of my life. It would show only the light of understanding that burned within me and, as far as it could consumed and purified all the rest.' In this statement, I think, Santayana expresses something akin to what Berenson would have liked to achieve.

Santayana enthroned Reason transcendentally above perception and feeling.[2] But there was no such hierarchy in Berenson. The severity of Santayana's philosophy inevitably made for increasing isolation.

Even for Berenson who kept his eyes alive, and refreshed and revised his views and interest in the historical events of the world around him, the loneliness of old age was great. It is for that loneliness that all life would seem to be a preparation. By that time a

---

[1] It was published in the *Saturday Review*, New York, May 15, 1954.

[2] 'Reason differs from perception and sentiment precisely in transcending our human egotism and aspiring to understand things as they are in themselves, and to love in them the good that they love' (*The Idler and his Works*).

philosophy must have been acquired and peace made with inevitable death. Santayana's philosophy is stoic: the cool, bright light of understanding consumes him. Berenson's ideal is Epicurean, a word which contemporary adventurers have pounded into pulp and emptied of all its true meaning. Women played a rich part in Berenson's life, not a very rich part in Santayana's, so that life, for Berenson, was a more complete experience.

*   *   *

Arturo Loria ventures into this last field with much insight. In the article, 'B. B. Umanista' in the Florence monthly *Il Ponte*, to celebrate the conferring of Honorary Citizenship by Florence on Berenson, he says:

'With women, he admits, he is more expansive than with men, freer, more imaginative. I think more than one beautiful and intelligent woman, visiting him with other people, received the impression of being received like the Queen of Sheba, while all around seemed to be presented to her as a gift—the landscape, the pictures, the books, the words of the host. Feminine grace at "I Tatti" receives homage which seemed like an ancient tribute: the feeling that a mutual expectancy has at last been happily fulfilled gives a poetic importance to the gestures of ecstatic courtesy. These are moments of course, but they are sufficient for a woman's memory to be coloured by the intimacy of the occasion and for the young man in the company to make a resolution to try to learn, at least in later years, how to praise the spirit of a woman in such a pleasing way as to make her superior to herself. Perhaps the gift is inimitable, the fruit of a refinement of the senses and of a love for all that intensifies life, and permits the discovery of joyful novelties in the course of the most ordinary of life's days. He would rejoice among the women of his own household if one had dressed her hair more becomingly to her face, if another was wearing a special flower, or if another was the bearer of some good news which she had not yet told him, but which he could read on her face.'

Undoubtedly, to intelligent women, Berenson found he could say an enormous number of things more easily than to men. This is surely an excellent and a natural state of affairs. It works both ways in intelligent men and women. Berenson had a great many intelligent women friends of various nationalities, Italian, French, English, American (hardly any German so far as one knows), and with them, provided they knew how to write a good letter, he would keep up very long and regular correspondence.[1] With Lady Colefax he corresponded for over forty years. She wrote him all the gossip of London, and since she gathered all the chief political, literary and journalistic figures round her lunch table, it was good gossip. There were other friends in England like Sir George Lewis's daughter, Miss Katie Lewis, with whom he corresponded for almost as long a period. The art of letter writing has almost died out in England and elsewhere, like the art of conversation. The telephone and the cocktail party kill these arts. Berenson never used a telephone after 1920. Nothing as noisy and barbarous as a cocktail party ever took place at 'I Tatti'.

Since the nationality of his visitors and friends was not a matter of primary importance, he devised a term, *unsereiner*, to describe the honorary citizens of his little kingdom. 'One of us' was the whole extent of his snobbishness. It was a visa on the passport of friends, conferred even on the passing visitor with the flash of an attribution. How did one qualify? The variety of those who qualified was very wide. The decks were cleared for royalty whose ritualistic upbringing fascinated him. The King and Queen of Sweden came regularly to stay after 1945.[2] Long before the war he had known the King as Crown Prince. In those days Marie-José, then Crown Princess of Italy, often called. Prince Paul of Jugoslavia was another guest, and so was another Florentine neighbour, ex-Queen Marie of Rumania. On more ordinary occasions it did not much matter if you failed to shine, provided you were not vicious, boring, or rude. He was very ruthless with those three categories. To a beautiful but dull young woman at lunch he would suddenly say, 'Tell me, my dear, what do you do that is useful?' To a solemn professor who had talked much he would say when at last the conversation flagged, 'Academic life is full of a lot of humbug, don't you think?' To anyone who seemed to receive their inspiration through alcohol or drugs, he could be devastating. Berenson was very well informed about Modigliani's habits of taking hashish, about Utrillo's drunkenness, and about Picasso's 'long, boorish silences with Braque when they planned cubism', and would call it all 'inspiration through dissipation'. To a young house guest at dinner (for which everyone changed into evening dress) who was clearly a little drunk he would say, looking

[1] See Plate XX.   [2] See Plate XV.

at him intently, 'Are you quite sure that you shaved this morning?' To another who had failed to get into a dinner jacket and apologized, he said, 'I don't mind at all. I do it as a discipline. You have no idea how wild I am. I need such disciplines.'

His views on Soviet communism were much more interesting than the late Senator McCarthy's. 'If you pile one abstraction on another, you reach the Moscow Empyrean', was his brief summary. He would not sever acquaintance with a man because he was a communist, but if he thought that an *unsereiner* or anyone who had enjoyed all the advantages of education, political contacts, wide reading, travel and culture, was toying with the Moscow Empyrean, he became almost physically upset. It happened after the Second War that one or two friends, especially Italians, published articles in near-communist newspapers, and he could not fathom it, and worried and worried over it. He was very fond of Renato Guttuso,[1] the painter, and of the Siena art historian, Count Ranuccio Bianchi-Bandinelli, both fully-fledged Comrades. Artists he held to be politically irresponsible. Politically he thought that all the Bianchi-Bandinellis of Italy were the products of what he called 'the conceptualistic mis-education which German-mindedness has induced in Italy'. With such friends, and they were devoted friends, he would never talk politics at all. With that side of his friends which was (to his mind) inappropriate, exacting or dissatisfying, he used the most ancient of all weapons, that of mute delay. It always worked. Sometimes it worked too well, and the friends reverted to acquaintanceship.

A famous elderly art historian who arrived one evening for dinner announced that on the journey he had suddenly begun to enjoy trees. Telling the story Berenson said, 'A tree had jumped out of his books at last, into life, after all these years'. Someone asked Berenson, 'What did *you* say?' Berenson replied, 'I congratulated him heartily'.

Numbers of museum directors called from every town in the United States for a gossip, a talk, an opinion. He would always help a museum director if he could. Some of them were strange enough, and not easy for the other guests or the members of the household. Berenson would always find a kind word for them. When someone complained of one of these many directors, he said of him: 'He has made a very fine small museum. His talk is like all society talk, anecdotal. He is an innocent snob, a homosexual, a bore. I hope you go to his town and visit his museum next time you go to America.'

[1] See Plate XVII.

One or two visitors came with ulterior motives, mainly with what Berenson called 'a plot to Boswellize me'. They had to leave sooner than expected. The very learned visitor who might be an expert in the period from A.D. 300 to 900. Berenson would affectionately call a Muddyevilist, more clearly defined as 'one who makes sly glances at the Middle Ages'. If they were (and they usually were) devoted students of the obscurer symbolism of the period, he would sometimes say that they were engaged in Ico-nonsense. High-flown philosophical talk or writing he would call metafuzzical. When some completely incongruous visitor arrived, to whom he alone took a fancy, Berenson would meet the criticism of his household and friends after the visitor had gone with, 'You know, as in that story of the Scotchman whom an Englishman observed eating asparagus at the wrong end, "I preferrr it this way".'

He would warn the household about some of the visitors, which helped quite a lot. Thus, describing a woman guest who was expected to lunch, a member of a famous European family, he would predict, 'She is made entirely of steel and asbestos—quite hard'. A gentle inquiry from his sister Bessie (who came over every summer, travelling 7,000 miles well on into her eighties, to see him): 'But, B.B., do you *like* her?' and Berenson would reply: 'That's not the point. She belongs to my world.'

After another visitor had left, Berenson asked a knowledgeable guest, 'But X *is* a dealer, isn't he?' The guest in turn asked, 'You don't like dealers?' and Berenson said, 'I don't like crypto-dealers. Plain dealers are all right.'

*   *   *

Every year since long before the Second War, when the heat of summer descended upon the valley of the Arno with overwhelming stillness, and the town of Florence filled with tourists, the household at 'I Tatti' would move up to a much higher hill, which Milton made famous throughout the English-speaking world as a place where Satan summoned

> . . . Angel Forms, who lay entrans't
> Thick as Autumnal Leaves that strow the Brooks
> In Vallombrosa, where the Etrurian shades
> High overarch't imbower. . . .

Travellers in the train from Florence to Rome, if they look out of a window on the left hand soon after leaving Florence, will for a long time glimpse a high village up above the station of S. Ellero (where their express will not stop) called Saltino, 'the little jump'. For a brief moment even the great monastery in a cleft high up in the mountain, to the left of Saltino, might be glimpsed on a clear day. But it is the view the other way from Vallombrosa, descending hill upon hill into the valley where the Arno winds like a silver streak beyond Pontassieve, and up again unendingly to the giant crags far away, the marble mountains of Carrara, that is unforgettable at all hours of the day and evening. It is one of the very great views of Italy, where great views are not rare. It is both grand and intimate. At night when the lights go on in a hundred villages, and sparkle in the valley towns of Figline, Rignano and Pontassieve, the whole view springs to new life. The sunsets of Vallombrosa, never the same on two evenings as sunsets never are, are the highlight of the mountain day.

It is always cool in Vallombrosa, however hot it may be elsewhere. At first the Berensons rented a small house on the Consuma road. Then Berenson purchased a solid little mountain house which he gave to Nicky Mariano, and there she built a small thatched summer house, whence the view in all its beauty and wide expanse met the eye. From July to September they would stay in this far place, without a telephone, but in touch with the world when the postman arrived twice a day with letters and telegrams. The cars went down to Florence two or three times a week, bringing back a few guests, fruit and vegetables from 'I Tatti' and other food from the town. One remembers the long ninety-minute car climb from the sweltering heat below into the rarefied atmosphere of the mountain. One remembers, too, looking back on the way down and finding how quickly, how irretrievably, the little house disappeared from view. The pines are very tall at Vallombrosa, taller than in the Black Forest; cathedral-like is the darkness between them, lit only by occasional shafts of sunlight. The trees whose autumnal leaves strewed the brooks in Milton's day were giant beeches and sweet chestnut, so big that some of their long since departed trunks have left circles fifteen feet across. These woods are springy with the leaves of centuries, and down the mountain still run a hundred very clear, translucent, sparkling brooks. One of them runs into the woodland garden of Casa al Dono.

Old Age

Every evening after tea, when the sun was about to set, Berenson would walk along with Nicky Mariano and his friends, if any were staying or visiting, to a small tree nursery of the State Forestry Commission where the youngest pines were sheltered under terraces of straw matting and the older ones already caught the slanting glow of the evening sun. The little walk through the woods to this small man-made amphitheatre, and indeed the whole of what might be called the sunset rite, was ever the occasion of delightful talk of a rather universal kind, as befitted the hour.

'It has always seemed a miracle to me [Berenson would say] that human life should have survived on this planet and reached the heights it has reached, considering how brittle and frail the body is, and how varied and difficult the circumstances can be.'

It was the kind of remark that would encourage a young visitor, hitherto silent, to put the despair of youth into words. Berenson would then go on:

'I have often been utterly despairing of myself, but never with the Show—the whole Show, no. My worst attack of despair, of almost daily and suicidal despair, came at the end of six months in New York, on my last visit [1929], when I was lionized morning, noon and night. Often it was a pleasure seeing friends I loved, but the whole experience reduced me to a state of neurasthenia. . . . New York has a dreadful character about it which seems to consider anything it has known for more than five minutes, as old.'

Another visitor might, in that evening hour, recall the woes of ill health, and Berenson, who always seemed the smallest and the most delicate person present, would stop a moment to say:

'I have never but been aware of my body as an instrument that was causing me some discomfort or difficulty. I learnt early to detach myself and so carry on, in spite of aches. Certain ills are not remediable either in the body or in the body politic, except by long practice. They have to be borne.'

The visitor who dwelt too long upon the awful complications and tragedies of life might hear this from Berenson:

271

'Every man carries his own dung hill around with him. I know when the vermin rears its ugly head, and then I have to beat it down back to where it belongs. That is a daily process and a continuous one.'

If, as often happened in the war-torn world of those days, some recent 'convert' to Communism was mentioned, Berenson would assess the matter with:

'The really revolutionary proletarian is the individual whose tether has given out, whatever social class he belongs to. Such people hate the very *Wesen* of the propertied classes, and one is rightly afraid of them.'

Inevitably, as one reached the scene from which the impending sunset was to be watched, the whole beauty of the Italian landscape, town and country, would spring to mind, or sometimes into words. Berenson would not let it lie there. He would add his afterthought:

'It is a wonder, you know, that Italy stands on her feet as she does, considering the lavish outlays on pretentious public buildings, the extravagant picnics in architecture, the wars and all the nonsense of Fascism.'

One had to be wary about all enthusiasms, for people, landscapes or pictures. Berenson was nothing if not a realist in conversation, aware of all the snags. Someone reported how a young English couple had purchased an Italian house with a splendid view, high above the sea:

'They are still young colts, galloping round. That house at X is the fruit of English romanticism—inaccessibility, cliffs, height, views. Such things are temporary. With age and infirmity they can no longer be a pleasure or practicable. They spring from an attempt to identify oneself with a piece of landscape, whereas it is the man within who must resolve his identification. Landscape cannot resolve it for him.'

With Berenson it was, of course, a completely natural occurrence to be serious. The surface of his talk rippled with humour, but the undercurrent was serious, and never more serious than in talking

PLATE XXII The green garden at 'I Tatti' in 1956, forty years after it had been planted with cyprus, juniper and box

PLATE XXIII   The corridor outside Mr and Mrs Berenson's studies at 'I Tatti'

Bernard Berenson and the author in the snow winter of 1951 at 'I Tatti'

about people. Sometimes, but not very often, he got people wrong. Sir Max Beerbohm was a case in point.

'I only met him twice and for five minutes. I got, both times, an impression of showy-ness, of the showman, to an absurd degree. He certainly excelled—he was a genius in both caricature and prose.'

In the company at Vallombrosa, moving slowly towards the sunset, there would, as often as not, be some friend (often a woman friend) who hung devotedly upon Berenson's every word, and another friend who noting the situation would suggest, 'B.B., you are a god in her eyes'. The evening hour, or just the inherited disposition to generalize and philosophize once brought this comment to that occasion:

'The concept of "God the Father" or "God the friend" or "God the inspiration" easily dissolves into a human being upon whom affection, respect, curiosity and interest are centred. Once dissolved, the concept cannot be reconstrued, and retains only archaeological and tribal interest. But this does not signify an end to all religious feeling.'

And then all conversation would cease as the little group gathered to face the immense landscape touched with the gold of the setting sun. There were stormy autumnal settings, grandiose 'like Götterdämmerung': others calm and superb beneath a greeny-pink mother-of-pearl sky: others mysterious in the mist of what might have been a rare wet day: others simply spectacular, with immense rays of clouds drifting towards the ball of fire. So varied and splendid was each of these sunsets that it became quite natural not to talk much until the last tip of the sun had disappeared below the distant hilly horizon. Almost immediately afterwards the lights began to twinkle in the deep valley towns and all over the hillsides, wherever the little farms lay.

Upon the way home the conversation would often turn to reminiscences, and Berenson's reminiscences were vivid and accurate across the span of nearly three generations. Someone asked whether he had ever known Cavalcaselle. And Berenson recalled the meeting in Rome in 1889, 'Very handsome and tall he was, and by far the

273

most knowledgeable Italian about pictures. But he had no method, and of course no photographs. He drew finely, and he compared his drawings.' I remember asking about Morelli. Berenson said, 'Morelli had the method. He was Cavalcaselle's enemy-friend. But Morelli's method lacked something. I gave it what it lacked—the psychology of art.'

It would be unfair to rely on Berenson's view of his own contribution to the enjoyment of things seen. No one ever quite knows the nature of his contribution to the general treasure. Berenson is no exception. His recent remarks upon the sunset, the landscape, the atmosphere, the line of a hill, revealed even to a stranger accompanying him for the first time upon such an occasion, that Berenson cared above all else for the seeing and understanding eye. If anyone else possessed it he was overjoyed. I think he believed that it lay dormant in everyone, and one will never know in how many people he coaxed it to life and to activity from the moment they met him. But that was only the beginning. To notice everything is the same as noticing nothing. To dwell on the ugly, the incongruous, the failure, was not his way. He seemed to find there was never time enough for all that was waiting to be discovered and appreciated, re-discovered and re-appreciated.

Someone asked him on one of these evenings at Vallombrosa about Santayana, and Berenson said: 'There was something philistine about him, above all about his catholicism . . . something without pity and without humanity. He was utterly intellectual.'

If a visitor from the art world was talking fluently about some school of painting such as the 'Mannerists', Berenson could be wonderfully innocent with a small question: 'What exactly *is* mannerism?' (although no one had ever drawn such a lucid distinction between Mannerism and Affectation).[1] Sometimes in the loneliness which exiles know, he could be monumentally disillusioned and say, 'All my friends have let me down'. It was not true. It was only that he expected a warmth in friendship which most of his friends, caught up in many public and private occupations, simply had not the energy to provide as constantly as he would have wished. But of course the 'letting down' in the art world, as in other professional fields, can be formidable. Berenson acknowledged what he owed to Morelli and Cavalcaselle, and expected younger men to acknowledge what they owed to him. That acknowledgement mostly

[1] See *Caravaggio, ed. cit.*, p. 97.

failed to find expression, but when acknowledgement was made, Berenson was overjoyed, whereas the spate of articles, essays, and tributes which appeared in 1955 to celebrate his ninetieth birthday did not really dispel that deep apprehension about himself which is such a striking feature of his *Sketch for a Self-Portrait*.

There was no skeleton in the cupboard—mistakes in attribution are not skeletons. There was the 'life-enhancing' vision of experiences, which dimmed as death approached. There was, I think, and only at times, that intense despair which all sensitive people feel about earning a living. Berenson could mock at himself—abuse himself—but he never could really laugh at himself. He could mock at others, but not laugh at them. Perhaps, for that, you have to be big and burly. He was small and too delicate, too elegant, too intelligent and in the end too mellowed to indulge in laughter at himself or anyone else. It was extraordinary to see him entering the room when some unwary visitor had unknowingly occupied the chair upon which Berenson would always sit. Habit would take him in that direction and then hesitation would take hold of him. He would say nothing. He would wonder where to go and look helpless for a second. Then he would find an unfamiliar chair.

In the mornings at Vallombrosa he would join the household on 'the tennis', as the Italians called the grass terrace which some previous owner had laid out in the shape of a court. There in the sunshine, with the guests sitting on the grass or on a rug, someone might read aloud, or Berenson might take out his magnifying glass and suggest that a visitor should examine a sprig of cow parsley under it. 'Have you ever seen anything like that?' he would ask, and as likely as not they were astonished and he might murmur a quotation:

> *Frage nicht, durch welche Pforte*
> *Du in Gottes Stadt gekommen,*
> *Sondern bleib am stillen Orte,*
> *Wo du einmal Platz genommen.*

and the catharsis was accomplished.

He was much too polite ever to display his immense erudition, and if others did display theirs, he was apt to become more deeply original than usual, to test their capacity for original thought. It was possible for old friends to go for a walk with him without saying anything on the grounds that 'there is no greater pleasure than to be

275

with a friend with whom talk is not necessary'. These were 'golden silences' for him.

'It is easy now to live in ecstasy. . . . All ambition spent . . . I can appreciate any and every gift to the point of worship . . . I only wish I had the will to passivity becoming to my age. At times I feel like many a one in the years of Hitler's power who always had a bag ready, in case the Gestapo or its local jackals came to carry him off. I am packed and, with Landor, "ready to depart", but not peppering to do so.'

So he wrote for a queer little anthology compiled by Samuel Duff McCoy called *How Prayer Helps Me,* in which some sixty Americans from Dean Acheson and Herbert Hoover to Adlai Stevenson, Marianne Moore and Harry Truman contributed a page or two each in 1955. An inaccurate footnote to Berenson's contribution says that he was born in Massachusetts in 1864, and that Ernest Hemingway, 'upon being notified that he was to receive the Nobel Prize in Literature in 1954, remarked that it should earlier have been awarded to Carl Sandburg and to Bernard Berenson, and to the latter in particular for the lucidity of his prose'.

*   *   *

On Sunday, December 12, 1954, Berenson and Nicky Mariano had driven up for the usual morning walk downhill, from above Vincigliata. As usual, the car, with the faithful Welsh driver Parry at the wheel, had stopped at a high point and both got out in the fine winter sun. Berenson's scarf had been left behind. Miss Mariano went to fetch it, closed the door of the car, and Berenson signalled to Parry to drive on. But the door was not fully closed. It flung open and knocked Berenson down, so that he fell over the steep edge of the hill, rolling down to a place some twenty-five feet below. As always in winter, he was wrapped in a heavy coat and wore his Russian fur cap.[1] Undoubtedly his lightness and these heavy wraps saved him from certain death.

He got up alone. The car drove back to 'I Tatti'. He walked upstairs clinging to the banisters and went to bed.

As usual there were guests to lunch. With unfailing courage and self-possession Miss Mariano presided over the lunch downstairs,

[1] See Plate XXIII.

returning to Berenson's room immediately afterwards. Berenson's assistant, Mr William Mostyn Owen, was left in charge of the guests and described afterwards how he suddenly heard the sound of running feet upstairs, and could bear it no longer. He went up and learned that Berenson had fainted—just after telling his personal maid that this was the end. The doctor gave him some strychnine injections, and the grand old heart revived. He lay in bed for a week and then wrote:

'I hope your papers have not said anything about what happened to me a few days ago. I was pushed by the car door over a steep hillside with twigs, stones and boulders. I rolled like a hoop three times and then bumped against a huge rock that stopped me. Since then I have been in bed licking my bruises, but nothing broken. Really *j'ai la veine dans la guigne* . . . I ought not to have written so much as I am still feverish.'[1]

The recovery was miraculous. Strength returned, but inevitably the severe accident left its mark. To the usual hardships of age, loss of memory, difficulty in hearing and seeing, was now added unusual frailty. Hardest of all to bear was the way in which the frailty impaired his fine will and his control. There were still wonderful moments with no less wonderful visitors, but in between there was great despondency, remorse for unfinished work, immense sorrow at the death of one close friend after another, his translator Arturo Loria; his most intimate brother-in-law Ralph Barton Perry, and the absence of that vitality which might overcome such moments.

Italy had survived and overcome the severest test which Berenson could conceive, with the overwhelming victory of the Christian Democrats against a formidable Communist Party, at the General Election of April 18, 1948. Now, nearly ten years later, the ill-starred expedition of Sir Anthony Eden's Government to Suez shook Berenson with an equal anxiety and apprehension. He was not against the expedition. He would have wished it to have taken place immediately upon the seizure of the Canal. He was horrified that the United States should have been found voting with Russia against the action. I have not touched on the intense concern with which he followed public events and policies after the Second War. They occupied several hours of his day. He became both privately and

---

[1] To the author.

through the Press extremely well informed about what was going on, so that leading political figures made a point of calling upon him if they were in the neighbourhood. One of the happiest of these visits was that of Mr Harry S. Truman in 1955.[1]

The despondency about England after Suez was so great that he would bitterly refer to 'ex-England', as though words could reverse the course of history. The quarrel with England was of far longer standing than Suez. He never believed that England's Arab policy could lead to anything but disaster, but then he also held the same view about the fate of the Welfare State. I think he had a dream picture of England, a passionate love and admiration of it, quite remote from the financially impoverished reality which emerged after the two world wars. He was always at his very best with English guests, and appreciated by them more thoroughly than by anyone else. At their best, they alone seemed to have the education, the learning, the humour and the wisdom which he most enjoyed. But he remained himself a citizen of the world. With Emerson he might have written:

> I trim myself to the storm of time,
> I man the rudder, reef the sail,
> Obey the voice at eve, obeyed at prime.
> The port, well worth the cruise, is near,
> And every wave is charmed.

[1] See Plate XV.

Postscript

October 6th, 1959

THIS morning at 9 o'clock the radio here gave the first news of B.B.'s death. To all of us who were fond of him it came as a relief. For nearly three years he had been much afflicted by the pains of age and latterly had been unable to communicate except by signs. Death was as keenly sought as life had once been. Only his faithful companion knew what he had to bear, and only his friends knew what hard years these had been for her.

Re-reading my book I feel much has been left out, and again much, almost defensively, put in. Were we all needlessly jealous of his reputation? Did I catch, did we not all catch, some of his anxieties about those 'who will be extreme to mark what is amiss', eating away piecemeal at the intention and the dream, at the innocence of the naked and the dead? They will come, no doubt, for none is so pitiless as the expert on the expert.

At this moment I think of his vision of 'I Tatti' as a place, not an institution, where men and women might stay for a time reading in that splendid library he collected book by book, walking in that lovely garden, talking as they never talked before and letting their projects, whether about art or kindred subjects, flower into some tangible and achievable shape.

But how can that be, I keep wondering, if he is not there to nip the falsehood and the affectation in the bud, going straight to the point, as he often did? What a span of life was his! What fires he kindled and may yet kindle among those with inclination to read, not surfeited with radio and with television and the urge to buy!

One wishes well to the house on the hillside at Settignano, under its new rule. Its founder rests where he belongs, in Italian soil; also in the quiet places of the heart. He found the earth good; the sun his light and life; the moon he greeted every night it shone, before going to bed; he always bowed three times to a new moon, when it was too cold or wet to go outside; and the woods, the grass, the flowers, the birds and the hills were his comfort. These, he seemed to say—these you shall care for and enjoy; the rest will come of itself. And he was right.

279

October 12th, 1959

This morning a letter from Umberto Morra from Cortona. He writes: 'So it is all over. You will have read the papers about the ceremony and the wonderful way BB was clad in white, in a large cashmere shawl with a hood, his ivory face and hands whiter than the garment. The light just before sunset was incredibly pure and golden. There was no fuss, no strict, ceremonial order . . .

Nicky seems to be in peace. She had a telephone call from Agnes Mongan in Cambridge, Mass. It seems they won't come to take over before five or six months.'

FINIS

INDEX

Index

287

BERENSON